BIBLIOGRAPHY AND MODERN BOOK PRODUCTION

'No bibliographer ... achieved his aim without resting heavily upon the assistance of others.'

DR LUTHER EVANS

Wits Press RE/PRESENTS

Wits University Press celebrated its centenary in 2022. Since its inception, the Press has been curating and publishing innovative research that informs debate to drive impactful change in society. Drawing on an extensive backlist dating from 1922, Wits Press Re/Presents is a new series that makes important research accessible to readers once again. While much of the content demonstrates its historical provenance, it remains of interest to researchers and students, and is re-published in e-book and print-on-demand formats.

BIBLIOGRAPHY AND MODERN BOOK PRODUCTION

NOTES AND SOURCES FOR STUDENT LIBRARIANS, PRINTERS, BOOKSELLERS STATIONERS, BOOK-COLLECTORS

ASSEMBLED BY
PERCY FREER B.A.HONS(BIRM.),
F.L.A., UNIVERSITY LIBRARIAN

WITH A FOREWORD BY
PRINCIPAL H. R. RAIKES, A.F.C., M.A.
VICE-CHANCELLOR, UNIVERSITY OF THE WITWATERSRAND

ELABORATED AND INDEXED BY
VIBEKE BERG-SONNE F.S.A.L.A.

WITS UNIVERSITY PRESS

Published in South Africa by
Wits University Press
1 Jan Smuts Avenue
Johannesburg 2001

www.witspress.co.za

First published by Witwatersrand University Press, 1954
Published edition © University of the Witwatersrand, 2024
Introduction © Veronica Klipp, 2024

http://dx.doi.org.10.18772/12024089094

978-1-77614-909-4 (Paperback)
978-1-77614-910-0 (Hardback)
978-1-77614-911-7 (Web PDF)
978-1-77614-912-4 (EPUB)

All rights reserved. No part of this publication may be reproduced, stored in a retrieval system, or transmitted in any form or by any means, electronic, mechanical, photocopying, recording or otherwise, without the written permission of the publisher, except in accordance with the provisions of the Copyright Act, Act 98 of 1978.

Project manager: Koliswa Moropa
Proofreader: Kate Whittaker
Cover design: Hybrid Creative
Typeset in 10.5 point Plantin

To
Charles
E.A.B. and H.M.R.
Matt

CONTENTS

Introduction by Veronica Klipp	ix
Acknowledgments	xvii
Foreword	xxi
Introductory Note	xxiii
Addenda	xxv
PART 1. BIBLIOGRAPHY	xxix
I. The Bibliographers Define Bibliography	1
II. Literature of Bibliography and Modern Book Production	15
III. Bibliographies	77
IV. Compilation and Arrangement	109
V. Collation and Description of Books (Old and New) Their Structure and Parts	117
PART 2. MODERN BOOK PRODUCTION	131
VI. Historical Introduction	133
VII. Paper	145
VIII. Printing	161

IX. Illustration	181
X. Facsimiles and Near-Print	209
XI. Bookbinding	229
XII. Practical Authorship	249
XIII. Modern Fine Printing	293
Appendix: Examination Questions	323
Index	333

INTRODUCTION

Veronica Klipp

Bibliography and Modern Book Production provides a fascinating journey through the historic practices of librarianship and publishing.[1] The sources and material assembled here allow one to trace key developments in both bibliographic practice and book production from 1494 to 1949. As such it serves as a rich compendium for librarians and information workers as well as students and book publishers.

How did it come about? Who was its 'assembler', Percy Freer, and why has Wits University Press chosen to digitise it now, 70 years after its first publication?

The 1954 book arose from Freer's encyclopaedic knowledge of the intertwined disciplines of bibliographic practice and book production. It reflected his passion for librarianship and his vision for a text which could be used in the library course he proposed to the University of the Witwatersrand (Wits) in 1953. As one of two titles he published during his tenure as librarian (1929–1953), it demonstrates Freer's contribution to the landscape of library sciences, academia and the nascent practice of scholarly publishing in South Africa during his lifetime.

Given the book's value as a historic record in an era in which digital advances are changing the nature of publishing, it seemed fitting to bring new life to this text and ensure that future scholars have access to the wealth of knowledge it contains.

Librarian

Freer was born in 1893 and although he played many roles, was first and foremost a librarian. According to Humphrey Raikes' foreword to this volume, he 'entered the library world as a boy, at the age of 14', though in what capacity is not clear.[2] After World War I he studied at the Universities of Birmingham and Heidelberg, graduating with a BA Honours in 1922, after which he worked at the Norfolk and Norwich Library. In 1926 he moved to Cape Town, where he took up the position of under-librarian at the South African Public Library. During this time, he helped establish the South African Library Association and became the editor of its official journal, *South African Libraries*.[3] In 1929 he was appointed as the first librarian at Wits University, where he remained until his retirement in 1953.

Although the University was incorporated and granted university status in 1922, the establishment of a central library was slow to follow. A number of departmental libraries existed, but most were loath to hand over their volumes (numbering between 8000 and 9000 books) to a central facility as long as there was no proper supervision, which would require the appointment of a librarian. A reading room staffed by senior students was established in 1925; this expanded as more departments began housing their books there and by 1928 an acting librarian was appointed. In 1929, when the Carnegie Corporation of New York offered a donation of £5000 to the Medical Library on condition that a qualified librarian was appointed to take care of its running and the cataloguing of its books, a fully functional central library was finally established under Freer's management in the university's Central Block.[4]

From the start, Freer carried a heavy workload filled with a number of competing tasks. He was a keen teacher and became involved in the training of new librarians in order to provide qualified staff for the cataloguing and classifying (following the Library of Congress model) of the rapidly expanding books collection; this included holding lunch hour seminars to help prepare graduates for Library Association examinations.

Following a catastrophic fire in the Central Block on 24 December 1931 that destroyed the library and its 35 000 volumes, the decision was taken to embark on an enthusiastic fundraising campaign for a new library. Freer, with support from the Carnegie Corporation, undertook a study tour of libraries in the United States, Canada and Britain. He then put forward the plan to model the new library on the Petit Trianon at Versailles and building was completed in 1934. In the 1970s this library was re-named after Dr William Cullen, President of the South African Association for the Advancement of

Science, in recognition of his enormous efforts to raise construction funds and book donations.⁵

Publisher

From 1932, Freer became involved in Witwatersrand University Press matters. Supported by the library's typists, he established standards and developed scholarly publishing practices. In September 1937 the university's Publications Committee recommended that he take on full responsibility for preparing all works for publication.

Margaret Hutchings describes the impact of the intolerable workload that ensued in her unpublished history of the Press.⁶ Although 'softspoken, gentlemanly', in 1944 Freer wrote a forceful letter to the university registrar, insisting that he and his staff could no longer carry on with their publishing duties and that it was time for specialists to take over his 'amateurish efforts'.⁷ Ever the perfectionist, he wrote:

> I am painfully aware that our W.U.P. accounts are in bad shape; that money is overdue on most of our titles; that our advertising needs revision and extension, etc. We are, however, quite unable to do more at present. The earlier suggestion of an extra Grade I Assistant, with her salary shared equally by Library and Publications still seems to me the most reasonable and practical one pending more funds and a better arrangement.⁸

When proposals for staff appointments at the Press were not accepted, he asked for six months' leave of absence. Undaunted, in 1945 he drafted the first memorandum of 'Duties of a Publications Officer', which included reading and editing of typescripts, the preparation of printer specifications, decisions regarding possible future reprints (in the days of metal type, these had to be made at the first print run), checking of proofs and author corrections, post-publication marketing, sales and bookkeeping, and correspondence with authors and booksellers.⁹ The processes he outlined here remained the key publishing functions until the advent of electronic publishing in the 1980s.

Only after a Publications Officer (or Publisher) was appointed in 1947 could Freer relinquish most of his publishing duties. Hutchings said of him: 'Although Mr P. Freer was never on the staff of the University Press, from 1937 to 1947 he *was* the University press.'¹⁰

Educator and Author

In 1949 Freer had proposed the establishment of a Library School at the university that would offer a four-year BA followed by a Diploma in Librarianship. *Bibliography and Modern Book Production* was written with this course in mind, though Freer stressed it was 'not a text-book of bibliography' but a guide to sources, which aimed to provide a 'logical course of study'. The eventual course outline – which was only established in 1958 by his successor, Elizabeth Hartmann – consisted of the following:

> Bibliography and Reference Methods; Cataloguing and Classification; Library Administration, Organisation and Routine; Literature and Librarianship; Historical Bibliography and Book Production; Compilation of Bibliography.[11]

This list demonstrates the overlapping skills required for bibliography, librarianship and book publishing. The subject of bibliography had become an important one in the first half of the twentieth century. New methodologies were developed to study texts and books as material objects and bibliography became 'the science of the material transmission of literary documents'.[12] Presumably Freer had been exposed to this 'New Bibliography' school as a student in the United Kingdom just after World War I and his breadth of knowledge and attention to detail are astonishing.

True to his vocation as a librarian, Freer starts with a seemingly exhaustive list of sources on bibliography in the first part. In the second, his attention turns to book production – or what we could also call the means of creating the (print) book as material object.

Freer's historic knowledge is on full display here. Beginning with the practice of writing and the early development of 'books' manufactured from papyrus, wax tablets and eventually paper, he moves on to the development of European printing by movable type in the 15th century.[13] He follows this up with explanations of all aspects related to book production, from editing to illustration, printing and the development of typefaces and fonts (or 'founts', as Freer calls them), book-binding and authorship. He illustrates each section with examples from England and North America and includes some references to South African publishing in the sections on printing, copyright and legal deposits.

Most contemporary readers will probably be unfamiliar with much of the terminology: 'incunabula'; 'half-stuff'; 'slugs'; 'gravers, spit sticks and scorpers'; and who knows the origins of the typesetting term 'leading'? It is clear that Freer's work as librarian and publisher relied on extensive knowledge of what we might call his primary subject, common to both: the book as print object. At the time, both libraries and publishers (along with printers and book binders) needed a thorough mastery of this subject in order to be successful. So, Wits was lucky to have found a person with expertise that could be put to use in both areas.

Conclusion

Shortly after this book was first published, bibliography was superseded by 'book history' – a field that developed from it but was based on the realisation that 'physical production of a text was very much dependent upon the conditions in which it was produced'.[14] The focus shifted to the social contexts of book production and dissemination as well as the sociology of reading. Around the same time, technological developments resulted first in electronic publishing, followed in the early part of this century by digital publishing, which requires a new kind of knowledge for librarian and publisher: metadata, ebooks, aggregation, dissemination and so on. 'Books' – as physical objects and as metonyms for texts – have morphed into 'content' transmitted by a number of different formats and media.

Why then should *Bibliography and Modern Book Production* be digitised and brought into circulation again? Perhaps because it combines in one volume a near encyclopaedic knowledge of the history of the print book while demonstrating the solid foundations of scholarly publishing and librarianship in South Africa. This makes it an excellent historical source for current students and practitioners of librarianship, information work and publishing.

When Percy Freer retired at the end of 1953, he left an important legacy that became the foundation for future expertise at Wits University:

> From a one room 'library' and a few scattered, uncoordinated collections in various departments, the Library, under Freer's guidance, had grown to a bookstock of some 250 000 volumes and a staff of 23. Freer was well-known in professional circles as

the compiler of the *Catalogue of Union Periodicals* (1943–1952) and as the author of *Bibliography and Modern Book Production* (1954).[15]

Given the scope and impact of his work, it felt appropriate to recognise Freer's contributions as scholar, librarian and publisher by guiding his publication from the era of print into the contemporary world of digital communications in order to inspire future scholarship.

Notes

1 Percy Freer, *Bibliography and Modern Book Production: Notes and Sources for Student Librarians, Printers, Booksellers, Stationers and Book Collectors.* (Johannesburg: Wits University Press,1954), 181.
2 Henry Raikes, 'Foreword', in *Bibliography and Modern Book Production*, Percy Freer (Johannesburg: Wits University Press,1954), ix.
3 Isaac Isaacson, 'Building a Library', in *Wits Library: A Centenary History*, eds. Reuben Musiker and Naomi Musiker, 9–21 (Johannesburg: Scarecrow Books,1998).
4 Isaacson, 'Building a Library', 17.
5 Isaac Isaacson and Naomi Musiker, 'The Fire and Its Aftermath', in *Wits Library: A Centenary History*, eds. Reuben Musiker and Naomi Musiker, (Johannesburg: Scarecrow Books,1998), 27–29.
6 Margaret Anne Hutchings, *'Witwatersrand Univerity Press 1922–1969. Compiled from Minutes and Notes'.* Unpublished manuscript. 1980–1984.
7 Gueroni Renzo Bozzoli 'Foreword', in *Wits Library: A Centenary History*, eds.Rueben Musiker and Naomi Musiker (Johannesburg: Scarecrow Press, 1998), ix.
8 Hutchings, 22–23.
9 Hutchings, 35–36.
10 Hutchings, 115.
11 Naomi Musiker and Clare Walker, 'Education for Librarianship', in *Wits Librarian: A Centenary History*, eds. Reuben Musiker and Naomi Musiker (Johannesburg: Scarecrow Press, 1998), 151–155. They note that the course was offered until 1975.
12 Walter Wilson Greg, 'What is Bibliography?' in *Transactions of the Bibliographical Society 12*: 29–53,1914, in *An Introduction to Book History*, 2nd ed., eds. David Finkelstein and Alistair McCleery (London and New York: Routledge, 2013), 8.

13 Freer, *Bibliography and Modern Book Production*, 133, 145, 161. He comments on the development of the first moveable type was created from earthernware type in China in about 1050, the invention of paper by the Chinese around 103AD and later, Peruvian knot-writing.
14 David Finkelstein and Alistair McCleery. *An Introduction to Book History*, 2nd ed. (London and New York: Routledge, 2013), 9.
15 Reuben Musiker, 'The Period 1939–1960', 40.

Bibliography

Finkelstein, David and Alistair McCleery. *An Introduction to Book History*. 2nd ed. London and New York: Routledge, 2013.

Freer, Percy. *Bibliography and Modern Book Production: Notes and Sources for Student Librarians, Printers, Booksellers, Stationers, Booksellers*. Johannesburg: Wits University Press, 1954.

Hutchings, Margaret Anne. *Witwatersrand University Press 1922–1969. Compiled from Minutes and Files'*. Unpublished manuscript, 1980–1984.

Musiker, Rueben and Naomi Musiker. *Wits Library: A Centenary History*. Johannesburg: Scarecrow Books, 1998.

ACKNOWLEDGMENTS

I must firstly record early and practical encouragement received from the late Dr Henry Guppy, and again acknowledge to Dr Arundell Esdaile, C.B.E., a set of his Library Association Correspondence Course Papers (1925/6) that adumbrated "A Student's Manual of Bibliography". My good luck continued, for my former colleague at Birmingham, Mr Herbert Woodbine (retired 1945) later sent out to me a set of his Papers, the best I have ever seen, meticulously prepared in 1931/2 for the Correspondence Course of the Association of Assistant Librarians. Had he shaped his "Notes" for publication then, mine would have been superfluous. Indeed any value that these may have retained is very largely due to Herbert Woodbine. Any defects are, of course, my responsibility. Also to Dr H.R.Raikes, Vice-Chancellor and Principal of the University of the Witwatersrand, I am deeply indebted for placing at my disposal our considerable bibliographical resources, for financial aid, and the Foreword.

So many books and articles have been consulted in the preparation of these "Notes" that it is impossible to refer to all sources of information, nevertheless, my grateful thanks are offered to all those who have contributed in any way to their content.

It was my friends of the Dedication who urged me to seek, and helped me to obtain the permission of the South African Library Association to publish these "Notes", and so to meet the continual demands of students, past, present and, I hope, future.

Dame Fortune felicitously sent Mrs Vibeke Berg-Sonne to play the big rôle indicated on the title-page, and Miss Ilva Meier to undertake the final typing. To them I again extend my warmest thanks.

Johannesburg.
1 March 1953.   Percy Freer.

ERRATA

[160]	for	CLEETON, Glen V…	read	… Glen U…
[170]	"	Osborne,B.N:	"	Osborn, B.N.
[220]	"	CAPELLI…	"	CAPPELLI…
[342]	"	DODSON, M…	"	DOBSON, M.S:
[532]		DILL…	"	[532a]…
[595a]	"	NORTON…	"	ORTON…
[746] 1.2,	for	Baralme,	"	Barcelona: Libr.Palau.
[786] 1.2,	"	R.A. Rips,	"	R.E. Rips.
p.114,1.4,	"	Husing,	"	Husung…
p.124,1.10,	"	[92]	"	[792]
p.129n(4)	"	MORGAN	"	DE MORGAN:
p.141n(4)	"	BORHARDT	"	BORCHARDT:
p.142,1.3	"	Methelin's	"	Mentelin's…
p.144,1.6	"	Georg	"	George…
p.146,1.4	"	chloride	"	chlorine
p.182,1.24	"	Mansions	"	Mansion…
p.186n(2)	"	FUST	"	FURST:
p.231,1.17	"	Catherine de	"	Catharine de
p.233,1.12	"	Revière	"	Rivière…

FOREWORD

It gives me very great pleasure to write a foreword to Mr Freer's "Bibliography and Modern Book Production". Naturally I make no pretence to being a bibliographer; but what I do know is Mr Freer's intense interest in his subject.

Mr Freer was born in 1893 and entered the library world as a boy, at the age of 14, in the Birmingham Reference Library, and in 1909 the University Library. He was there till War Service took him away in 1914. On his return from the war he entered the University of Birmingham as a student graduating B.A. with Honours in 1922. After a period at the Norfolk and Norwich Library, Norwich, he came to the Union as Under-Librarian, South African Public Library, Cape Town, in 1926 and in 1929 was appointed Librarian of this University. He is retiring at the end of this year at his own request after 46 years in library work.

Ever since I came to know him in 1929 I have realized his immense keenness not only as a working librarian, but also as a student and teacher of bibliography. After Mr Freer had been at the University for two years we lost almost the whole of our book collection in a disastrous fire, but nothing daunted, he set to work again and assisted with the design of the new building, funds for the erection of which were provided by generous donors. At the same time he began once more to build up a book collection of which the University is rightly proud.

But Mr Freer has not limited his activities to the service of the University. All South African scholars are deeply indebted to him for his "Catalogue of Union Periodicals". He was also one of the prime movers in the establishment of the South African Library Association and has at all times devoted special attention to its Education Committee and the instruction of its students in Bibliography.

The present book is the outcome of his studies and his lecture notes, and I commend them to librarians both here and overseas as the essence distilled from a lifetime of experience in the subject.

H.R. Raikes, M.A.(Oxon)
Vice-Chancellor
University of the Witwatersrand

Johannesburg.
14.11.53.

INTRODUCTORY NOTE

Why another book on Bibliography? Because these "Notes" result from long experience as student, tutor, and examiner; because no one available book quite meets our requirements; because Esdaile, McKerrow, and Van Hoesen are scarce; and finally, because mine may now fill a real need. Their primary <u>purpose</u> is to guide the student while preparing himself for the relevant examinations of the library associations and schools of librarianship at home and abroad. Their <u>scope</u> approximates to that of "Final Bibliography and Modern Book Production" of the South African Library Association's Syllabus, and covers much of the (British) Library Association's Final - Part I, except that Book Selection of subject content is excluded. Historical Bibliography, Reference Work proper, as well as Subject Bibliographies escape detailed attention, but Form Bibliographies are included. The <u>arrangement</u> of the book has been designed to introduce the student from the outset to the literature of his subject, including the essential bibliographies. Simultaneously it aims at providing both a convenient and yet logical course of study.

It cannot be too strongly emphasized that <u>this is not a text-book</u> of bibliography, but only a guide to sources. The text offers the merest outline of its subject field. The student must make his choice from the books enumerated in Chapter II, and from the articles cited in the footnotes. The main reason for so large a selection is, of course, to offer a wide choice to those far removed from the bigger centres.

Additions, comments, corrections, and suggestions towards an improved, possibly illustrated edition are cordially invited. Meanwhile Papers. Type Faces, Methods of Illustration, Facsimiles, and Modern Fine Printing, are liberally <u>exemplified</u> in their respective chapters, and chosen mainly from the professional literature.

ADDENDA

p.18
[32a] BOSWELL, David B: Text-book on B. Grafton 1952.

p.20
[45a] ASSISTANT Librarian. See [80]

p.32
[151a] BINNS, Norman E: Introduction to historical B. Association of Assist.Librns. 1953.

p.33
[170a] MYRICK, Frank B: Primer of book production. N.Y: <u>Bookb.Bk Prod.</u> 1945.

p.34
[179a] GELB, Ignace Jay: Study of writing: the foundations of grammatology. Routledge (1952)
[181a] MOORHOUSE, Alfred Chas: Triumph of the alphabet; a history of writing. N.Y: Schuman [1953]
Enlarged version of his "Writing & the alphabet".

p.35
[192a] ĆERNÝ, Jaroslav: Papers & books in ancient Egypt… inaugural lecture, <u>etc</u>. H.K. Lewis (1952)

p.36
[204b] DIRINGER, D: The hand produced book. Hutchinson [1953?]

p.39
[247a] LANGWELL, W.H: Permanence of paper. Paper & Board Makers Res.Ass. T.B. 1 & 2. 1952.

p.41
[266a] ASSOCIATION Suisse des compositeurs… Guide du typographe romand… 2ed. Lausanne: L'Association 1948.
[272a] NEWELL, Leslie Fredk: Stereotyping & electrotyping. Pitman 1953. (<u>Printing Theory & Practice</u>)

p.42
[276a] ZUERCHER, Georges: Allgemeine Berufskunde für Buchdrucker; 3.verb…illus.Aufl. Bern: Verfasser 1947.
[283a] HOSTETTLER, Rudolf: Type: a selection of types - une selection de caractères d'imprimerie - eine Auswahl guter Drucktypen. St Gallen: The Author (1949) (<u>S.G.M. Books 2</u>)

p.43
[289a] STEER, Vincent: Printing design & layout…including…500 typefaces…with a foreword by Beatrice L. Warde; 4ed. Virtue 1951.
[296] COWELL, W.S., <u>firm</u>: Handbook of printing types (designed & written by John N.C. Lewis). The Firm (1947)

xxv

p.48
[360a] WEEKLEY, Montague: Oxford Univ.Pr. 1953.
[360b] BUCKLAND-WRIGHT, John: Etching & engraving: techniques & the modern trend. The Studio 1953.

p.51
[405a] BLUNT, Wilfrid: Art of botanical illustration. Collins 1950. (New Naturalist Ser.14)
[408a] STANILAND, Lancelot Norman: Principles of line illustration; with emphasis on the requirements of...scientific workers. Burke 1952.
[410a] GREENWOOD, Herbert Wm: Document photography. Focal Pr. (1943)

p.52
[411a] BRITISH Standards Institution: Recommendations for sizes...of sensitized photographic paper & materials...for document reproduction. The Instn. (B.S.1896: 1952)

p.57
[467a] BURBRIDGE, Peter Geo: Notes and references. Cambridge Univ. Pr. 1952. (Cambr.Authors' & Printers' Guides 4)
[470a] COLLISON, Rbt Lewis: Indexes & indexing, etc. Benn 1953.
[474a] ROYAL Society: General notes on the preparation of scientific papers. Publd for the R.SOC. by Cambridge Univ.Pr. 1950.

p.58
[486a] JOY, Thos: Bookselling. Pitman (1952)

p.59
[501a] GREAT BRITAIN. Board of Trade. [Text of the Universal copyright Convention] H.M.S.O. 1953. (Cmd 8912)
[502a] PINNER, H.L., ed: World's copyright; an encyclopaedia. Leyden: Sijthoff 1953- . 4v. In progress.
[505a] EWART, K: Copyright. Cambridge Univ.Pr. 1952. (Cambr. Authors' & Printers' Guides 5)

p.61
[521a] MCCOLVIN, Lionel: The personal library; a guide for the bookbuyer. Phoenix Ho. (1953)

P.66
[584a] MOORE, T. Sturge: Brief account of the origin of the Eragny Press. The Press 1903.

p.70
[629]   LINDSAY, W.M: Latin abbreviations.
"In 1908 he published as a St Andrews Univ...Publ.[V] Contractions in Early Latin Minuscule MSS, embodying partly his (subsequent) Sandars Lectures..."(H.J.Rose)[1]

p.75
[682a] LEWIS, Freeman: Paper-bound books in America. N.Y: Publ.Libr. 1952.

---

1   (Proc.Brit.Acad. 23:497,1937)

p.75
[683] ROSENBACH Abraham Simon Wolf, 1876-1952. Founded Fellowship...at the University of Pennsylvania.

p.83
[695] LONDON. Stationers' Company... Transcripts, etc;
[695a] repr. N.Y: P. Smith 1950. 5v. & 3v.

p.87
[717a] SOUTH African Public Library, Cape Town: Bibliography of African Bs; rev. to Feb.1948. Cape Town: The Libr. 1948. (Grey Bs 2)
Originally comp. in 1937 by P. Freer; expanded by D.H. Varley, & published in S.Afr.Libr. 10(2-3)38-42, 66-73 Oct. & Jan.1942-3 & maintained in Q.Bull.S.Afr. Libr.

p.92
ITALY
[745a] PAGLIAINI, Attilio: Catalogo generale della libreria italiana 1847-99. Milano: Associazione Tip.-Libr.Ital. 1901-22. 6v.
- 1 + Suppl. 1900-10+ ib.1912+

p.95
[763] MALCLÈS... Reviewed by A.D. Roberts in J.Document. 7(1) 188-91 Mar.1951; 9(1)63-9 Mar.1953.

p.98
[781a] COOK, Dorothy Elizabeth, & Monro, Isabel S., comp: Short story index...to 60,000 stories in 4,320 collections. N.Y: Wilson 1953. Supersedes Firkins.
[781b] COTTON, G.B., & Glencross, Alan: Fiction index: a guide to over 10,000 works of fiction, incl. short story collections, anthologies, & omnibus volumes...arranged under 2,000 subject headings, etc. Association of Assist.Librns 1953.

p.105
[820a] DOBELL, Bertram: Catalogue of books printed for private circulation. The Author 1906.
Privately Printed Books - Not for sale; German Nicht im Handel, privately printed & published. (cf. Harrod: Librarians'...[25] p.121) See also Bibliography. Chapter XIII here.

p.107
[830a] RECORD, P.D., ed: Index to theses accepted for higher degrees in (20) universities of Great Britain & Ireland. Aslib 1953+
v.1,1950-1, with 2,182 titles.

p.202n
(3) HARTNETT, John B: Xerography. (Print 7(5)9-15 Nov.1952)

p.206n
STRAUSS, Victor: Modern silk screen printing. (Print 7(5)21-36 Nov.1952)

xxvii

PART 1

BIBLIOGRAPHY

"...We are still more indebted to that neglected race, the BIBLIOGRAPHERS!"[1]

I

THE BIBLIOGRAPHERS DEFINE BIBLIOGRAPHY

The word BIBLIOGRAPHY comes from the Greek bibliographia. meaning book-writing.

The pioneer bibliographer, Johannes Tritheim, a cloistered monk, published his Liber de scriptoribus ecclesiasticis. Basle: Amberbach 1494. 300p. It is the first bio-bibliography (and a select, national bibliography) recording about 7,000 titles by about 1,000 medieval authors; arranged in chronological order, with a short account of each, followed by a list of their writings, and supplemented with an author index (by Christian names). This catalogue of ecclesiastical writers was used by Konrad Gesner in his Bibliotheca universalis, etc. Tiguri [Zürich] Froschauer 1545-55. v.1-3 and Appendix. About 2,600p.[2] This work was the most notable early attempt at an

---

1 D'ISRAELI: Curiosities of literature. Routledge 1886. P.502(1).
2 "The abridgers of Gesner's Bibliotheca ascribe the romance of Amadis to one Acuerdo Olvido: Remembrance, Oblivion. Not knowing that these two words, placed on the title-page of the French version of that book, formed the translator's Spanish motto!"(ib. p.120(1)).

universal bibliography, covering about 15,000 titles in Greek, Latin, and Hebrew, by about 3,000 authors. (Note that some 40,000 incunabula have survived). The arrangement is alphabetical, likewise by Christian names, and is provided with author and subject indexes.

	Sir James Murray[1] gives four meanings to the word Bibliography: 1. The writing of books. First so used in 1678
1678	by J. Phillips; 2. The systematic description and history of books, their authorship, printing, publication, editions, etc.
1814	First so used in 1814 by T.F. Dibdin; 3. A book containing
1838	such details. First so used in 1838 by Henry Hallam; 4. A list of the books of a particular author, printer, or country, or of those dealing with any particular theme; the literature of a
1869	subject. First so used in 1869 by W. Rowlands.

Below we have given other definitions in chronological order:

1802	A Bibliographer is one who makes a special study of the knowledge of books, of literary history, and of all that relates to the art of printing.[2]
1814	...Bibliography...denotes the knowledge of books, as it regards, 1, the <u>materials</u> of which they are composed, 2. the <u>subjects</u> discussed... 3. the knowledge of the different editions... and lastly...[their] classification.[3]

---

1 MURRAY: New English dictionary. Oxford: Clarendon Pr. 1888-1928. 10v. v.1 p.846(3).
2 PEIGNOT: Dictionnaire raisonné de bibliologie, &c. Paris: Renouard [1802-4] 3v. v.1 p.50.
3 HORNE: Introduction to the study of B., &c. Cadell & Davies 1814. p.viii, 27.

1821   In Germany bibliography belonged to literature alone and was treated as its handmaid and attendant.¹

1877   Bibliography as yet is a mere jackal, or packhorse, or some other patient beast of burden doomed to work for other arts and sciences, content with small emoluments for itself and smaller praise... Bibliography is fast becoming an exact science, and not a whit too soon.²

Bibliography...a well from which sprang, green and dripping, the living tree of knowledge. Unless bibliography is practised in the spirit of that conception it becomes a species of research which closely approaches sterility.³

To the two divisions of bibliography which are generally recognized, viz: Material, or Practical, and Intellectual, another is added which I term His- torical bibliography and place first as introductory. We have, then, these main divisions of the general subject: I. Historical bibliography. 1. Writing materials. 2. Classical MSS. 3. Revival of learning. 4. MSS of the Middle Ages and the beginnings of modern literature. 5. Invention of printing. 6. The early printers. 7. Libraries. II. Material, or Practical bibliography. 1. Denominations and sizes of books. 2. Mechanical execution of books (paper, type, illustrations, bindings, &c.). 3. Editions. 4. Catalogues. 5. The care of books. III. Intellectual bibliography. There are 8 lectures: 1. Classifications of knowledge... In the seven remaining lectures the main classes into which literature is divided are sub-divided to as great an extent as possible, and endeavor is made to name the best books in each of the

1866   sub-divisions...⁴

---

1 EBERT: Allgemeines bl. Lexikon. Leipzig: Brockhaus 1821-30. 2v. v.1 p.10. [687]
2 STEVENS: Photo-bibliography, &c. The Author 1878. p.16 & 44. (Also in: Trans.Conf.Libr. 1:70-81,1877, & Libr.J. 2:162-73,1877).
3 STEVENS as quoted by Wroth: (In: Standards...[125] p.106-7).
4 DAVIS: Teaching B. in colleges. (Libr.J. 11(8/9)p.290-2, 1886).

1892   "Bibliography" may be defined to be the study of the bodies of books and "Bibliology" as the study of their minds.[1]

Bibliography has been called the grammar of literary investigation.[2]

Dr Copinger in this article explained the two main branches of his day: the one referring to the contents of books he termed "Intellectual bibliography" or "Bibliology"; the other, treating of their external character and correct description, he termed "Material bibliography".

1893

1893   The object of bibliography is to bring a book, or a set of books, in their absence, as much as possible before the student. A perfect bibliography will not only give a full and exact description of a book...but also set before the student...an idea of the correspondence of the title with the contents, of the plan and arrangement, of the circumstances of production and of the place of the volume in the literature of the subject.[3]

1896   Bibliography is the science of books having relation to their production and most advantageous use and enjoyment, as connected with the successive stages of compilation, publication, registration and the more final stages of book-lists, special bibliographies, catalogues, indexes, etc. ...the arts of printing and binding are here included under the general term of "Publication".[4]

...The word bibliography is used in two somewhat different senses. In one it denotes technical book description; in the other it signifies enumeration of books treating of a subject... The former signification includes the latter...

---

1   THOMAS as quoted in Copinger: Inaugural address. (Trans.bl Soc. 1(1/2)p.3,1893)

2   COPINGER: Inaugural address. (ib.1(1/2)p.31-4)

3   MADAN: On method in B. (ib.p.91)

4   CAMPBELL: Theory of national & international B., &c. Libr.Bur. 1896. p.217.

1899 ...Just, then as biography follows from the existence of human beings, bibliography is the result of the existence of printed books. Bibliography is, in fact, the biography of books...[1]

1900 Two main divisions underlie the general study of bibliography...variously described as the intellectual and the material, the internal and the external, the literary and the mechanical. The first has reference to the contents of books. The second treats of their external characteristics - their forms, prices, names of printers, places of printing, history of particular copies, &c.[2]

1904 Bibliography: a list of books of a particular author, printer, place or period, or on any particular theme; the literature of a subject...as distinguished from a bibliography... Catalog; a list of books in some library or collaction.[3]

1906 For the purpose of this book the definition of bibliography as the science which treats of the description, cataloguing and presentation of books is ample... Bibliography is the science which relates to the history, materials and description of books in general...is universal, and considers the personal history of all the books.[4]

Present custom...recognizes as coming within its [Bibliography's] scope...the history of printing...bookbinding...book-illustration...and bookcollecting... The present article is only concerned with bibliography as the art of the examination, collation and description of books, their

---

1 FERGUSON: Some aspects of B. (Publ.Edinb.bl Soc. 4(1) p.9, 1899/1901). Also as Repr. Edinb: Johnston 1900.
2 GUPPY: Science of B. & what it embraces, &c. (Libr.Ass. Rec. 2:174,1900)
3 CUTTER: ...Rules for a dictionary catalog; 4ed. Washington: Govt Print.Off. 1904. p.15.
4 BROWN: Manual...[113]p.3–4.

1910- enumeration and arrangement...and...with the bibliography of bibliography.[1]

Whether such enumeration is a process in a science or not has never greatly troubled me, so long as it is done in a scientific spirit. It is essential work, and long usage has decided that the man who does it is called a bibliographer... What then is the business of the bibliographer? Primarily and essentially, I should say, the enumeration of books. His is the lowly task of finding out what books exist, and thereby helping to secure their preservation, and helping the specialist with information as to the extent of the subject-matter with which he has to deal.[2]

1911- Dr Greg divided bibliography into 3 branches: 1. Elements of bibliography... 2. Systematic bibliography... 3. Critical bibliography. The elements of bibliography include all the technical knowledge which is required for unravelling the history of books... Systematic bibliography consists of the description and classification of books according to some guiding principle... Systematic bibliography is often regarded as bibliography par excellence, but this is a mistake... For the contents of a book are no proper concern of the bibliographer... Critical bibliography is very nearly what is commonly meant by textual criticism... It is this branch of the science, Critical bibliography, which best deserves the name of "The grammar of literature"... Before the editor and student of literature can hope to win the favours of his mistress, Literature, he will have to win the favours of his mistress, Literature, he will have to seek good graces of her handmaid, bibliography...[3] (cf. Ebert,p.3 here).

---

1   POLLARD: B. & bibliology. (In: Encycl.Brit. 11ed. vol.3, p.908a)
2   - The aims of B. -Note. (Libr. s4,13(3)p.256-7,1932)
3   JOURNAL of the 20th session. (Trans.bl Soc. 12:10-2, 1911/3)

DEFINITIONS

1911-
The only bibliography which is really the business of the bibliographer is a bibliography of bibliographies... Strictly bibliographical investigations form three-fourth of textual criticism... Critical Bibliography is the science of the material transmission of literary texts...¹

Bibliography is an historical study, or...rather...a method of historical investigation.²

Bibliography is in no way particularly or primarily concerned with the enumeration or description of books... Bibliography has nothing to do with the subject matter of books, but only with their formal aspect... Bibliography is the study of books as material objects... Books are the material means by which literature is transmitted; therefore bibliography, the study of books, is essentially the science of the transmission of literary documents.³

I...regard bibliography as an inductive rather than a deductive science, with some analogy to biology... It is the end that enumeration is to subserve that determines whether a work is bibliographical or not... The work of enumeration is the task of students and specialists... it is not the task of the bibliographer.⁴

...the cataloguer...must come in the end to realize that it is this life-history of books that is the true study of the bibliographer, and that actual enumeration and description are only incidental... For in the ultimate resort the object of bibliographical study is...to reconstruct for each particular book the history of its life, to make it reveal in its most intimate detail the story of its birth and adventures as the material vehicle of the living word. As an extension of this follows the investigation of the methods of production in general and of the conditions of survival... Bibliography and textual criticism appear to interlock in a

---

1 GREG: What is B.? (Trans bl Soc. 12:46-8,1911/3)
2 - Present position of B. (Libr. s4,11(3)p.256.1930)
3 - B. - An apologia. (ib. s4,13(2)p.114-5.1932)
4 - The aims of B. (ib. s4,13(3)p.252-4)

manner that makes it difficult if not impossible to separate their respective fields and leads one to wonder whether it may not in the end be necessary to bring most textual criticism within the province of bibliography.[1]

(a) The science, that treats of books, their materials, authors, typography, editions, subjects, history, &c. and a bibliographer is one who has a knowledge of that science. (b) The art of the examination collation and description of books. (c) The science of the systematic description of recording of books, which have either a period, regional, subject, author, or other recognized relation to each other.[2]

1915

Bibliography claims as its province the consideration of all methods by which thought is transmitted from the mind of the author to the public, but more especially the perpetuation of thought, in these latter days, by means of the printing press.[3]

1916-

...modern bibliography becomes comparative as well as anatomical...Bibliography has at last come to stand upon a scientific basis...the time has come for a change in bibliographical methods...the work of "comparative bibliography" is that which we must now take up...[4]

Material Bibliography, by which we mean more particularly a detailed description of the work produced by the printer in converting the MS. of an author into the printed work...The ideal bibliography is that in which the author, as well as the printer, is recognized as having claims upon one's attention.[5]

---

1   GREG: The aims of B. (In: Bibliographical Soc...[600] p.27,30).
2   MUDGE: B. Chicago: Amer.Libr.Ass. 1915. p.2-3. (Prepr. of Man.of Libr.Econ. Chap.27).
3   COLE: Bl problems with a few solutions. (Pap.bl Soc.Amer. 10(3) p.124,1916).
4   - B. - A forecast. (ib. 14(1)p.16-8,1920).
5   - Bl method. (Atti Congr.mond.Bibl.Bibliogr. 1: Roma-Venezia. 2:288, 1929). 24 copies repr.1931.

1916
Bibliography may be defined as 1. the art of discovering book information and imparting this...to others; 2. by derivation, the...mass of compiled literature which contains this information, and 3.specifically, a compilation of book information relating to a particular person, place, thing, or period.[1]

1917
...Bibliography...is the foundation not only of the history of literature itself, but of all history, of science, and of the philosophy.[2]
He divides bibliography into Material bibliography and Literary, or Intellectual bibliography.

1922
...Bibliography can in no sense be described as a craft, it is rather a science...which treats of the description, cataloguing and preservation of books.[3]

1923
...Bibliography, i.e. the science of the organization of recorded knowledge [the records of knowledge]...Education, and Research...bibliography can play a humble but useful part.[4]

1926
We...define bibliography as the study of lists of literature; the lists themselves are generally termed bibliographies, and their use is called bibliographing (the action of consulting bibliographies).[5]

1927
There is much more in these modern methods of research than used to be understood by "bibliography"...but they belong rather to the sphere of textual criticism than to formal bibliography.[6]

---

1 FEIPEL: Elements of B. (Pap.bl Soc.Amer. 10(4)p.177,1916) Also pubd as a separate by Univ.of Chi.Pr.
2 MURRAY: B: its scope & methods, &c. Glasgow: Maclehose 1917. P.9.
3 HODGSON: B. (Stationers' Co. Craft Lectures. 1 ser. p.62, 1922/3)
4 HULME: Statistical .... [635] p.9 & 44.
5 SCHNEIDER: Theory... 1926.[131] p.16.
6 MCKERROW: Introduction... [36] p.2-3.

1928
Bibliography is the science of books...the organization of the records of knowledge, but not the philosophic, encyclopedic, scientific organization of knowledge itself...rather a subordinate, an auxiliary to each individual branch of study...Bibliography is divided into 1. Historical, dealing with the history of book production...2. Bibliothecal, concerned with the collection, preservation and organisation of books in libraries...3. Enumerative, including lists of books...4. Practical, dealing with the methods of work of student and author...[1]

1929
...it has become clear...that the historian and critic of literature ignores the science of bibliography at his peril... Bibliography is a systematic study of the writing, printing and binding of books, their formats, editions, dates, relationships, and textual problems. Latterly indeed the science of bibliography has been used as a new instrument of precision in resolving the authority of variant texts.[2]

1931
Bibliography is an art and also a science. The art is that of recording books; the science, necessary to it, is of the making of books and of their extant record...Bibliographical method falls into two halves. The first is analytical, the second systematic...Dr Greg uses the term "critical", I have preferred "analytical" as not so liable to suggest that the bibliographer's function includes appraisal of the contents of books...Historical bibliography is beyond [my] scope...But some idea should be given of its great importance.[3]

Although not entirely satisfactory, bibliography is a preferable designation for the science of organizing knowledge.[4]

---

1 VAN HOESEN & WALTER: B...[38] p.1,3.
2 WILLIAMS: Book clubs...[603] p.104.
3 ESDAILE: Student's...[34] p.13,18,20.
4 VAN PATTEN: Future of cataloging. (Bull.Amer.Libr.Ass. 25(9) p.506,1931)

1932

Bibliography: 1. The study or account of the history of books from the external side as distinct from their subject matter; description of the making up of books, the various editions and impressions and the differences which distinguish these. 2. List of books and writings dealing with a particular subject, or written by a particular author.[1]

1935

I define...a bibliography as 'a list of books arranged according to some permanent principle'.[2]

1939

We have three kinds of study involving the description of books...first, textual bibliography or the detailed study of the material form...secondly historical bibliography or the study of book production...in general; and thirdly subject bibliography or the cataloguing...of material as preliminary to the study of a subject.[3]

Bibliography is the correct description of books, and not all the many other things unmercifully linked with it.[4]

1941

...if bibliography is the study of "the material transmission of literary texts" [Greg, p.6 here] it is concerned both with the material objects by which they are transmitted - printers' tools as well as books and their components, and with the human activities which transmit them...and it is to the group of organized human activities...loosely known as "history and the social sciences" that bibliography belongs...The nearest approximation to a scientific law in bibliography is probably the principle of the forme-unit.[5]

---

1 WYLD: Universal dictionary of the English language. Routledge 1932. p.100(1)
2 BESTERMAN: Beginnings...[105] p.2.(cf. Greg, p.6-7 here)
3 COWLEY: B1...[126] p.7.
4 PALTSITS: B., the correct description of books. (Proc. inter-Amer.bl & Libr.Ass. 2:39,1939)
5 BALD: Evidence & inference in B. (Eng.Inst.Annu. 1941. p.162-4)

BIBLIOGRAPHY

1945

To a certainty a bibliographical critic seldom aspires, but by the exercise of his critical skill he can at least say where the possibilities lie, and give an honest reason for the faith, that is in him; nor will he rest content until by the use of this Novum Organum of critical bibliography he has deduced from the available evidence all that can be discovered about the material means of textual transmission and has presented his conclusions for an editor to build on.[1]

1948-

Perhaps we can compile enumerative but write descriptive bibliographies...The bibliography assimilated in the usual library school course is of a different nature from the training necessary to answer with exactness the numerous questions which a descriptive bibliographer has to ask...[2]

The methods of descriptive bibliography seem to have evolved from a triple purpose: (a) to furnish a detailed, analytical record of the physical characteristics of a book... (b) to provide an analytical investigation and an ordered arrangement of these physical facts...(c) to approach both literary and printing or publishing history through the investigation and recording of appropriate details in a related series of books. Descriptive bibliographies serve as the permanent repository not merely for the "important"...but for the relatively complete facts about the physical dress of a text...They are the foundation for literary history, and may indeed be literary histories in themselves...Analytical bibliography deals with books and their relations solely as material objects, and in a strict sense has nothing to do with the historical or literary considerations of their subject matter or content...It is...the basic function of a descriptive bibliography to present all the evidence about a book which can be determined by analytical bibliography applied to a material object. Supplementary to this primary function is the presentation of collateral "bibliographical" evidence without confusion between the two.[3]

Bibliography, pure B. &. literary studies.[4]

---

1 WILSON: Shakespeare & the 'new B.' (In: Bibliographical Soc... [600] p.121)
2 BOWERS: Certain basic problems in descriptive B. (Pap.bl Soc.Amer. 42(3)p.212,216, 1948)
3 - Principles... [124] p.vii,14-5,31,34.
4 - (Pap.bl Soc.Amer. 46(3)186-208 July/Sep.1952)

1949

A bibliography is a compilation of information regarding recorded sources of information.[1]
(cf. Hulme, p.9 here).

"Librarianship is that branch of learning which has to do with the recognition, collection, organisation, preservation and utilisation of graphic and printed records..." What is this in a single word? Surely the answer is bibliography. Bibliography indeed is the alpha and omega of all that is comprised in our definition...Bibliography is the study of the book throughout its life...[2]

Bibliography is not so much an end in itself as it is an ancillary investigation to the study of the text (be it literary, historical, or scientific)...the bibliographer...expects to be informed of three basic facts: 1. what edition does the book belong to, 2. what are the principles of its physical construction, and 3. what does the volume contain...the subject-matter itself...can be valuable bibliographical evidence.[3]

...the end of bibliographical analysis is the elucidation of the history of texts. It follows that bibliography is not an end but a means, a process in the study of the transmission of texts...'Fulldress bibliography' is the complete listing and analysis of the literature of a subject, the works of an individual, the production of a press the possessions of a private collector, or of a small library.[4]

---

1 EVANS: B. by co-operation. (Bull.med.Libr.Ass. 37(3) p.198,1949)
2 IRWIN: Librarianship; essays on applied bibliography. Grafton 1949. p.62.
3 BUHLER: (In: Standards...[125] p.8-9,38)
4 WROTH: (ib. p.105,107)

"We have never seen a perfect catalogue."[1]

II

LITERATURE OF BIBLIOGRAPHY AND MODERN BOOK PRODUCTION

This chapter is arranged as the main body of the <u>Note-book</u>. Books only are entered here; periodical articles are entered as footnotes.

GENERAL.

1. Bibliographies.

[1]   BURTON, Margaret, and Vosburgh, Marion E: Bibliography of librarianship, <u>etc.</u> Library Ass. 1934.
      Excludes material in Slavonic & Oriental languages.

[2]   CANNONS, Harry G.T: Bibliography of library economy; a classified index to the professional periodical literature...1876-1920. Chicago: American Libr.Ass. 1927.
      Superseded by <u>Libr.Lit</u>.[10]. led. published 1910.

[3]   COLE, George Watson: Index to bibliographical papers published by the Bibliographical Society and the Library Association...1877-1932. Chicago: Bibliographical Soc.of Amer. (1933)

---

1   STEVENS: Historical nuggets. Stevens 1862-85. 3v. v.3 p.[?]

[4] CROSS, Tom Peete, comp. Bibliographical guide to English studies; 10ed. Chicago Univ.Pr. 1951.

[5] GRAHAM, Bessie: Bookman's manual; a guide to literature; 6ed.,rev...by Hester R. Hoffman. N.Y: Bowker 1948.

[6] HANDBUCH der Bibliothekswissenschaft; hrsg. von Georg Leyh; 2Aufl. Stuttgart: Koehler 1950+
lAufl. by Fritz Milkau was published 1931-40. 3v.

[7] HART, Horace: Bibliotheca typographica...a list of books about books...introd. by G.P. Winship.
Rochester, N.Y: Hart 1933.

[8] INTERNATIONALE Bibliographie des Buch- und Bibliothekswesens. Neue Folge. Leipzig: Harrassowitz 1,1926+ Erste Folge (Bibliographie des Bibliotheks- und Buchwesens 1904-12; 1922-5 (published 1925-7) was published as a Suppl. to Zbl.BiblWesen.[104]. None published since 15,1940.

[9] LEXIKON des (gesamten) Buchwesens; hrsg. von Karl Löffler und Joachim Kirchner, unter Mitwirkung von Wilhelm Olbrich. Leipzig: Hiersemann 1935-7. 3v.
"Manul" reprint advertised by Breslauer in 1952.

[10] LIBRARY Literature. N.Y: Wilson 1921/32+ 1921/32 published by the Amer.Libr.Ass. Abstracts books, pamphlets & articles from about 100 professional periodicals. 3-yearly cumulation (except 1940/6 published in 1 vol.). Dictionary arrangement.

[11] LIBRARY Science Abstracts. Library Ass. 1950+
Quarterly. Each number contains about 50 abstracts arranged under broad subject headings. Abstracts about 50 periodicals. Annual author and subject index.

[12] NATIONAL Book League: Catalogue of the library. Cambridge Univ.Pr. 1944.
Ed. 1-er3 called: Books about books.

[13] ULRICH, Carolyn F., and Küp, Karl: Books and printing; a selected list of periodicals 1800-1942. Woodstock, Vt: Rudge; N.Y: Public Library 1943.

[14] VEREENIGING ter Bevordering van de Belangen des Boekhandels: Catalogus der bibliotheek. Amsterdam: Nijhoff 1920-49. 6v.

[15] VORSTIUS, Joris: Ergebnisse und Fortschritte der Bibliographie in Deutschland seit dem ersten Weltkrieg. Leipzig: Harrassowitz 1948.
Also as Zbl.BiblWesen.[104] Beiheft 74.

[16] YEAR'S Work in Librarianship. Library Ass. 1928+
Not a formal B. but essays on what the reviewers thought best in the preceding year's professional literature at home & abroad.

See also BiblLeven.[51]; J.Docum.[77]; Rev.Docum.[97]; & Zbl.BiblWesen.[104].

2. Study and Teaching.

[17] BROWN, James Duff, ed: Guide to librarianship; a series of reading lists, etc. Libraco 1909.

[18] COLUMBIA University. School of Library Service: Syllabus for the study of bibliography, etc; 4ed. prepared by M. Hutchins. N.Y: The School 1947.

[19] GREENHOOD, David, and Gentry, Helen: Chronology of books and printing; rev.ed. N.Y: Macmillan 1936.

[20] KRABBE, Wilhelm: Bibliographie, etc; 6Aufl. Hamburg: Stichnote 1951.

[21] WILLIAMS, Reginald Gordon: Courses of study in library science; being the assistants' guide to librarianship; 2.rev. & enl. ed. Bolton: Central Press 1926.

3. Terminology.

[22] BOOKMAN'S Glossary; 3ed. N.Y: Bowker 1951. 2ed. 1931 by J.A. Holden; 3ed. re-written by a committee of 6 experts. Gives definitions. Includes list of city & trade names, & list of proof-readers' marks.

[23] COWLES, Barbara, ed: Bibliographers' glossary of foreign words and phrases...comp. from 20 languages. N.Y: Bowker 1935.
In one alphabet. Gives translations only.

[24] FUMAGALLI, Giuseppe, ed: Vocabolario bibliografico. Firenze: Olschki 1940. (Biblioteca di bibliografia italiana 16)
Gives definitions.

[25]   HARROD, Leonard Montague, <u>ed</u>: Librarians' glossary, <u>etc.</u> Grafton 1938.
Gives definitions.

[26]   INTERNATIONAL Congress of Publishers: Vocabulaire technique de l'editeur en sept langues: français, deutsch, English, español, hollandisch, italiano, magyar. Berne: Congrès int.des Editeurs 1913.
Contains about 3,500 words.

[27]   MOTH, Axel, ed: Glossary of library terms, English, Danish, Dutch, French, German, Italian, Spanish, Swedish. Boston Book Co. 1915. (<u>Useful reference series</u> 10)
Definitions in the English part.

[28]   - Technical terms used in bibliographies and by the book and printing trades. Boston Book Co. 1915.
Definitions in English part. Bound with Walter [32]

[29]   PINTO, Olga, <u>ed</u>: Termini d'uso nelle bibliografie dei periodici; saggio comp. in 38 lingue. Roma: Bardi 1929.
Comp. for first Congresso mondiale delle biblioteche e di bibliografia.

[30]   THOMPSON, Elizabeth Hardy, <u>ed</u>: A.L.A. Glossary of library terms, <u>etc</u>. Chicago: American Libr.Ass. 1943.
Gives definitions.

[31]   UNESCO: Vocabularium bibliothecarii; begun by Henri Lemaître, rev. & enl. by Anthony Thompson. Paris: Unesco 1953. (<u>Unesco bl Hdbks 2</u>)
First classified dictionary for librarians, containing about 2,500 terms, in 3 parallel columns, English, French, & German, with separate alphabetical index for each language.

[32]   WALTER, Frank Keller, <u>ed</u>: Abbreviations and technical terms used in book catalogs and in bibliographies; rev. ed. Boston Book Co. [1919]
First issued 1912; 1915, 1917, 1919 eds bound with Moth [28].

4. **Books covering the whole Subject.**

[33]   CIM, Albert: Le livre, <u>etc</u>. Paris: Flammarion 1905-8. 5v.
An enlargement of: Une bibliothèque.

[34] ESDAILE, Arundell: Student's manual of bibliography; (2ed.). Allen & Unwin; Library Association 1932.
New ed., rev. by Roy Stokes, announced 1952.

[35] LIBRARY Association: Book construction. Library Ass. 1931.

[36] MCKERROW, Ronald Brunlees: Introduction to bibliography for literary students; repr. Oxford: Clarendon Pr. 1948.

[37] MALLABER, K.A: Bibliography. A.A.L. In preparation.

[38] VAN HOESEN, Henry Bartlett, and Walter, Frank Keller: Bibliography, practical, enumerative, historical, etc. N.Y: Scribner's 1928.
Repr. 1929 & 1937. Being revised by Van Hoesen.

5. Periodicals.

Periodicals covering all subjects of the Note-book, except Copyright and Publishing, are entered here.

[39] ALPHABET and Image. Art & Technics 1945-8. 8 nos.
Alph.Image.
A. & I. was to be split up into 2 periodicals: Alphabet, covering the typographic arts, and Image, to cover the arts, the first of which has not yet appeared. Superseded Typography [102]. Analysed in St Bride: Fdn Cat...[150].

[40] AMERICAN Documentation. Cambridge, Mass: American Inst. of Docum. 1,1950+ Amer.Docum.
Each no. contains abstracts.

[41] AMERICAN Library Association. A.L.A. Bulletin. Chicago: American Libr.Ass. 1,1907+ A.L.A.Bull.
1-32, 1907-38: Bulletin. Appears 11 times a year, mainly on administrative aspects of public libraries.

[42] - Proceedings. Chicago: American Libr.Ass. 1,1876+
Proc.Amer.Libr.Ass.
1-51,1876-1929: Papers & proceedings. 1-28 also in Libr.J. [82] 1876-9,1883; 29+ in the above. Not issued for 1878, 1880, 1884.

[43]   ANNUAL of Bookmaking. N.Y: The Colophon 1928/37-38. 2v.   Colophon.
Contemporary American bookmaking; affiliated with Colophon [63]

[44]   ASLIB Information. Association of Spec.Libr. & Inform. Bur. 1,1929+   ASLIB Inform.
Each no. contains Recent Papers & Library Accessions.

[45]   ASLIB Proceedings. Association of Spec.Libr. & Inform. Bur. 1,1948+   ASLIB Proc.
Published jointly by ASLIB & the British Society for international Bibliography after their amalgamation. Supersedes the Proceedings published by these bodies before 1948. Quarterly. Papers usually followed by extensive Bs. 1948-51 contained papers presented at ASLIB meetings only.

BIBLIO. See [745]

BIBLIOGRAPHIC Index. See [767]

[46]   BIBLIOGRAPHICA. K. Paul 1895-7. 3v.   Bibliographica.
"A classic of the book arts". (Ulrich)

[47]   BIBLIOGRAPHICAL Society: Illustrated monographs. The Soc. 1,1894+   Illus.Monogr.bibliogr.Soc.

[48]   - Transactions. The Soc. 1892-1919. 15v; s2 1,1920+ s2 published in Libr.[79].   Trans.bibliogr.Soc.
- Cole: Index...See [3]

[49]   BIBLIOGRAPHICAL Society of America: News sheet. N.Y: The Soc. 1,1926+   News sheet.bibliogr.Soc.Amer.
Includes notes of Bibliographies in preparation, and its Proceedings.

[50]   - Papers. N.Y: The Soc. 1,1904/6+   Pap.bibliogr.Soc.Amer.
1-3 as its Proceedings & Papers. Americana mostly. Published Quarterly. Good reviews.

[51]   BIBLIOTHEEKLEVEN. Rotterdam: Centrale Ver. voor openbare Leeszalen en Bibl. 1,1916+   BiblLeven.
Supersedes Maandbl.BiblWesen. Each no. contains reviews of professional literature, resumé of contents of about 20 professional journals & list of professional literature added to the K.Bibliotheek.

[52] BOEK. Den Haag: Nijhoff 1912+ Boek.
Dutch bibliography & fine printing; ns27 contains an index of Boek, Bibliogr.Adversaria, & Tijdschr.voor Boek- en BiblWesen from their beginnings.

[53] BOOK Collector. Book Centre 1,1947+ Book Coll.
Quarterly. 1947-51: Handb.

[54] BOOK Collector's Packet; a monthly review of fine books, bibliography, typography and kindred literary matters. Chicago: Black Cat Pr. 1932/3-1945/6. 4v. Book Coll.Packet.
1-2 also as (1-20); suspended Aug.-Nov.1933, 1934- Mar.1938, 1940-5.

[55] BOOK-Collector's Quarterly. First Ed.Cl. 1930-5. 17 nos.
Book-Coll.Quart.
Ed. by A.J.A. Symons & D. Flower. "One of the great bibliographical periodicals" (Ulrich)

[56] BOOKBINDING and Book Production. N.Y: Bookbinding and Book Prod. 1,1925+ Bookb.Bk.Prod.
1-24(2)1925-Aug.1937: Bookbinding Mag. Monthly. Contains reviews of books on bookbinding & book production, & of specimens.

[57] BOOKMAN. Hodder & Stoughton 1891-1934. 87v.
Bookman.
Merged into London mercury, later merged into Life & letters. Contained reviews of contemporary literature, but also articles on aspects of book production.

[58] BOOKS. National Book Leag. 1,1929+ Books.
(1-183)1929-44 as the League's News sheet. Contains N.B.L. announcements, articles on specific subjects, in reality informal Bibliographies, also including foreign writers. 1950-1 had a series of articles by J. Thorp called "A beginner's guide to bookmaking".

BOOKSELLER. See [703]

BRITISH Book News. See [752]

[59] BRITISH Printer. MacLean-Hunter 1,1888+ Brit.Print.
Issued 6 times a year. Sub-title varies. Contains reviews of new books for the printer, & of specimens.

[60] BRITISH Society for international Bibliography: Proceedings. The Soc. 1939-47. 9v. Proc.Brit.Soc.int.Bibliogr.

Merged into ASLIB Proc.[45]

[61]　　BULLETIN for Libraries. Paris: UNESCO 1,1947+
　　　　　　　　　　　　　　　　　　　　　　　Bull.Libr.
　　　　Issued monthly with English & French text on opposite pages.
　　　　Contains UNESCO announcements (also a Reader's guide
　　　　to UNESCO Publ.), reviews, publications wanted, exchanges
　　　　wanted, copies for free distribution.
　　　　1951+ contains: Progress in bibliographical services.

　　　　BULLETIN de Documentation bibliographique. See [766]

　　　　BULLETIN of Bibliography. See [764]

[62]　　CAMBRIDGE Bibliographical Society: Transactions. The
　　　　Soc. 1,1949+　　　　　　　　　　　Trans.Cambr.bibliogr.Soc.

[63]　　COLOPHON; a quarterly for bookmen. N.Y: Pynson Printers
　　　　1-5(1-20)1930-5; ns 1-3(4)1935-8; ns(s3)1(1-4)1939/40.
　　　　　　　　　　　　　　　　　　　　　　　Colophon.
　　　　Sub-title varies; superseded by New Colophon [87]

　　　　CURRENT Lit... See [704]

[64]　　DOCUMENT Reproductie. Oegstgeest: Nederlands Genoot.
　　　　voor Docum.Repr. 1,1947+　　　　　　　　Docum.Repr.
　　　　Much technical information.

[65]　　DOLPHIN; a periodical for all people who find pleasure in fine
　　　　books. N.Y: Limited Ed.Cl. 1933-41. 4v.　　　　Dolphin.
　　　　"The outstanding American publication on the book" (Ulrich).
　　　　1-3 analysed in St Bride Fdn: Cat... [150]

[66]　　ERASMUS; international bulletin of contemporary scholar-
　　　　ship. Basel: Prometheus Druck 1947+　　　　　Erasmus.
　　　　Published 6 times a year. Reviews in the main languages
　　　　publications in the humanities arranged under broad subject
　　　　headings.

　　　　F.I.D. Communications. See Rev.Docum. [97]

[67]　　F.I.D. Informations. Fédération Int.de Docum. 1951+ News
　　　　items.　　　　　　　　　　　　　　　　　　F.I.D.Inform.

[68]　　FLEURON; a journal of typography. Cambridge Univ.Pr.
　　　　1923-30, 7v.　　　　　　　　　　　　　　　　Fleuron.
　　　　Annual; not published 1929; 1923-5 ed. by Oliver Simon;
　　　　1926-30 by Stanley Morison. Index to all vols at end of vol.7.
　　　　"A significant, learned and copiously documented periodical"
　　　　(Ulrich). Analysed in St Bride Fdn: Cat... [150]

[69] GRAPHIS; international journal for graphic and applied art. Zürich: Graphis Pr. 1,1944+   Graphis.
Published 6 times a year.

[70] GUTENBERG Jahrbuch. Mainz: Gutenberg Ges. 1,1926+
Gutenberg Jb.
Articles on rare books, fine printing, calligraphy, & binding, in the main languages.

[71] IMPRIMATUR; a literary quarterly for bibliophiles. Cinncinnati: Evanston Stat. 1,1947+ Imprimatur. (Cinn.)

[72] IMPRIMATUR; ein Jahrbuch für Bücherfreunde. Hamburg: Gesellschaft der Bibliophilen 1,1930+ ?   Imprimatur.(Hamb.)

[73] IMPRINT. Imprint Publishing Co. 1913. 9 nos.   Imprint.
No issues for Sep.-Oct. Gerard Meynell of the Westminster Press (founded by Lord Douglas 1878) started the Imprint, "Short-lived but influential periodical, for which a type-face of the same name was made, & in which Stanley Morison...makes his first appearance." (Greenhood: Chron... [19])

[74] INLAND Printer. Chicago: MacLean-Hunter 1,1883+
Reviews of specimens.   Inl.Print.

[75] INTERNATIONAL Printing. Norwich: Jarrold 1,1945+
Int.Print.
Irregular, each no. being devoted to a specific subject.

INTERNATIONALE B.d.Buch- u. BiblWesens. See [8]

INTERNATIONALER Jber.d.B. See [765]

[76] JOHN Rylands Library: Bulletin. Manchester: The Libr. 1903-8,1914+   Bull.John Rylands Libr.
1:Quart.Bull; 1904-8 annu; 1914+ half-yearly. Of value for bibliographers, palaeographers & literary students. Very often contains bibliographies of material in the Library.

[77] JOURNAL of Documentation. Association of Spec.Libr.& Inform.Bur. 1,1945+   J.Docum.
Quarterly. Long articles on bibliography & special library problems. Reviews of reference books & professional literature. Each no. contains the "Documentation Survey" of articles on documentation, excluding those dealing with public libraries & school libraries, with short abstracts.

[78] LIBRARIAN and Book World. Clarke & Co. 1,1910+
<u>Libr.& Bk World.</u>
1-2(9)1910-Apr.1912: <u>Libr.</u>; suspended Oct.1919-Sep. 1920. Appears monthly & contains short reviews of books for libraries as well as longer ones of professional literature, also gramophone notes.

[79] LIBRARY. Oxford Univ.Pr. 1-10 1889-99; ns 1-10 1899-1909; s3, 1-10 1910-9; s4,1-26 1920-46; s5,1,1946+ <u>Libr.</u>
Supersedes <u>Libr.Chron.</u>; sub-title varies. June 1920+ contains <u>Trans.bibliogr.Soc.</u> [48]. A scholarly, quarterly review, mainly dealing with bibliography. Reviews of books on bibliography.

[80] LIBRARY Assistant. Association of Assistant Librarians. 1, 1898+ <u>Libr.Assistant.</u>
Mainly of interest for students & young librarians; about 10 times a year. Reviews professional literature & examination papers. 46(1)1953+ <u>Assistant Librn.</u>

LIBRARY Association. Cole: Index... See [3]

[81] LIBRARY Association Record. Library Ass. 1-24 1899-1922; ns 1-8 1923-30; s3 1-3 1931-3; s4 1,1934+ <u>Libr.Ass.Rec.</u>
Supersedes the Ass's <u>Monthly notes.</u> Mainly on problems of interest to public libraries. Some reviews of books on public library problems.

[82] LIBRARY Journal. N.Y: Bowker 1,1876+ <u>Libr.J.</u>
Fortnightly. Reviews books for the library (also children's books), current films, audio-visual material, & gramophone records. V.1-25 also available on microcards.

LIBRARY Literature. See [10]

[83] LIBRARY Quarterly. Chicago Univ.Grad.Library School 1,1931+ <u>Libr.Quart.</u>
Scholarly, long reviews.

LIBRARY Science Abstracts. See [11]

[84] LIBRI. Copenhagen: Munksgaard 1951+ <u>Libri.</u>
Treats of great & learned libraries, history & collecting of books. Reviews.

[85] LONDON School of Printing and kindred Trades: Yearbook. The Sch. 1922/3+   Yearb.Ldn Sch.Print.
Includes the Suppl: Printing trade craft lectures, which supersedes Stationers' Co's craft lectures (sl-10 1922-30?). Analysed in St Bride Fdn: Cat... [150]

[86] MONOTYPE Recorder. Monotype Corp. 1901+
    Monotype Rec.
For the users of monotype machines. Useful for the history of printing types. 1923-40 analysed in St Bride Fdn: Cat... [150]

[87] NEW Colophon; a book-collectors' quarterly. N.Y: Duschnes Crawford 1,1948+   New Colophon.
Supersedes Colophon [63]

[88] NEW York. Public Library: Bulletin. N.Y: The Libr. 1,1897+
    Bull.N.Y.publ.Libr.
Monthly. Nearly every no. contains a list of new periodicals added to the Library. Many Bs of American & general interest appeared here first, & later as reprints. Index 1-40,1897-1936.

[89] OXFORD Bibliographical Society: Proceedings and papers. Oxford: The Soc. 1,1922+   Proc.Pap.Oxf.bibliogr.Soc.

[90] PAPER and Print. Stonhill & Gillis 1,1928+   Paper & Print.
Sub-title varies. Articles on papermaking, paper in its relation to printing, & the uses of boards, etc. Some reviews. Samples of papers.

[91] PENROSE Annual; a review of the graphic arts. Lund Humphries 1,1895+   Penrose Annu.
1: Process work yearbook; 2-3,7-8: Process yearbook; 4-6,9-19: Penrose's pictorial annual; suspended 1917-9, 1941-8. In short articles treats new developments in printing processes, new types, illustrative processes, etc.

[92] PRINT; a quarterly journal of the graphic arts. Hartsdale, N.Y: Rudge 1,1940+   Print.
From 6(4) incl. The Print collector's quarterly. Analysed in St Bride Fdn: Cat... [150]

[93] PRINTING, Packaging & Allied Trades Research Association: Bulletin. The Ass. 1,1938+   PATRA Bull.
Irregular. Research in progress.

[94]   PRINTING, Packaging & Allied Trades Research Association: PATRA journal. The Association 1,1937+   PATRA J.
- Printing abstracts. See [149]

[95]   PRINTING Review. Printing Rev. 1td. 1,1931+   Print.Rev.
Quarterly.

[96]   PRODUCTION Yearbook; the reference manual of the graphicarts. N.Y: Colton Pr. 1,1934+   Prod.Yearb.
Title varies. The American equivalent of Penrose's Annu. [91]

PUBLISHERS' Circular. See [700]

PUBLISHERS' Weekly. See [711]

[97]   REVUE de la Documentation/Review of documentation. Den Haag: Fédération Int. de Docum. 1,1934+   Rev.Docum.
1-5 1934-8: I.I.D. Communications; 6-13 1939-46: F.I.D. Communications. Pubd about 6 times a year. Articles on international documentation in English, French & German. Each no. contains "Bibliographia": abstracts of books & periodical articles dealing with Documentation & Bibliography in all subjects.

[98]   SIGNATURE; a quadrimestrial of typography and graphic arts. Signature (1-15)1935-40; ns 1,1946+   Signature.
Ed. by Oliver Simon & printed at the Curwen Press.

[99]   SOUTH African Libraries/Suid-Afrikaanse Biblioteke. Johannesburg: South Afr.Libr.Ass. 1,1933+   S.Afr.Libr.
Quarterly.

[100] TIMES, The: Times literary supplement. The Times 1,1902+
Weekly. Reviews.   Tms lit.Suppl.

[101] TYPOGRAPHICA; contemporary typography and graphic arts. Lund Humphries 1,1949+   Typographica.
3 issues p.a.

[102] TYPOGRAPHY. Shenval Pr. 1936-9. 8 nos.   Typography.
Superseded by Alph.Image.[39]. Analysed in St Bride Fdn: Cat...[150]

[103] WILSON Library Bulletin. N.Y: Wilson 1,1914+
                                               Wilson Libr.Bull.
1-13(10)1914-Jun.1939: Wilson Bull. 10 nos a year. "Current reference books" in each.

YEAR'S Work in Librarianship. See [16]

[104] ZENTRALBLATT für Bibliothekswesen. Leipzig: Harrassowitz 1,1884+ <u>Zbl.BiblWesen.</u>
"Neue Bücher und Aufsätze zum Bibliotheks- und Buchwesen" (Rudolf Blum, <u>comp.</u>) as a current feature; ed. by Joris Vorstius.

BIBLIOGRAPHIES (Chapter III)

[105] BESTERMAN, Theodore: Beginnings of systematic bibliography; 2.rev.ed. Oxford Univ.Pr. [1936]

[106] COLLISON, Rbt L: Bibliographies. Crosby Lockwood 1951.

[107] PINTO, Olga: Bibliografie nazionali; 2ed. Firenze: Olschki 1951. (<u>Biblioteca di bibliografia italiana</u> 20)

[108] SHORES, Louis: Basic reference books; 2ed. Chicago: American Libr.Ass. 1939.
3ed. <u>in preparation.</u>

[109] UNESCO. <u>International conference on the improvement of bibliographical Services</u>: General report. Paris: UNESCO 1950.

[110] - Library of Congress bibliographical Survey: (1) Bibliographical services, their present state & possibilities of improvement, ib. 1950.

[111] - (2) National development and international planning of bibliographical services, ib. 1950.
These 2 reports contain summaries of reports only. Complete text available on microfilm.

See also Cowley: B1...[126] p.214-8; Esdaile: Student's ...[34] p.272-348; Schneider: Theory...[131]; Van Hoesen: B...[38] p.180-258, as well as the relevant Bs listed in chapter III.

COMPILATION AND ARRANGEMENT OF BIBLIOGRAPHIES (Chapter IV)

1. <u>General.</u>

[112] BRITISH Standards Institution: Bibliographical references. (<u>B.S.</u> 1629:1950).

[113] BROWN, Jas Duff: Manual of practical bibliography. Routledge [1906]

[114] BROWN, Zaidee: Library key, etc; 7ed. N.Y: Wilson 1948. p.81-91.

[115] CONNER, Martha: Practical bibliography making, etc; rev. by M.V. Higgins. ib. 1938.

[116] HIGGINS, Marion Villiers: Bibliography, ib. 1941.

[117] HURT, Peyton: Bibliography and footnotes; 2ed. rev. by Margaret L. Hurt Richmond. Berkeley: University of Calif.Pr. 1949.

[118] LIBRARY of Congress. Bibliography and Publications Committee: Manual for bibliographers in the Library of Congress, by Mortimer Taube and Helen F. Conover. Washington: The Libr. 1944.

[119] POLLARD, Alfred Wm: The arrangement of bibliographies. Association of Assistant Libr. 1950. (A.A.L. Repr. 2)
Also in Libr...[79] ns 10:168-87,1909.

[120] SHAW, Thos Shuler: Bibliography and reference materials. Berkeley: University of Calif.Pr. 1949.

[121] WYER, Jas Ingersoll: Reference work. Chicago: American Libr.Ass. 1930. p.25-8.

See also Clarke: Manual...[470] p.26-90,138-9; Cowley: Bl... [126] p.10-20,178-94; Van Hoesen: B...[38] p.12-26.

2. Abbreviations of Titles of Periodicals.

[122] LEAGUE of Nations. International Institute of intellectual Co-operation: ...International code of abbreviations for titles of periodicals, etc. Paris: International Inst. of Intellectual Co-oper. 1930.

[123] - - Supplement. ib. 1932.
The code used in the World list... [804] & in Catalogue of Union Periodicals [807]

COLLATION AND DESCRIPTION OF BOOKS...
(Chapter V)

1. Collation and Description.

[124] BOWERS, Fredson Thayer: Principles of bibliographical description. Princeton Univ.Pr. 1949.

[125] BÜHLER, Curt Ferdinand, and others: Standards of bibliographical description. Philadelphia: University of Penn.Pr. 1949. (A.S.W. Rosenbach Fellowship in Bibliogr.)

[126] COWLEY, John Duncan: Bibliographical description and cataloguing. Grafton 1939.

[127] DELISLE, Léopold Victor: Instructions pour la rédaction d'un catalogue des manuscrits et...des incunables, etc. Paris: Champion [1910]

[128] HAEBLER, Konrad: Typenrepertorium der Wiegendrucke. Leipzig: Harrassowitz 1905-24. 5 Pts in 6.

[129] POLLARD, Alfred Wm and Greg, Walter Wilson: Some points in bibliographical descriptions. Association of Assistant Libr. 1950. (A.A.L. Repr. 3) Also in Trans.bibliogr.Soc.[48] 9:31-52,1908.

[130] SCHNEIDER, Georg: Handbuch der Bibliographie; 4Aufl. Leipzig: Hiersemann 1930.

[131] - Theory and history of bibliography; transl. by Ralph R. Shaw. N.Y: Columbia Univ.Pr. 1934.
A translation of the historical & theoretical part of the above; 3ed.

[132] STILLWELL, Margaret Bingham: Incunabula and Americana 1450-1800; a key to bibliographical study. N.Y: Columbia Univ. Pr. 1931.

See also Esdaile: Student's...[34] p.215-71; McKerrow: Introduction...[36] p.145-238.

2. Parts and Structure of a Book. General.

See Aldis: Printed...[156]; Brown: Manual... [113] p.21-44; Esdaile: Student's...[34]; McKerrow: Introduction...[36] p.25-8,73-96; Van Hoesen: B...[38] p.29-34.

3. Special.

Cancels.

[133] CHAPMAN, Rbt Wm: Cancels. Constable 1930. (Bibliographia 3).

Colophons.

[134] GARNETT, Richard: Essays in librarianship and bibliography. G. Allen 1899. p.197-209.
Also in Libr. s1,2:125-32,1890.

See also Pollard: Last...[142].

Chronograms.

[135] HILTON, Jas: Chronograms. Stock 1882-95. 3v.

Dedications.

[136] GEBERT, Clara, ed: Anthology of Elizabethan dedications and prefaces. Philadelphia: University of Penn. Pr. 1933.

Printers' Devices.

[137] DAVIES, Hugh Wm: Devices of the early printers 1457-1560, etc. Grafton 1935.

[138] MCKERROW, Ronald Brunlees: Printers' & publishers' devices in England and Scotland 1485-1640. Bibliographical Soc. 1913. (Illus.Monogr.bibliogr.Soc. 16)

[139] ROBERTS, Wm: Printers' marks, etc. Bell 1893.

Title-Pages.

[140] DE Vinne, Theodore Low: Title-pages as seen by a printer. N.Y: Grolier Cl. 1901.

[141] JOHNSON, Alfred Forbes, comp: 100 title-pages, 1500-1800, etc. Lane (1928)

[142] POLLARD, Alfred Wm: Last words on the history of the title-page, with notes...on...colophons, etc. Nimmo 1891.

MODERN BOOK PRODUCTION.
(Part II. Chapters VI-XIII)

1. Bibliographies.

[143]   BATESON, Fredk Wilse, ed: Cambridge bibliography of English literature. Cambridge Univ.Pr. 1941. 4v.
Book production & distribution: 1:3-9,345-64; 2:81-107; 3:70-106.

[144]   BIGMORE, Edw. Clements, and Wyman, Chas Wm Henry, comp: Bibliography of printing, etc. Quaritch 1880-6. 3v. Repr. N.Y: Duschnes 1945. 2v.
Arranged alphabetically by authors, with some form headings for periodicals, parliamentary papers, &c. Annotated.

[145]   BRITISH Federation of Master Printers: 100 technical books... for a printing works library. The Fed. 1948.

- Selected list of graphic arts literature, books and periodicals, etc; (rev.). ib. 1948.

[146]   CARNEGIE Institute of Technology. Dep. of Printing Administration: Books on the graphic arts. Pittsburgh: The Inst. 1949.

[147]   INDEX to the Printing Trade Periodicals. Printing Ind. Res. Ass. 1930-2. 3 nos.

[148]   LEHMANN-HAUPT, Hellmut: 100 books about bookmaking; a guide to the study and appreciation of printing. N.Y: Columbia Univ.Pr. 1949.
Supersedes the same author's 50 books...1933, & 70 books... 1941.

[149]   PRINTING, Packaging & allied Trades Research Association: Printing abstracts. The Ass. 1,1945+
1 in PATRA J.[94]

[150]   SAINT BRIDE Foundation: Catalogue of the periodicals relating to printing, etc. The Fdn 1951.

[151]   - Catalogue of the technical reference library of works on printing and the allied arts. ib. 1919.
A supplement for 1920-50 to be published shortly.

2. Study and Teaching.

[152] COLUMBIA University. <u>School of Library Service</u>: Syllabus for the study of the history of books and printing...prepared by Bertha M. Frick; 4ed. N.Y: Columbia Univ.Pr. 1943.

3. Terminology.

[153] DICTIONARY of printing terms; 5ed. Salt Lake City: Porte Publ.Co. [1950]

[154] HOSTETTLER, Rudolf: Printer's terms. (German, English, French, Italian, Dutch). St Gallen: R. Hostettler, E. Kopley, H. Strehler 1949. (<u>S.G.M. Bks</u>)

[155] LINOTYPE and Machinery, ltd: Dictionary of terms used in the printing and allied trades. Linotype & Machinery ltd [1940]

See also Bookman's...[22]; International...[26]; Moth: Technical...[28]; Fisher: Compendium...[161] p.119-44; Simon: Printing...[172] p.141-58; Thorp: Printing...[175] p.146-52.

4. General Books.

[156] ALDIS, Harry Gidney: The printed book; 3ed...by J. Carter and Brooke Crutchley. Cambridge Univ.Pr. 1951.

[157] The ART of the Book. The Studio 1914,1938,1951. 1914 ed. by Ch. Holme; 1938 by B.H. Newdigate; 1951 by Ch. Ede.

[158] BENNETT, Paul A. ed: Books and printing. Cleveland: World Publ.Co. (1951)

[159] CAMBRIDGE. <u>University. Fitzwilliam Museum</u>: Catalogue; an exhibition of printing 1940. Cambridge Univ.Pr. 1940.
Illustrates the uses to which printing has been put since Gutenberg.

[160] CLEETON, Glen V. and Pitkin, Chas W: General printing. Bloomington: McKnight (1941)

LITERATURE: BOOK PRODUCTION

[161] FISHER, A. Rigby, ed: Compendium for printers and buyers of printing. Hutchinson Print.Trust [1937]

[162] HACKLEMAN, Chas Wm: Commercial engraving and printing. Indianapolis: Commercial Engr.Publ.Co. [1924]

[163] HARRISON, Fredk: Book about books; new ed. Murray 1950.

[164] JENNETT, Sean: The making of books. Faber (1951)

[165] JOHNSON, Wm Harding, and Newkirk, Louis Vest: The graphic arts. N.Y: Macmillan Co. 1942.

[166] KARCH, Rbt Randolph: Graphic arts procedures. Chicago: Technical Pr. ltd. 1950.

[167] KNIGHTS, Chas C: Printing, reproductive means and materials. Butterworth 1932.

[168] MCMURTRIE, Douglas C: The book; 3ed. N.Y: Oxford Univ. Pr. (1943).
Ed. 1-4 as "The golden book".

[169] MANN, Geo: Print. Grafton 1952.

[170] MARINACCIO, Anthony and Osborne, B.N: Exploring the graphic arts. Scranton, Pa: International Textbook Co. 1942.

[171] POORTENAAR, Jan: Art of the book. Harrap 1935.

[172] SIMON, Herbert and Carter, Harry: Printing explained. Leicester: Dryad Pr. 1931.

[173] SIMON, Oliver: Introduction to typography. Faber 1945.

[174] TARR, John C: Printing to-day; 3ed. Oxford Univ.Pr. 1949.

[175] THORP, Jos: Printing for business. Hogg 1919.

[176] WHETTON, Harry, ed: Practical printing and binding. Odhams 1946.

[177] WHITEHOUSE, John Howard: Craftmanship of books. Allen & Unwin 1929.

FROM PICTOGRAPHY TO TYPOGRAPHY.
(Chapter VI)

1. The Alphabet.

[178]   CLODD, Edw: The story of the alphabet; new ed. N.Y: Appleton 1938.

[179]   DIRINGER, David: The alphabet. Hutchinson's Sci. & Tech .Publ. [1948]

[180]   MAGGS Bros: Art of writing, 2800 B.C. to 1930 A.D.; illus., etc. The Firm [1930]. (Catalogue 542)

[181]   MOORHOUSE, Alfred Chas: Writing and the alphabet. Cobbett Pr. 1946.

[182]   OGG, Oscar: The 26 letters. Harrap [1948]

[183]   PARKER, Bertha Morris: Story of writing. Washington: American Coun. on Educ. 1932.

[184]   TSCHICHOLD, Jan: History of writing in pictures. Basel: Holbein 1945.

[185]   - Illustrated history of writing and lettering. Zwemmer 1946; Allen & Unwin 1951.

[186]   ULLMAN, Berthold Louis: Ancient writing and its influence. N.Y: Longmans 1932.

[187]   WILLIAMS, Henry Smith: History of the art of writing; a series of 97 plates. Cambridge: Heffer [1910]
See also Van Hoesen: B...[38] p.259-315.

2. Special.

[188]   CARTER, Thos Francis: The invention of printing, etc. N.Y: Columbia Univ.Pr. 1931.

[189]   DRIVER, Godfrey Rolles: Semitic writing from pictography to alphabet. Oxford Univ.Pr. 1948. (Schweich Lectures of the Brit.Acad. 1944)

[190]   GRONINGEN, Bernhard Abraham van: Short manual of Greek palaeography. Leyden: Sijthoff 1940.

LITERATURE: CALLIGRAPHY

[191] THOMPSON, Edw. Maunde: Introduction to Greek and Latin palaeography. Oxford: Clarendon Pr. 1912.

3. World of Books in Classical Antiquity.

[192] BETHE, Erich: Buch und Bild im Altertum; hrsg...von E. Kirsten. Leipzig: Harrassowits 1945.

[193] KENYON, Fredc G: Books and readers in ancient Greece and Rome. Oxford Univ.Pr. 1932.

[194] PINNER, H.L: World of books in classical antiquity. Leyden: Sijthoff 1948.

4. Calligraphy.

[195] BENSON, John Howard, and Carey, Arthur Graham: Elements of lettering. Newport, R.I: Stevens 1940.
2ed.(McGraw-Hill) in preparation.

[195a] BLUNT, Wilfrid: Sweet Roman hand; 500 years of italic cursive script. Barrie 1952.

[196] CHAPPELL, Warren. Anatomy of lettering; rev.ed. N.Y: Loring & Mussey 1940.

[197] DEIGHTON, Harold: Art of lettering. Batsford (1947)

[198] FAIRBANK, Alfred J: Book of scripts; (rev.ed.). Harmondsworth: Penguin Books (1952). (King Penguin)

[199] - Handwriting manual; 2.rev.ed. Leicester: Dryad Pr. 1947.

[200] FRY, R.E., and others: Handwriting. 1926-7. 2 pts. (Soc.for pure Eng. Tracts 23,28)

[201] GOUDY, Fredc Wm: The alphabet & Elements of lettering; rev.ed. Berkeley: Univ.of Calif.Pr. 1942.

[202] JOHNSTON, Edw: Writing and illuminating and lettering. Pitman 1939.

[203] MORISON, Stanley: Art of printing.
Merged into his Typographic arts [271]

[204] TARR, John C: Lettering. Crosby Lockwood 1951.

[204a] WEST, Aubrey: Written by hand. Allen & Unwin (1951)

5. Manuscripts.

[205] MADAN, Falconer: Books in manuscript...2ed. K. Paul 1920.

6. Illuminated Manuscripts.

[206] ENGLISH Romanesque Illumination. Oxford: Bodleian Libr. (1951). (Bodleian Picture Bks 1)

[207] HERBERT, John Alexander: Illuminated manuscripts; 2ed. Methuen [1912]

[208] MIDDLETON, John Henry: Illuminated MSS in classical and mediaeval times... Cambridge Univ.Pr. 1892.

[209] WEITZMANN, Kurt: Illustrations in roll and codex. Princeton Univ.Pr. 1947.

7. Early Printing. Bibliographies.

[210] CHICAGO Club of Printing House Craftsmen. Committee on Invention of Printing: Contributions to the bibliography of printing. Chicago: The Club 1940-1. 6 pts.

[211] MCMURTRIE, Douglas Crawford, ed: Invention of printing; a bibliography, etc. ib. 1942.
3,228 items.

8. Early Printing. General.

[212] DUFF, Edw. Gordon: Early printed books. K. Paul 1893.

[213] GOLDSCHMIDT, Ernst Philip: Medieval texts and their first appearance in print. Bibliographical Soc. 1943.

[214] - Printed book of the Renaissance...type, illustration, ornament. Cambridge Univ.Pr. 1950.

[215] HAEBLER, Konrad: Study of incunabula, etc. N.Y: Grolier Cl. 1933.

[216] LEHMANN-HAUPT, Hellmut: Peter Schoeffer of Gernsheim. N.Y: Leo Hart 1950.

[217] SCHOLDERER, Victor: Printers and readers in Italy in the fifteenth century. Oxford Univ.Pr. [1949] (Annu. Italian Lecture of the Brit. Acad. 1949)

[218] STILLWELL, Margaret Bingham: Incunabula and Americana 1450-1800. N.Y: Columbia Univ.Pr. 1931.

[219] WINSHIP, Geo. Parker: Printing in the 15th century. Philadelphia: University of Penn. Pr. 1940.

See also Haebler: Typenrepertorium...[128]

9. Abbreviations used in MSS and early Printing.

[220] CAPELLI, Adriano: ...Lexicon abbreviaturarum; dizionario di abbreviature latine ed italiano, etc; 4ed. Milano: Hoepli 1949.

[221] CHASSANT, Alphonse Antoine Louis: Dictionnaire des abréviations latines et françaises usitées dans les inscriptions, les manuscrits, etc; 4ed. Paris: Aubry 1876.

10. South African Early Printing.

[222] MORRISON, Wm R: A brief history of South African printing and catalogue of exhibition of early South African printing. Johannesburg: Hortors [1935]

PAPER. (Chapter VII)

1. Bibliographies.

[223] APPLETON, Wis. Institute of Paper Chemistry: Guide to the literature of the pulp and paper industry. The Inst. 1936.

[224] KANTROWITZ, Morris Samuel, and others: ...Permanence and durability of paper; an annotated bibliography...1885-1939. Washington: Government Print.Off. 1940. (Tech.Bull. 22)

[225] WEST, Clarence Jay, comp: Bibliography of pulp and paper making. Crosby Lockwood 1937.

[226]   WEST, Clarence Jay, comp: Paper and its relation to printing. Appleton, Wis: Institute of Paper Chem. 1944. (Bibliogr. Ser. 164)

See also Lafontaine: Dict...[229] p.xi-xii.

2. Terminology.

[227]   AMERICAN Paper and Pulp Association: Dictionary of paper, etc; 2ed. N.Y: The Ass. 1952.

[228]   LABARRE, E.J: Dictionary...of paper and paper-making, etc; 2ed., rev. & enl. Oxford Univ.Pr. 1952.

[229]   LAFONTAINE, Gerard H., comp: Dictionary of terms used in the paper, printing and allied industries. Toronto: Howard Smith Paper Mills 1949.

[230]   WHEELWRIGHT, Wm Bond, comp: Paper trade terms; a glossary for the allied trades; rev. and enl. Boston: Callaway Associates (1947)

See also Day: Paper...[236] p.75–99; Morris: Paper...[241] p.293–332.

3. General.

[231]   CLAPPERTON, Rbt Henderson: Paper and its relationship to books. Dent 1934.

[232]   — and Henderson, Wm: Modern paper-making; 3ed. Blackwell 1952.

[233]   CROSS, Chas Fredk, and Bevan, E.J: Text-book of paper making; 5ed. Spon 1936.
Chapter 13: Qualities of paper.

[234]   DAWE, Edw: Paper and its uses; 4ed. Technical Pr. 1939. 2v.

[235]   — Paper for printers. Pitman 1949.

[236]   DAY, Fredk T: Paper and printing manual. Trade Journals 1950.

[237]   ENCYCLOPAEDIA Britannica: Articles: Fibre, Paper.

LITERATURE: PAPER

[238] HUNTER, Dard: Paper-making; 2.rev.ed. Pleiades 1948.

[239] JOINT Executive Committee of the Vocational Education Committees of the Pulp and Paper Industry of the U.S. and Canada: Manufacture of pulp and paper; a text-book of modern pulp and paper mill practice. N.Y: McGraw–Hill 1921–39. 5v.

[240] MADDOX, Harry Alfred: ...Paper; 6ed. Pitman 1945.

[241] NORRIS, F.H: Paper and papermaking. Oxford Univ.Pr. 1952.

[242] PAPER Makers' Association. <u>Technical Section. Education Committee</u>: Paper making; repr. Kenley, Surrey: The Ass. 1950.

[243] RENKER, Arnim: Das Buch vom Papier; 3Ausg. Wiesbaden: Insel-Verlag 1950.

[244] SINDALL, Rbt Walter: Manufacture of paper. Constable 1919.

[245] TULLIS Russell and Co., <u>firm</u>: Papermaking fibres. Markinch: The Firm 1950.

[246] WHEELWRIGHT, Wm Bond: Printing papers. Chicago Univ. Pr. 1936.

See also Carter & Pollard: Enquiry...[415]; Cim: Livre...[33]; Esdaile: Student's...[34] p.33–48; Hackleman: Commercial... [162]; Ass: Book...[35]; McKerrow: Introd...[36]; McMurtrie: Book...[168]; Poortenaar: Art...[171].

4. Permanence.

[247] GRANT, Julius: Books and documents. Grafton 1937.

[248] LEAGUE of Nations. <u>Committee of Experts for the Conservation of MSS and Books</u>: Report. Geneva: The Leag. 1928.
See also at end of Parley...Footnote (1), p.153 here.

[249] LIBRARY Association: Durability of paper. The Ass. [1930]

[250] PRINTING, Packaging and allied Trades Research Association: Durability of paper. The Ass. 1931.

[251] R.SOCIETY of Arts. Committee on the Deterioration of Paper: Report. The Soc. 1898.

5. History.

[252] BLUM, André: On the origin of paper; transl. by H.M. Lydenburg. N.Y: Bowker 1934.

[253] CLAPPERTON, Rbt Henderson: Paper; an historical account of its making by hand, etc. Oxford: Shakespeare Head Pr. 1934.

[254] HUNTER, Dard: Papermaking; the history and technique of an ancient craft; 2.rev.ed. Pleiades 1948.

[255] — Paper-making through 18 centuries. N.Y: Rudge 1930.

6. Samples.

[256] ASSOCIATION of Makers of Esparto Papers: Esparto paper. Edinburgh: The Ass. 1933.

[257] DICKINSON and Co., firm: The "de luxe" book of printing. The Firm [190?]

[258] HAMMERMILL Paper Co: How Hammermill bond is made... Erie, Pa: The Firm 1930.

[259] HOLLISTON [Paper] Mills: Permanent papers, etc. Norwood, Mass: The Firm 1934.
Samples & history of paper-making.

[260] NATIONAL Association of Paper Merchants: Students' sample book. The Ass. 1950.

[261] SOUTH African Pulp and Paper Industries, Ltd. Enstra [194?].

[262] SPALDING and Hodge, firm: Specimen book of printing papers. The Firm 1906.

See also Dawe: Paper &...[234]; Esdaile: Student's...[34]; Jacobi: Printing...[267]; Labarre: Diet...[228]; Simon & Carter: Printing...[172].

7. Watermarks.

[263] BRIQUET, Chas Moïse: Les filigranes...1282–1600; 2ed. Leipzig: Hiersemann 1923. 4v.

[264] CHURCHILL, Wm Algernon: Watermarks in paper...17th and 18th centuries. Amsterdam: Hertzberger 1935.

[265] ENCYCLOPAEDIA Britannica. Article: Watermarks.

[266] HEAWOOD, Edw: Watermarks...17th and 18th centuries. Hilversum: Paper Publ.Soc. 1950. (Monumenta Chartae Papyraceae Historiam Illustrantia I)

Periodicals see Paper and Print.[90]; Printing...Ass; PATRA J.[94].

PRINTING. (Chapter VIII)

1. General.

[267] JACOBI, Chas Thos: Printing; 6ed. Bell 1919.

[268] LUKER, Leslie G: Science for printers. Griffin 1951.

[269] MORISON, Stanley: First principles of typography. Cambridge Univ.Pr. 1951. (Cambridge Authors' and Printers' Guides 1) Drafted first as article Typography in Encycl.Brit. rewritten for no.7 of Fleuron. First published separately in 1936.

[270] – Printing.
Article in Encycl.Brit.

[271] –Typographic arts. Edinburgh: Thin 1944.

[272] – – Sylvan Pr. 1949.
Includes the above & the Author's Art...[203] with an appendix bringing it up-to-date.

[273] ROSNER, Charles: Printer's progress. Sylvan Pr. 1951.

[274] TIMES. The: Printing in the 20th century. The Times 1930.

[275] UNITED States. Government Printing Office: Typography and design. Washington: Govt Print.Off. 1951. (Apprentice Training Ser. Intermediate Period)

[276]   WARDE, Beatrice: Crystal goblets: invitation to typography. Sylvan Pr. 1947.

See also Esdaile: Student's...[34] p.49–92; McKerrow: Introd... [36] p.6–52; Van Hoesen: B...[38] p.316–72.

2. Foundries.

[277]   REED, Talbot Baines: History of the old English letter foundries...n.ed., rev.& enl.by A.F. Johnson. Faber 1952. led. Stock 1887.

3. Inks.

[278]   KLAETSCH, Hermann: Druckfarbe in vergangenen Zeiten. Mainz: Gutenberg–Ges. 1940.

4. Type Faces.

[279]   AMERICAN Institute of Graphic Arts: Type faces and paper surfaces. New York: The Inst. [1941?]

[280]   BIGGS, John R: An approach to type. Blandford Pr. 1949.

[281]   GOUDY, Frederic W: Typologia. Berkeley: University of Calif. Pr. 1940.

[282]   GRONENDAAL, M.H: Drukletters. Amsterdam: Stam 1944.

[283]   HLASTA, Stanley C: Printing types and how to use them. Pittsburgh: Carnegie Inst. of Tech. 1951.

[284]   JOHNSON, A.F: Type designs. Grafton 1934.

[285]   JONES, Herbert: Type in action; 2.rev.ed. Sidgwick & Jackson 1950.

[286]   MIDDLETON, Rbt Hunter: Creating type. New York: Diamant Typographic Serv. 1949.
First ed. as: Making printers' type faces.

[287]   MORISON, Stanley: On type faces. Medici Soc. 1923.

[288]   – Printing type.
Article in Encycl.Brit.
Also as Introd. to Berry...: Catalogue...[295]

[289]   MORISON, Stanley: Type designs of the past and present. Fleuron Pr. 1926.
Also in <u>Monotype Rec</u>. 24(209/10) p.5-56 Nov./Dec.1925.

[290]   THOMAS, David: Type for print; 2ed. Whitaker 1950.

[291]   UPDIKE, D.B: Printing types; 2ed. Harvard Univ.Pr. 1937. 2v.

[292]   VOLK, K.H: Using type correctly. New York: Volk inc. (1947)

[293]   WHITEHILL, C: Moods of type. New York: Barnes & Noble (1947)
See also Aldis: The printed...[156] p.21-8; Esdaile: Student's...[34] p.93-147; McKerrow: Introduction...[36] p.288-308.
You will often find articles on printing types in <u>Alph. Image</u> [39] (defunct); <u>Penrose'sAnnu</u>.[91]; <u>Print. Rev</u>.[95]; <u>Signature</u> [98]; <u>Typography</u> [102] (defunct).

5. <u>Specimens.</u>

[294]   BASTIEN, Alfred, <u>ed</u>: Type lettering: some contemporary alphabets. West Drayton: Typographical Centre 1950.

[295]   BERRY, W. Turner, and Johnson, A.F., <u>comp</u>: Catalogue of specimens of printing types by English and Scottish founders 1665–1830. Oxford Univ.Pr. 1935.

[296]   COWELL, <u>firm</u>: Handbook of printing types. The Firm 1947.

[297]   – Book of type-faces. ib. 1952.

[298]   CLOWES, Wm & Sons, <u>firm</u>: Book types from Clowes; 2ed. The Firm (1950)

[299]   EASTERN Corporation, <u>firm</u>: Type specimen sheets. Bangor, Maine: The Firm [195?]

[300]   MONOTYPE Corporation: 21 classic type faces. [1946] On various types of paper, by letterpress, or reprinted by photo-offset, or by photogravure.

[301]   OLIVER Burridge & Co., <u>firm</u>: Burridge broadsheets. The Firm [195?]

[302] TARR, J.C: Book of alphabets. Pitman 1951.

[303] TILLOTSON'S (Bolton) Ltd., firm: Tillotson's specimen book of type-faces. Bolton [195?]

[304] TYPOGRAPHIC Standard Type Catalogue. Typographia 1950+ 60 cards a year issued on a subscription basis.

See also B.M: Cat...[792] Introds; Tarr: How...[544]

ILLUSTRATION. (Chapter IX)

1. Bibliographies.

[305] STEEVES, H. Allan: Index to graphic arts printing processes. N.Y: Public Libr. 1943.
Also in the library's Bull.[88] 47(5) p.323-44, 1943.

[306] WEITENKAMPF, Frank. The illustrated book. Cambridge: Harvard Univ.Pr. 1938. p.267–88.

2. General.

[307] ARMS, John Taylor: Handbook of print making and print makers. N.Y: Macmillan Co. 1934.

[308] BIGGS, John R: Illustration and reproduction. Blandford Pr. (1950)

[309] BLAND, David: The illustration of books. Faber 1951.

[310] ENCYCLOPEDIA Britannica Co., Ltd: Graphic arts. N.Y: Garden City Publ.Co. 1934.
The text consists of articles from the Encycl.Brit.

[311] HIND, Arthur Mayger: Processes & schools of engraving...4ed. British Museum 1952.

[312] HOLMAN, Louis Arthur: Graphic processes: intaglio, relief and planographic, with a collection of actual prints. Boston: Goodspeed 1929.

[313] IVINS, William: ...How prints look. N.Y: Metropolitan Mus. of Art 1943.

[314] KAUFFMANN, Désiré: Graphic arts crafts. N.Y: Van Nostrand 1948.

[315] PETRINA, John: Art work, how produced, how reproduced. Pitman [1934]

[316] POORTENAAR, Jan: Technique of prints and art reproduction processes. Lane [1934]

[317] WHITMAN, Alfred: Whitman's print collector's handbook. Bell 1918.

See also Aldis: The printed...[156] p.75–98; Esdaile: Student's... [34] p.148–77; Hackleman: Commercial...[162]; Jennett: The making...[164]; Knights: Printing...[167]; McKerrow: Introduction...[36] p.329–36; Poortenaar: Art...[171]; Tarr: Printing...[174]

3. History. General.

[318] BENESCH, Otto: Artistic and intellectual trends from Rubens to Daumier as shown in book illustration. Cambridge: Harvard Coll.Libr. 1943.

[319] CRANE, Walter: Of the decorative illustration of books, old and new; 3ed. (repr.). Bell 1921.

[320] DARTON, F.J.H: Modern book illustration in Great Britain and America. Studio 1931. (Special Winter No.)

[321] – Modern book illustrators and their work. Studio 1914.

[322] POLLARD, Alfred William: Early illustrated books, etc. 3ed. Kegan Paul [1926]

[323] WEITENKAMPF, Frank: Illustrated books of the past four centuries. N.Y: Public Libr. 1920.

[324] ZIGROSSER, C: Six centuries of fine prints. Williamson [1938]

See also McKerrow: Introduction...[36]; Van Hoesen: B...[38] p.383-8.

4. History. British.

[325] GRAY, B: The English print. Black 1937.

[326] HARDIE, M: English coloured books. Methuen [1906] (Connoisseur's Libr.)

[327]　JACKSON, Holbrook: The 1890's...n.ed. Penguin 1950.

[328]　JAMES, Philip Brutton: English book illustration 1800–1900. King Penguin books 1947.

[329]　LEWIS, C.T.C: Story of picture printing in England...19th century. Sampson Low [1928]

[330]　NATIONAL Book League: British book illustration 1935–45; a catalogue of an exhibition. Cambridge Univ.Pr. [1946]

[331]　NATIONAL Gallery, Millbank: Catalogue: book illustration of the 60's. The Trustees 1923.

[332]　REID, Forest: Illustrators of the 60's. Faber [1928] Printed at the Chiswick Pr; identifying notes in "List of illustrations".

[333]　SALAMAN, Malcolm Chas: British book illustration yesterday and to-day. Studio 1923.

[334]　SKETCHLEY, R.E.D: British book-illustration of to-day; introd. by A.W. Pollard. Kegan Paul 1903.

[335]　THORPE, James: English illustration; the 90's. Faber [1935?]

[336]　WHITE, Joseph W. Gleeson: English illustration; the 60's: 1855–70. Constable 1897.

5. **Methods. Autographic, Relief.**

(a) Bibliography.

[337]　HASSALL, Joan: Wood engraving. National Book Leag. 1949. (Reader's Guides)

(b) General.

[338]　BALSTON, Thos: Wood engraving in modem English books. National Book Leag. 1949.

[339]　BEEDHAM, R. John: Wood engraving...introd. and appendix by Eric Gill; 3ed. Faber 1947.

[340]　BLISS, Douglas Percy: History of wood-engraving. Dent 1928.

LITERATURE: WOODENGRAVING

[341] CRAIG, Edward Gordon: Woodcuts and some words; introd. by C. Dodson. Dent 1924.

[342] DODSON, M: Blockcutting and print-making by hand. Pitman 1930.

[343] FARLEIGH, John: Graven image; an autobiographical text-book. MacMillan 1940.

[344] FURST, Herbert: Modern woodcut. Lane 1924.

[345] HIND, Arthur M: Introduction to a history of the woodcut. Constable 1935. 2v.

[346] LEIGHTON, Clare Veronica Hope: ...Wood-engraving and wood-cuts. Studio 1948.

[347] – Wood-engraving of the 1930's. ib. [1936] (Special Winter No.)

[348] MACNAB, Iain: Student's book of wood-engraving. Pitman 1938.

[349] PLATT, J.E: Colour woodcuts: a book of reproductions and a handbook of method. Pitman 1938.

[350] REIMER, Imre: Woodcut/wood engraving. St Gall: Zollikofer 1947.

[351] SALAMAN, Malcolm Chas: The woodcut of to-day at home and abroad. Studio 1927.

[352] SLEIGH, Bernhard: Wood–engraving since 1890. Pitman 1932.

[353] WATSON, E.W. and Kent, N., ed: The relief print. N.Y: Watson–Guptill 1945.

(c) Individual Engravers.

[354] BALSTON, Thos: The wood-engravings of Robert Gibbings. Art & Technics 1949.

[355] CLEVERDON, Douglas: The engravings of Eric Gill. Faber 1934.

[356] IMAGE, Selwyn: Thomas Bewick. Print Coll. Cl. 1932.

[357]   MUELLER, Hans Alexander: Woodcuts and wood engravings; how I make them. N.Y: Pynson Printers 1939.

[358]   PIPER, Myfanwy: Reynolds Stone. Art & Technics 1951.

[359]   REYNOLDS, Graham: Thomas Bewick. Art & Technics 1949.

[360]   RUZICKA, R: Thomas Bewick, engraver. N.Y: Typophiles 1943.

6. Autographic. Intaglio.

[361]   CUTNER, Herbert: Teach yourself etching. English Univ. Pr. 1947.

[362]   DAVENPORT, Cyril Jas Humphries: Mezzotints. Methuen 1904. (Connoisseur's Libr.)

[363]   FURST, Herbert Ernest Augustus: Original engraving and etching. Nelson 1931.

[364]   HAYTER, Stanley W: New ways of gravure. Routledge (1949)

[365]   HOLME, Chas: Modern etching and engraving. Studio 1902.

[366]   – Modern etchings, mezzotints and drypoints. ib. 1913. (Special Winter No.)

[367]   HUBBARD, Eric Hesketh: On making and collecting etchings. Batsford: Print Soc. (1923)

[368]   LAVER, Jas: History of British and American etching. Benn 1929.

[369]   LIPPMANN, F: ...Engraving and etching...3ed., transl. by M. Hardie. Grevel 1906.

[370]   LUMSDEN, Ernest S. Art of etching. Seeley, Service 1929.

[371]   PATON, Hugh: Etching, drypoint, mezzotint. Raithby, Lawrence 1895.

[372]   PENNELL, Jos: Etchers and etching...3ed. Fisher Unwin (1925)

[373]   PRIDEAUX, Sarah Treverbian: Aquatint engraving. Duckworth (1909)
Of considerable South African interest.

LITERATURE: ETCHING

[374] ROBINS, W.P:. Etching craft. Bookman's J.1923.

[375] SHORT, F: ...Etchings and engravings. R.Soc.of Painter-Etchers 1911.

[376] SINGER, H.W. and Strang, W: Etching, engraving and the other methods of printing pictures. Kegan Paul 1897.

[377] STEEL, Kenneth: Line engraving. Pitman 1938.

[378] VICTORIA and Albert Museum. <u>Dep. of Engraving, Illustration and Design</u>: Tools and materials used in etching and engraving; 4ed. The Mus. 1925.

[379] WEDMORE, Fredk: Etchings. Methuen (1911) (<u>Connoisseur's Libr.</u>)

[380] WEST, Levon: Making an etching. Studio [1941?]

7. <u>Auto-Lithography.</u>

[381] CUMMING, David: Handbook of lithography; 3ed. Black 1932.

[382] HARTRICK, Archibald Standish: ...Lithography as a fine art. Oxford Univ.Pr. 1932. (<u>Little Craft Books</u>)

[383] MAYNE, J: Barnett Freedman. Art & Technics 1948.

[384] WENGENROTH, Stow: ...Making a lithograph. Studio 1936. (<u>How to make it Ser.</u>)

8. <u>Photographic. General.</u>

[385] CLERC, Louis Philippic: The Ilford manual of process work; 7ed. Ilford ltd 1951.

[386] CURWEN, Harold: Processes of graphic reproduction in printing; 2ed. Faber (1947)

[387] FEDERATION of Master Process Engravers: Process engraver's compendium, <u>etc</u>. The Fed. 1932.

[388] SMITH, Frank H: Photographs and the printer. Focal Pr. (1948)

[389]   SMITH, Wn Jos and others: Photo–engraving in relief; 2ed. Pitman 1948.

[390]   ULLYETT, Kenneth: Pictorial printing processes. Pitman 1949.

9. Photographic. Relief.

[391]   BALSTON, Thos: English book illustrations 1880–1900. (In Carter: New paths...[518] p.163-90).
Mainly about zincos.

10. Photographic. Intaglio.

[392]   BENNETT, Colin Noël: Elements of photogravure...3ed. Technical Pr. 1935.

[393]   BULL, Alfred J: Photo–engraving. Arnold 1934.

11. Photographic. Planographic.

[394]   LITHO-Media, inc., N.Y: Litho-media; a demonstration of the selling power of lithography. N.Y: The Firm 1939.

[395]   MERTLE, Jos Stephen and Keusch, Harry: Photolithography & offset printing... Chicago: Graphic Arts Publ.Co. 1940.

[396]   NICOLSON, Donald: Photo–offset lithography. N.Y: Chemical Publ.Co. 1941.

[397]   WILLY, Clifford Mason: Practical photo–lithography; 4ed. Pitman 1952.

[398]   WILSON, T.A: Practice of collotype. Chapman & Hall 1935.

12. Colour Illustration. General.

For colour illustration by means of one process only, see under that process.

[399]   BURCH, Rbt M: Colour printing and colour printers. Birman 1910.

[400] GRIFFITS, Thos Edgar: Colour printing. Faber (1949)

[401] RAYMOND & Raymond, firm: Catalogue of selected color reproductions; prepared for the Carnegie Corporation. N.Y: The Firm 1936. 2v.
Preliminary pages of v.1 offer a brief description of the various methods employed, collotype largely.

13. Special Methods.

[402] BIEGELEISEN, Jacob Israel and Busenbark, E.J: Silk screen printing process; 2ed. N.Y: McGraw–Hill 1941.

[403] – and Cohn, M.A: Silk screen stencilling as a fine art; with an introd, by Rockwell Kent. ib. 1942.

[404] STERNBERG Harry: Silk screen color printing... serigraphy. ib. 1942.

[405] DI GEMMA, J: Lumiprinting; a new graphic art. N.Y: Watson–Guptill 1942.
See also McKerrow: Introduction...[36]

14. Scientific Illustration.

[406] CANNON, Herbert Graham: Method of illustration for zoological papers. Association of Brit. Zool. 1936.

[407] HILL, Thos Geo: Essentials of illustration. Wesley 1915.

[408] RIDGWAY, John L: Scientific illustration. Stanford Univ. Pr. 1938.

[409] WISTAR Institute of Anatomy and Biology: Style brief. Philadelphia: The Inst. 1934.

FACSIMILES AND NEAR–PRINT. (Chapter X)

1. General.

[410] BINKLEY, Rbt C: Manual on methods of reproducing research materials. Ann Arbor: Edwards Bros 1936.

2. Microfilms and -Cards.

[411] BRITISH Standards Institution: Storage of microfilm. (B.S. 1153:1944)

[412] DIRECTORY of microfilm and photocopying services. The Hague: F.I.D. 1951. (F.I.D. Publ. 244)

[413] LIBRARY of Congress. General Reference and Bibliography Div: Microfilms and microcards; their use in research; a selected list of references; comp. by Blanche McCrum. Washington: The Libr. 1950.

[414] RIDER, Fremont: The scholar and the future of the research library. N.Y: Hadham Pr. 1944.

3. Fakes.

[415] CARTER, John, and Pollard, Graham: Enquiry into the nature of certain 19th century pamphlets. Constable 1934.

[416] – The firm of Charles Ottley, Landon & Co; footnote to an Enquiry. Hart-Davis 1948.

[417] PARTINGTON, W: Forging ahead. N.Y: Putnam 1939.

[418] RATCHFORD, Fanny E: Between the lines; letters and memoranda interchanged between H. Buxton Forman and Thomas J. Wise. Austin: Univ. of Texas Pr. 1945.

[419] WISE, Thos J: Letters...to John Henry Wrenn; ed. by Fanny E. Ratchford. N.Y: Knopf 1944.

See also Esdaile: Student's...[34] p.24–7; Hazen: B...[575]; Grant: Books...[247] p.8,11–5,32; McKerrow: Introduction...[36] p.231–8.

BOOKBINDING. (Chapter XI)

1. Bibliography.

[420] HOBSON, G.D: Books on book-binding. (Book-Coll. Quart. [55] 7:70–84, 1932)

[421] MEJER, Wolfgang: Bibliographie der Buchbinderei-Literatur. Leipzig: Hiersemann 1925.

[421a] MEJER, W: - Ergänzungsband 1924–32 [von] Hermann Herbst. ib. 1933.

[422]   PRIDEAUX, Sarah Treverbian: Historical sketch of bookbinding. Lawrence and Bullen 1893. p.251–94.

See also Diehl: Bookbinding [429] 1:205–19; Stillwell: Incunabula...[218] p.198–201; U.S: Theory...[444]

2. Terminology.

See Cockerell: Bookbinding...[427] p.313–7; Coutts: Manual... [428] p.221–44; Diehl: Bookbinding [429] 1:223–34; 2:375–91.

3. General.

[423]   AMERICAN Library Association. Committee on Bookbinding: Care and binding of books and magazines. Chicago: American Libr.Ass. 1928.

[424]   BINDERS Board Manufacturers Association: Bound to last, etc. N.Y: The Ass. 1926.

[425]   BUCK, Mitchell Starrett: Book repair and restoration. Philadelphia: Brown 1918.

[426]   CHIVERS, Cedric: Paper for lending library books. Bath: Chivers [1909?]

[427]   COCKERELL, Douglas: Bookbinding and the care of books; 5ed. Pitman 1953.

[427a] – Some notes on bookbinding. 2 impr. Oxford Univ.Pr. 1948. Includes his 'Note on bookbinding' 1904.

[428]   COUTTS, Henry Thos and Stephen, Geo.A: Manual of library bookbinding. Libraco 1911.

[429]   DIEHL, Edith: Bookbinding. N.Y: Rinehart 1946. 2v. 1: Background; B; 2: Technique; Glossary.

[430]   DONNELLY, R.R. and Sons, firm: Rod for the back of the binder. Chicago: Lakeside Pr. 1928.

[431]   DREWERY, R.F: Library binderies. Library Ass. 1950. (Libr. Ass.Pamphl. 3)

[432] FEIPEL, Louis N., and Browning, Earl W: Library binding manual. Chicago: American Libr.Ass. 1951.
Contains the latest, July 1950 rev. of the Amer.Libr. Ass.'s "Minimum specification for class "A" library binding", first published in the Amer.Libr.Ass.Proc. [42] 56, 1934.

[433] GAYLORD Bros, firm: Bookcraft... Syracuse: The Firm 1947.

[434] GRONEMAN, Chris. Harold: General bookbinding. Bloomington: McKnight and McKnight 1946.

[435] HARTHAN, J.P: Bookbindings: Victoria and Albert Museum. The Mus. 1950.

[436] HORNE, Herbert Percy: Binding of books; 2ed. Kegan Paul 1915. Chap.1 & Conclusion.

[437] LEIGHTON, Douglas: Modern bookbinding. Dent 1935.

[438] MATTHEWS, W: Modern bookbinding practically considered. N.Y: Grolier Cl. 1889.
Still good for handbinding & its Illus.

[439] MATTHEWS, Wm F: Bookbinding. Gollancz 1929.

[440] PHILIP, Alex. John: Business of bookbinding, etc: 2ed. Gravesend: The Author 1935.
Contains specimens.

[441] PRIDEAUX, Sarah Treverbian: Bookbinders and their craft. Zaehnsdorf 1903.

[442] RILEY & Co., firm: Modern library bindery. Huddersfield: The Firm [1946]

[443] TOWN, Laurence: Bookbinding by hand. Faber (1951)

[444] UNITED States. Printing Office: Theory and practice of bookbinding. Washington: Govt Print.Off. 1950.

[445] VAUGHAN, Alex. J: Modern bookbinding. Leicester: Raithby, Lawrence & Co. 1929.

[446]   ZAEHNSDORF, Joseph W: The art of bookbinding; 2ed. Bell 1900.

See also Curwen: Processes...[386]; Esdaile: Student's...[34] p.178–214; Grant: Books...[247]; Jennett: Making...[164] p.154–78; L.A: Book...[35] p.32–43; McMurtrie: The Book [168]; Van Hoesen: B...[38]

4. <u>Decay and Preservation.</u>

[447]   FREY, R.W., and Veitch, F.P: Preservation of leather bookbindings. Washington: Govt Print.Off. 1933.
(<u>U.S. Dep.of Agric. Leafl.69</u>)

[448]   GAYLORD Bros, <u>firm</u>: Bookcraft, <u>etc</u>. Syracuse: The Firm 1947.

[449]   - Toronto method of book repairing; 3ed., rev. and enl. ib. 1928.

[450]   LYDENBERG, Harry Miller, and Archer, John: Care and repair of books; 2ed. N.Y: Bowker 1945.

[451]   PLENDERLEITH, Harold Jas: Preservation of leather bookbindings; repr. British Mus. 1950.

[452]   PRINTING Industry Research Association and British Leather Manufacturers' Research Association. <u>Bookbinding Leather Committee</u>: Causes and prevention of decay of bookbinding leather. Interim (and second interim) report. The Ass. 1933–6. 2pts.

[453]   R.Society of Arts. <u>Committee on Leather for Bookbindings</u>. [Report]. The Soc. 1905.
A much extended version of the Rep. pubd in 5. July 1901 in its J. and as a separate. Contains specimens.

5. <u>Samples.</u>

[454]   LIBRARY Association. <u>Sound Leather Committee</u>. Leather for libraries. Libraco 1905.
Contains specimens.

See also Coutts: Manual...[428]; R.Society...[Report] [453]

6. Special.

[455]　OXFORD. Bodleian Library: Gold-tooled bookbindings. The Library (1951). (Bodleian Picture Bks 2)

[456]　LEIGHTON, D: Canvas bookcloth, etc. Bibliographical Soc. 1948.

[457]　BRITISH Federation of Master Printers. Observations on library binding, with special reference to the unsewn method. The Fed. 1951. (Libr.Binders' Memo. No.1)

[458]　ROSNER, Chas: The art of the book-jacket. Victoria & Albert Mus. 1949.

[459]　SADLEIR, Michael: The evolution of publishers' binding styles, 1770–1900. Constable 1930.

[460]　WEBER, Carl J: 1001 fore-edge paintings, etc. Waterville, Maine: Colby College Pr. 1949. (Colby Coll. Monogr. 16)

PRACTICAL AUTHORSHIP, etc. (Chapter III)

1. Terminology.

[461]　BEECK, Peter: Fachausdrück der Presse/Vocabulaire de presse/Vocabulary of the press; 3ed. Frankfurt a.M: Polygraph 1950.

[462]　COLLINS, Fredk Howard: Authors' and printers' dictionary...w. full list of abbreviations, etc; 9ed. Oxford Univ. Pr (1950)

[463]　ORNE, Jerrold: Language of the foreign book trade. Chicago: American Libr .Ass. 1949.

2. Author and Printer.

[464]　AMERICAN Standards Association: Abbreviations for periodicals. In preparation.

[465]　BENBOW, John: Manuscript and proof, etc. New York: Oxford Univ.Pr. 1937.

[466] BRITISH Standards Institution: Alphabetical arrangement. (B.S. 1749:1951)

[467] – Printers' and authors' proof corrections. (B.S. 1219: 1945)

[468] CAMBRIDGE University Press: Preparation of manuscripts and correction of proofs. Cambridge Univ.Pr. 1951. (Cambr.Authors' and Printers' Guides 2)

[469] CAREY, G.V: Making an index. ib. 1951. (Cambr.Authors' and Printers' Guides 3)

[470] CLARKE, Archibald Leycester: Manual of practical indexing, etc. Grafton 1933.

[471] FOWLER, Henry Watson: A dictionary of modern English usage; repr. Milford 1940.

[472] HART, Horace: Rules for compositors and readers at the University Press, Oxford; 36ed. Oxford Univ.Pr. 1952.

[473] LASKY, Joseph: Proofreading and copy-preparation, etc. New York: Mentor Pr. 1946.

[474] QUILLER–Couch, Sir Arthur: On the art of writing, etc; repr. Cambridge Univ.Pr. 1928.

[475] WILEY & Sons, firm: Author's guide, etc. New York: The Firm 1950.

[476] WILLIAMS, G.E: Technical literature, its preparation and presentation. Allen & Unwin 1948.

[477] WILSON Co., firm: Style book, etc; (3ed.) New York: The Firm 1936.

[478] WORDS into type; a guide in the preparation of manuscripts. N.Y: Appleton [1948]

See also Cowley: B1...[126] p.195–202; Van Hoesen: B...[38] p.26–45.

3. Author and Printer - South Africa.

[479] ASSOCIATED Scientific and Technical Societies of South Africa. Honorary Editors' Committee: Information for authors, editors, and printers. Johannesburg: A.S. & T.S. 1948.

[480] GOULD, Chas J.B: Author and printer in South Africa. Johannesburg: Imprint Soc. 1945.

4. Periodicals.

[481] AUTHOR. Society of Authors. 1890+

[482] BOOK Trade Handbook 1937; comp. and ed. by Wm G. Corp. Lane [1936]

5. Publishing and Bookselling.

[483] BENN, John: Publishing as a craft. Benn 1948.

[484] ENCYCLOPEDIE française. v.18. La civilisation écrite; ed. Julien Cain. Paris: Société de gestion de l'Encyclopedie française [1939]

[485] HAMPDEN, John, ed: The book world, etc. Nelson 1935.

[486] JOSEPH, Michael: Adventure of publishing. Wingate 1949.

[487] LANGDON–Davies, Bernhard Noël: The practice of bookselling, etc. Phoenix House [1951]

[488] LAWLER, John: The H.W. Wilson Co. Minneapolis: University of Minn.Pr. 1950.

[489] LONDON School of Economics and Political Science: Catalogue of a collection of works on publishing and bookselling, etc. The School 1936.

[490] MILLER, Wm: The book industry. N.Y: Columbia Univ.Pr. 1950.

[491] MILNE, James: Printers devil; or, how books happen. Epworth Pr. (1949)

[492] MUMBY, Frank Arthur: Publishing and bookselling; (rev. ed.) Cape (1949)

[493] PUBLISHERS Association. The Council: Royalty agreements: a guide for the use of publishers...rev. The Assoc. 1946.

[494] PUBLISHERS' Weekly: Selling books: a series of discussions for the staff. N.Y: Bowker 1941.

[495] PUTNAM, George Haven: Books and their makers during the Middle Ages. N.Y: Putnam 1896.

[496] PLANT, Marjorie: The English book trade. Allen & Unwin 1939.

[497] SANDERS, F.D., ed: British book trade organisation. Allen & Unwin (1939)

[498] UNWIN, Stanley: Truth about publishing; 6ed. Allen & Unwin 1950.

[499] WILSON, John G: The business of bookselling: three lectures, etc. Associated Bksellere of Gt Brit. and Ireland 1930.

See also McCormick: Editors...[679]

6. Copyright. International.

[500] GREAT Britain. Board of Trade: Report of the Departmental Committee on international copyright. H.M.S.O. 1935.

[501] – – Brussels copyright convention 1948. H.M.S.O. 1949.

[502] LADAS, S.P: International protection of literary and artistic property. N.Y: Macmillan Co. 1938. 2v.

7. Copyright. Great Britain.

[503] CLOUTMAN, Brett, and Luck, F.W: Law for printers and publishers; 2ed. by E.H. Hale. Staples Pr.(1949)

[504] COPINGER, Walter Arthur: Copinger and Skone James on the law of copyright...8ed. by F.E. Skone James. Sweet & Maxwell 1948.

[505] DAWSON, Thos: Law of the press; (2ed). Staples Pr. (1947)

[506] GREAT Britain: Correspondence respecting the revised Convention of Berne. H.M.S.O. 1909. (Misc. No.2. Cd 4467)

[507] NICHOLSON, Margaret: Manual of copyright practice for writers, publishers and agents. Oxford 1945.
American title of [512]

8. Copyright. U.S.A.

[508] DE WOLF, Richard Crosby: Law of copyright. Washington: Govt Print.Off. 1942.

[509] –Outline of copyright law. Boston: Luce 1925.

[510] HOWELL, Herbert A: Copyright law...of the United States; 2ed. Washington: Govt Print.Off. 1948.

[511] LIBRARY of Congress. Copyright Office: ...Copyright law of the U.S.A., being the Act of March 4, 1909, as amended, together with rules for practice and procedure. Washington: Govt Print.Off. 1953. (Bull. No.14)

[512] NICHOLSON, Margaret: Manual of American copyright practice. Oxford Univ.Pr. 1946.
Same as [507]

9. Copyright. Periodicals.

[513] UNESCO: Copyright Bulletin/Bull.du droit d'auteur. Paris: UNESCO 1948+

See also Evans: Copyright...[680]; Van Hoesen: B...[38] p.402–4.

10. BookCollecting.

[514] AUNGERVILLE, Richard, known as Richard de Bury: The love of books, the Philobiblon...transl...by E.C. Thomas. Chatto & Windus 1925.

[515] CARTER, John: A.B.C. for book-collectors. Hart–Davis 1952.

[516] – ed: New paths in book collecting. Constable 1934. Contains: Winterich, John T. Expansion of an author collection; Carter, John. Detective fiction; Muir, P.H. Ignoring the flag; Oldmor, C.B. Musical first editions; Sadleir, M. Yellow backs; Balston, T. English book illustration 1880–1900; Randall, David A. American first editions 1900–33; Muir, P.H. War books; Pollard, Graham. Serial fiction. Some of these have been published separately with serial title: Aspects of book collecting.

LITERATURE: BOOK-COLLECTING

[517]   CHAPMAN, R.W., <u>& others</u>: Book collecting: 4 broadcast talks by R.W. Chapman, John Hayward, John Carter, and Michael Sadleir. Cambridge: Bowes (1951)

[518]   EDMONDSTON, Elizabeth: Books of your own; suggestions for running a personal library. National Bk Leag. 1951.

[519]   FARMER, Bernhard Jas: The gentle art of book-collecting. Thorsons (1950)

[520]   GRAVES, Haslehurst: The personal library. Grafton 1928.

[521]   JACKSON, Holbrook: The anatomy of bibliomania; repr. N.Y: Farrar, Straus 1950.

[522]   MUIR, Percy H: Book-collecting as a hobby. Gramol Publications 1945.

[523]   –Book-collecting: more letters to everyman. Cassell 1949.

[524]   – <u>ed</u>: Talks on book–collecting. Cassell 1952.

[525]   SADLEIR, Michael: Book–collecting. National Bk Leag. 1947. (<u>Reader's Guides</u>)

[526]   SMITH, F. Seymour: An English library (4ed.) ib. 1950.

[527]   STORM, Cotton, and Packman, Howard: Invitation to book–collecting. N.Y: Bowker 1947.

[528]   WILLIAMS, I.A: Elements of book–collecting. Mathews & Marrot 1927.

[529]   WINTERICH, John Tracy, and Randall, David A: Primer of book collecting; new ed. N.Y: Greenberg 1946.

See also Carter: Taste...[654]

FINE PRINTING. (Chapter XIII)

1. Book Design.

[530]   BRITISH Standards Institution: Booksizes and dating of books. (<u>B.S</u>. 1413:1947)

[531]   COBDEN–SANDERSON, T.J: The ideal book. Doves Pr. 1900.

[532]   COBDEN-SANDERSON, T.J: The ideal book; repr. San Francisco; J.H. Nash 1929; also in: Carrousel...[608]

[532]   DILL, F.P., and Garnett, P: The ideal book. N.Y: Limited Ed. Cl. 1931.

[533]   DWIGGINS, Wm Addison: Form letters: illustrator to author. N.Y: Rudge 1930.
Repr. in: MSS by WAD. N.Y: Typophiles 1947. p.113–23.

[534]   – Layout in advertising; rev.ed. N.Y: Harper (1948)

[535]   GILL, Eric: Essay on typography; 2ed. Sheed & Ward 1936.

[536]   HOWE, Ellic, ed: "The trade"; passages from the literature of the printing craft 1550–1935. Hutchinson 1943.
Contents include passages from Rogers, Updike, Morison, & others.

[537]   JACKSON, Holbrook: The printing of books; 2ed. Cassell 1948.

[538]   MCLEAN, R: Modern book design. British Coun. 1951. (<u>Arts in Brit.Ser.</u>)

[539]   MEYNELL, Sir Francis: National design in printing. N.–W. Polytechnic Print.Dep. 1943.

[540]   MONOTYPE Corporation: Leaves out of books. The Corp. 1938.

[540a] – Pages from books. ib. 1931.

[541]   MORISON, Stanley: Four centuries of fine printing. Benn 1924.
About 600 examples covering 1470– 1914.

[541a] – – 2 rev.ed. ib. 1949.
272 examples only, covering 1465–1924.

[542]   ORCUTT, W.D: Master makers of the book. Allen & Unwin (1928) Chaps 6, 8–9.

[543]   TARR, John Chas: Design in typography. Phoenix House 1951.

[544]   – How to plan print (2 rev.ed.) Crosby Lockwood (1949)

[545]   THORP, Joseph, ed: Design in modern printing. Benn (1928) (<u>Design & Ind.Ass.Yearb.</u>)

[546] TSCHICHOLD, Jan: Designing books. N.Y: Wittenborn [1951]

[547] UPDIKE, Daniel Berkeley: In the day's work. Cambridge, Mass: Harvard Univ.Pr. 1924. p.5–-70.

[548] – Some aspects of printing, old and new. New Haven: Rudge 1941. p.23–40.

[549] WADE, Arthur Cecil: Modern lettering and layout. Pitman 1950.

[550] WILLIAMSON, Hugh: Some notes on book design. National Bk Leag. (1950)

See also De la Mare: A publisher...[664] Jennett: Making ...[164] p.181–453; Johnson: The printer...[661] McMurtrie: The book. [168] p.451–508; Morison: First... [269] Morison: Typographic arts [272] Simon: Introduction...[173] Updike: Printing...[291]

2. Private and Select Presses, Bibliography.

[551] HAAS, I: Bibliography of material relating to private presses. Chicago: Black Cat Pr. 1937.
Supplement to [554]

[552] – Bibliography of modern American presses. ib. 1935.
Supplement to [554]

[553] INTERNATIONALE Bibliographic der Haus–Druckereien. (Bibliotheca Bibliographica 15)
In preparation.

[554] RANSOM, Will: Private presses and their books. N.Y: Bowker 1929.

[555] – Selective check lists of press books. N.Y: Duschnes 1945–6. Pts 1–4.

[556] STEELE, R: Revival of printing; a bibliographical catalogue of works issued by the chief modern English presses...imprinted in the Riccardi Press fount by Charles J. Jacobi, with (collotype) facs. Macmillan 1912.

[557] TOMKINSON, G.S: Select bibliography of the principal modern presses, public and private, in Great Britain and Ireland, with an introd. by B.H. Newdigate. First Ed.Cl. 1928.

Bibliographies of the products of particular presses will be found under their names on p.65–6.

3. **General.**

[558] ARMITAGE, Merle: Notes on modern printing. N.Y: Rudge [1945]

[559] BENNETT, Paul A., <u>ed</u>: Books & printing; a treasury for bibliophiles. Cleveland: World Publ.Co. (1951)

[560] BRITISH Museum: Catalogue of an exhibition of books illustrating British and foreign printing 1919–29. The Museum 1929.

[561] – Guide to the exhibition in the King's library. ib. 1939.

[562] GIBSON, S: English printing 1700– 1925. Dulau 1925.

[563] HAINES, Helen Elizabeth: Living with books; 2ed. N.Y: Columbia Univ.Pr. 1950. (<u>Columbia Univ.Stud.in Libr. Sci. 2</u>) p.185–218.

[564] HENRY Huntington Library: Fine books; an exhibition. San Marino: The Libr. 1936.

[565] MEYNELL, <u>Sir</u> Francis: The English printed book. Collins 1946. (<u>Britain in Pictures</u>)

[566] MORISON, Stanley: Modern fine printing; an exhibition. Benn 1925.
Supplement to [541]

[567] – Review of recent typography. <u>Fleuron</u> 1927.

[568] OSWALD, John Clyde: History of printing. N.Y: Appleton 1928. p.243– 85.

[569] POLLARD, Alfred Wm: Fine books. Methuen (1912) (<u>Connoisseur's Libr.</u>) p.297–308.

[570] POTTINGER, David Thos: Printers and printing. Cambridge, Mass: Harvard Univ.Pr. 1941. p.109– 30.

[571] SIMON, Oliver, and Rodenberg, J: Printing of to-day. P. Davies 1928.

See also Aldis: The printed...[156] p.48–61; Art...1951 [157] <u>The Times</u>: Printing...[274]

4. Individual Private and Select Presses.

Foulis.

[572]   MURRAY, D: Robert and Andrew Foulis. Glasgow: Maclehose 1913.

Baskerville.

[573]   BENNETT, Wm: John Baskerville. Birmingham: Central Sch. of Arts & Crafts 1937–9. 2v.

[574]   STRAUS, Ralph, and Dent, Rbt K: John Baskerville. Chatto & Windus 1907.
Corrections & additions to be published in Trans.Cambr. bl Soc. [62] & a new volume will be published in 1957 by R.J.L. Kingsford & John Dreyfus.

Strawberry Hill Press.

[575]   HAZEN, A.T: Bibliography of the Strawberry Hill Press. New Haven: Yale Univ.Pr. 1942.

[575a] LEWIS, Wilmarth Sheldon: Collector's progress. Constable 1952.

Bell.

[576]   MORISON, Stanley: John Bell 1745-1831; bookseller, printer, publisher, typefounder, journalist, etc. Cambridge Univ.Pr. 1930. Set in Bell type.

Bensley.

[577]   MARROT, H.V: William Bulmer [and] Thomas Bensley. Fleuron 1930.

Bulmer.
See [577]

Chiswick Press.

[578]   KEYNES, G: William Pickering, publisher. Fleuron 1924.

[579]   WARREN, Arthur: The Charles Whittinghams, printers. N.Y: Grolier Cl. 1896.

Daniel Press.

[580]   MEMORIALS of C.H.O. Daniel; with a bibliography of the press 1845-1919. Oxford: Bodleian 1921.

The Revival of the 90's.

[581]   BALSTON, Thos: The Cambridge University Press collection of private press types. Cambridge Univ.Pr. 1951.

[582]   RICKETTS, C: Defence of the revival of printing. Ballantyne Pr. 1899.

Kelmscott Press.

[583]   SPARLING, H.H: Kelmscott Press and William Morris. Macmillan 1924.
Contains Morris's Aims in founding the Kelmscott Press.

Eragny Press.

[584]   EXHIBITION of designs and engravings for the Eragny Press 1894–1914. Arts Coun. of Gt Br. [1950]

Ashendene Press.

[585]   HORNBY, C.H.StJ: Descriptive bibliography of the Ashendene Press. The Press 1935.

Nonesuch Press.

[586]   MEYNELL, Francis, and others: The Nonesuch century. The Press 1936.

Golden Cockerel.

[587]   Chanticleer...Apr.1921-Aug.1936. The Press 1936.

[588]   Pertelote...1936-Apr.1943. ib. 1943.

[589]   Cockalorum...Jun.1943-Dec.1948. ib.[1951]

5. Modern Fine Printing in America.

[590]   ANTHOENSEN, Fred: Types and bookmaking. Portland, Me: Southworth-Anthoensen Pr. 1943.

[591]   GRESS, Edmund Geiger: Art and practice of typography. N.Y: Harper 1931. p.62–74.

[592]   LEHMANN–HAUPT, Hellmut: The book in America; 2ed. N.Y: Bowker 1951.

[593]   WROTH, Lawrence C: Typographic heritage. Portland, Me: Southworth-Anthoensen Pr. 1950.

6. Individuals.

Coudy.

[594] GOUDY, Fred W: A half-century of type design and typography. N.Y: The Typophiles. 1946. 2v.

[594a] – Typologia. Berkeley; University of Calif.Pr. 1940. p.157–70.

[595] LEWIS, B: Behind the type. Pittsburgh: Carnegie Inst. of Tech. Dep. of Print. 1941.

[595a] NORTON, V: Goudy, master of letters. Chicago: Black Cat Pr. 1939.

Morison.

[596] CARTER, John, comp: A handlist of the writings of Stanley Morison. Cambridge Univ.Pr. 1950.

Newdigate.

[597] THORP, Joseph: B.H. Newdigate, scholar-printer 1869–1944. Blackwell 1950.

Rogers.

[598] ROGERS, Bruce: Account of the making of the Oxford lectern Bible. Monotype Corp. [1937]

[598a] – Paragraphs on printing. N.Y: Rudge 1943.

[599] UPDIKE, D.B: The work of Bruce Rogers. Oxford Univ.Pr. 1939.

7. Bibliographical Societies.

[600] BIBLIOGRAPHICAL Society 1892–1942; studies in retrospect. The Soc. 1945.

[601] BIGHAM, Clive: The Roxburghe Club 1812-1927. Oxford Univ. Pr. 1928.

[602] GRANNISS, R.S. Work of a book club. N.Y: University Bk Cl. 1937.

[603] WILLIAMS, Harold: Book clubs & printing societies of Great Britain and Ireland. First Ed.Cl. 1929.

[604] WINTERICH, John Tracy: The Grolier Club 1884–1950. N.Y: The Cl. 1950.

LIGHT READING.

[605] ALTICK, Richard D: The scholar adventurers. N.Y: Macmillan Co. 1950.

[606] BEWICK, Thos: Memoirs...by himself. 1862.

[607] BUTLER, Samuel: Quis desiderio...? (In his Collected Essays 11:105–13. Cape 1925)
First published in Universal Rev.(3) Jul.1888.

[608] CARROUSEL for bibliophiles...ed. by William Targ. N.Y: Duschnes 1947.

[609] GARNETT, R.S: Some book hunting adventures. Blackwood 1931.

[610] – Odd memories. ib. 1932.

[611] KIPLING, Rudyard: The press. (In Rudyard Kipling's Verse. Hodder (1933) p.521-2)

[612] MARSHAK, I.I: Black on white. Routledge 1932.

[613] POE, Edgar Allan: The gold bug. (In his Works. Harper 1852.v.1)

[614] ROWLES, Geo.E: The "Line" is on. London Soc. of Compositors (1948)

[615] SYMONS, Julian: Bland beginning. Gollancz 1949.

[616] ZWEIG, Stefan: The invisible collection. (In his Kaleidescope. N.Y: Viking Pr. 1934. p.303-17)

READERSHIPS IN BIBLIOGRAPHY.

1. The Sandars Lectures.

Instituted by Samuel Sandars in his will in 1894. The Sandars reader is appointed by the Vice-Chancellor of Cambridge University, the Master of Trinity College, and the other members of the Syndicate of the Cambridge University Library. He must deliver his lecture(s) annually (or biennially) during term and his subject shall be bibliography, typography, bookbinding, book illustration, the science of books and manuscripts, and the arts relating thereto.[1]

---

1 Middleton-Wake: The invention...[618] p.v-vii.

LITERATURE: SANDARS LECTURES

1895
[617] THOMPSON, Edw. Maunde: Greek, Latin, and English hand-writing.

1896
[618] MIDDLETON-WAKE, Chas Henry: The invention of printing: a series of 4 lectures delivered in the Lent term of 1897. Murray 1897.
Privately printed.

1897
[619] STEVENSON, Wm Henry: Anglo-Saxon chancery.

1898 and 1903
[620] DUFF, Edw. Gordon: Printers, stationers and bookbinders of Westminster and London, from 1476 to 1535. Cambridge Univ. Pr. 1906.

1899
[621] CLARK, John Willis: The care of books, etc. 2ed. ib. 1902.

1900
[622] KENYON, Frederic Geo: Development of Greek writing, B.C.300–A.D.900.

1901
[623] THOMPSON, Henry Yates: Lecture on some English illuminated MSS. Chiswick Pr. 1902.

1902
[624] JAMES, Montague Rhodes: Manuscripts in Cambridge.

1903
See 1898.

1904
[625] –THOMPSON, Henry Yates: Illustrated MSS of the 11.–15. centuries.

1905
[626] THOMPSON, Edw. Maunde: The history of illumination and ornamentation of MSS.

1906
MAITLAND, Fredc Wm. [Did not lecture]

1907
[627] JENKINSON, Francis John Henry: Ulrich Zell's early quartos. (Libr. [79] s4, 7:46–66 1926)

1909
[628] MADAN, Falconer: Localization and dating of MSS.

1910
[629] 'LINDSAY, Wallace Martin: Latin abbreviations.

1911
[630] 'DUFF, Edw. Gordon: English provincial printers, stationers and bookbinders to 1557. Cambridge Univ.Pr. 1912.

1912
[631] COWLEY, Arthur Ernest: The papyri of Elephantine.

1913
[632] GREG, Walter Wilson: Bibliographical and textual problems of the English miracle play cycles. (Libr. [79] s3, 5: 1–30, 168–205, 280–319, 365–99, 1914) Subsequently issued in book form. Moring 1914.

1914
[633] LOWE, Elias Avery: Characteristics of the so-called national scripts, punctuation and critical marks as aids in dating and placing MSS; Graeco-Latin MSS; the codex Bezae and the codex Laudianus.

1915
[634] POLLARD, Alfred Wm: Authors, players and pirates in Shakespeare's plays; the MSS of Shakespeare's plays; the improvers of Shakespeare. (Libr. [79] s3, 7:73–101; 198–226, 265–90, 1916)

1916–20 Lectures suspended.

1921
[635] HULME, Edw. Wyndham: Statistical bibliography in relation to the growth of modern civilization, etc. Grafton 1923. Privately printed. Includes lectures 3–4 only.

1922
[636] BOLLAND, W.C: Manual of year book studies. Cambridge Univ.Pr. 1925.

1923
[637] JAMES, Montague Rhodes: Pictorial illustration of the Old Testament from the 4.–16. centuries.
Printed as: A book of O.T. illustrations in the middle of the 13th century, etc. ib. 1927.

LITERATURE: SANDARS LECTURES

1924
[638] WALKER, Emery: Printing for book production.

1925
[639] MINNS, E.H: The influence of materials and instruments upon writing.

1926
[640] ESDAILE, Arundell: The sources of English literature: a bibliographical guide for students. Cambridge Univ.Pr. 1929.

1927
[641] HOBSON, Geoffrey Dudley: English binding before 1500. ib. 1929.

1928
[642] MCKERROW, Ronald Brunlees: Relationship of English printed books to authors' MSS in the 16. and 17. centuries.

1929
[643] DE RICCI, Seymour: English collectors of books and MSS [1530–1930] and their marks of ownership. Cambridge Univ. Pr. 1930.

1930
[644] SCHOLDERER, Victor: Invention of printing: facts and theories.
cf.his Invention of printing. (Libr. [79] s4,21(1)1–25

1931
[645] MORISON, Stanley: The English newspaper...physical developments of journals printed in London between 1622 and the present day. Cambridge Univ.Pr. 1932.

1932
[646] WILSON, John Dover: The manuscript of Shakespeare's Hamlet and the problems of its transmission; an essay in critical bibliography. ib. 1934. 2v.

1933
[647] KEYNES, Geoffrey Langdon: John Evelyn; a study in bibliography and a bibliography of his writings. ib. 1937.

1934
[648] MILLAR, Eric Geo: Some aspects of the comparative study of illuminated MSS.

1935
[649] GASELEE, Stephen: Bibliography and the classics.

1936
[650] GORDON, Cosmo Alexander: Manuscript missals; some English uses.

1937
[651] SADLEIR, Michael: Bibliographical aspects of the Victorian novel.

1938
[652] SISSON, Chas Jasper: Judicious marriage of Mr Hooker and the birth of "The laws of ecclesiastical polity". Cambridge Univ.Pr. 1940.

1939
[653] CRESWICK, Harry Richardson: Some recent work on early English printed books.

1940–6 Lectures suspended.

1947
[654] CARTER, John Waynflete: Taste and technique in bookcollecting, etc. (2nd impr., corrected). Cambridge Univ. Pr. 1949.

1948
[655] WOMALD, F: St Augustine's gospels and English mediaeval drawings.

1949
[656] OLDHAM, J.B: English blind-stamped bindings. C.U.P. 1952.

1950
[657] WILLIAMS, Sir Harold: New light on the publication of Gulliver's Travels, 1726; Swift's part in the revision of the 1735 text of Gulliver's Travels; Swift's corrected copy of the Miscellanies, 1727–32. ib. 1952.

1951
[658] BENNETT, H.S: Books and readers in early Tudor England. (From his English books & readers 1475–1557. ib. 1952)

1952
[658a] OATES, J.C.T: The history of the collection of incunabula in the University Library.

2. J.M. Dent Memorial Lectures.

In memory of the late J.M.Dent. Established by his son, arranged annually from 1931-8 by the Educational department of the London County Council. Subject: any connected with the book trade.

	1
[659]	BLACKWELL, Basil: The world of books. Dent (1932)
	2
[660]	SADLEIR, Michael: Authors and publishers. (1932)
	3
[661]	JOHNSON, John: The printer. (1933)
	4
[662]	CLAPPERTON, Rbt Henderson: Paper and its relationship to books. (1934)
	5
[663]	LEIGHTON, Douglas: Modern bookbinding. (1935)
	6
[664]	DE LA MARE, Richard: A publisher on book production. (1936)
	7
[665]	GOSSOP, Rbt Percy: Book illustration. (1937)
	8
[666]	RAYMOND, Harold: Publishing and bookselling. (1938)
	9
[667]	SWINNERTON, Frank Arthur: Reviewing and criticism of books. (1939)

3. James P.R.Lyell Readership in Bibliography.

A readership in the subjects of palaeography, typography, book illustration and bookbinding, and the whole 'science of books and manuscripts'. The reader is appointed by the Vice-Chancellor of Oxford university, Bodley's Librarian, and representatives of the Boards of the Faculties of Literae Humaniores, Modern History, English Language and Literature, and of the Oxford bibliographical Society. Assistance for the publication and illustration of the lectures is also envisaged. First lecture will be given by N.K. Ker on MSS.

4. Richard Rogers Bowker Memorial Lectures.

Established by the New York Public Library. Subject: book publishing in the United States and mutual problems of authors, publishers, librarians, readers, all makers and users of books.

They have all been published by the New York Public Library, in its Bulletin and as separates. The first 12 have been reprinted in 3 v. by the Typophiles.

[668] 1 STOKES, Fredk Abbot: A publisher's random notes 1880–1935. 1937.

[669] 2 HARCOURT, Alfred: Publishing since 1900. 1937.

[670] 3 CROFTS, Fredk S: Textbooks are not absolutely dead things. 1938.

[671] 4 COMPTON, Frank Elbert: Subscription books. 1939.

[672] 5 DAVIS, Elmer Holmes: Some aspects of the economics of authorship. 1940.

[673] 6 WATKINS, Ann: Literature for sale. 1941.

[674] 7 THOMPSON, Jas S: The technical book publisher in wartimes. 1942.

[675] 8 BAY, Helmuth: The history and technique of map making. 1943.

[676] 9 BRANDT, Joseph August: The university of every man. 1944.

[677] 10 BECHTEL, Louise Hunting Seaman: Books in search of children. 1946.

[678] 11 FISHER, Dorothy Canfield: Book-clubs. 1947.

[679] 12 MCCORMICK, Ken: Editors today. 1948.

13
[680] EVANS, Luther Harris: Copyright and the public interest. 1949.

14
[681] WEEKS, Edw: The schooling of an editor. 1950.

15
[682] EDMAN, Irwin: Unrequired reading. 1950.

5. A.S.W. Rosenbach Fellowship in Bibliography.

[683] FRANKLIN, Benjamin: Proposals relating to the education of youth in Pensilvania. Philadelphia: [University of Pa Pr. 1931]

[683a] MORLEY, Christopher D: Ex libris carissimis. ib. 1932.

[683b] WROTH, Lawrence C: An American bookshelf, 1755. ib. 1934.

[683c] LESLIE, Shane: The script of Jonathan Swift, and other essays. ib. 1935.

[683d] NEWTON, Alfred Edw: Bibliography and pseudo-bibliography, etc. ib, 1936.

[683e] ADAMS, Randolph Greenfield: Three Americanists. ib. 1939. WINSHIP, Geo. Parker: Printing... See [219]

[683f] – The Cambridge Press, 1638– 1692. ib. 1945.

[683g] BÜHLER, Curt F., and others: Standards of bibliographical description. ib. 1949.

[683h] VAIL, Rbt Wm G: The voice of the old frontier. ib. 1949.

[683i] FULTON, John F: The great medical bibliographers, ib. 1951.

6. Windsor Lectures.

Named after Phineas L. Windsor, Librarian of University of Illinois 1910– 40. Given annually since 1948.

1
[684] WINTERICH, John T: Three lantern slides. Urbana: University of Ill.Pr. 1949.

2
[684a] RIDENAUER, Louis N., and others: Bibliography in an age of science. Urbana: University of Ill.Pr. 1950.

3
[684b] NINETEENTH-century English books; some problems in bibliography. ib. 1952.
Contents: Importance of original editions, by G.N. Ray; American editions of English authors, by C.J. Weber; Some bibliographical agenda, by J. Carter.

> "Knowledge is of two kinds. We know
> a subject ourselves, or we know where
> we can find information upon it".
> Dr Johnson.

III

BIBLIOGRAPHIES

Primary and Secondary Sources.

'The material of <u>historical bibliography</u> comprises primary and secondary sources of book information. <u>Primary sources</u> constitute the bulk of contemporary historical bibliography, while <u>Secondary sources</u> constitute the great body of antiquarian book knowledge. The <u>primary sources</u> are to be found in the private and public documents of the persons and institutions concerned in the production of books. They comprise journals and correspondence of authors and their friends, and subsequently the correspondence and documents exchanged between authors and publishers. Then follow, if the book is published, advertisements and announcements, including those carried by the book itself and such as appear elsewhere. These are finally supplemented by reviews and news items in the journals of the day. If the book continues to live in the minds of the people for any length of time, contemporary records of the book are apt to multiply indefinitely, and bibliographical lore is correspondingly increased. The aggregate of the foregoing constitute the storehouse from which succeeding ages must derive their bibliographical information, and without which antiquarian bibliography would be an impossibility'.[1]

'"Primary" bibliographies are those which are the original record of the whole or part of their contents, "secondary" those in which material elsewhere registered is rearranged for the convenience of research... primary, that is they are either in whole or in part the original, and it may be the contemporary, record of books... secondary bibliographies...in which works already

---

1   FEIPEL: Elements...[foot-note p.9]

recorded in primary bibliographies are selected, recombined, analysed, in a manner which will make them throw light on each other, either by subject-matter, or authorship, or period, or typography... Bibliographies of bibliographies are, of course, secondary...'[1]

'In the bibliography of an historical subject there should...be a clear division...between primary material, such as contemporary documents, letters, diaries, reports of commissions, minute books, archives, etc. on the one aide, and secondary material on the-other'.[2]

Primary sources: the source material itself, containing original contributions and unorganized data; Secondary sources: compilations of data, e.g: Abstracts, i.e: Guides to source material.[3]

'Primary bibliographies are those compiled at first hand (e.g: the national bibliographies of copyright libraries) whereas secondary bibliographies are essentially derivative, drawn from, and based on those primary sources; they are often subject lists'.[4]

Shores[5] divides bibliographies into the following types:

A. General Bibliographies.
   1. Universal, 2. Eclectic, or Educational.

B. Selected Bibliographies.
   1. Period, 2. National, or Regional, 3. Trade, 4. Form, 5. Subject (including the related type, 5a. Bio-bibliography)

Of these A.2 and 8.1, 4-5a fall wholly or partly under secondary bibliographies.

---

1   ESDAILE: Student's...[34] p.273, 335.
2   COWLEY. [126] p.187.
3   [?] 'When found, make a note of'.
4   ib.
5   SHORES, Louis: Basic reference books. 2ed. Chicago: American Libr. Ass. 1939. p.207-8. [108]

PRIMARY BIBLIOGRAPHIES

1. Universal.
2. National.

1. <u>Universal Bibliographies</u>... 'those in which the compiler lists every book he can lay his hands on'.[1] They aim to be comprehensive and to list everything that has ever been published - ambitious, but hopeless.

One of the attempts was by the Institut International de Bibliographie (Brussels Institute) which, beginning in 1895, by 1 April 1934 had 15,646,346 entries towards a world bibliography,[2] although Iwinski in 1911 had estimated the total then to be 25,000,000 titles.[3] The task becomes more and more hopeless, but could still be achieved for the first century after the invention of printing.

[685]   BRUNET, Jacques Chas: Manuel du libraire et de l'amateur de livres; 5ed. Paris: Firmin-Didot 1860-80. 6v. +
3 Suppl. Repr. Berlin: Altmann 1922. 6v.
Edition on microcards. Microcard Fdn 1950. First ed. published 1809; 5ed. contains 31,872 entries + about 10,000 in Suppl. Rare or important books in all languages, especially the Romance. For collectors.
Arrangement: author list + (vol.6) subject index (arranged according to his classification) which includes some less important titles not included in the alphabetical section. Annotated & includes auction prices. Part of the Supplement is <u>Deschamps: Dictionnaire de geographie</u>. 2v.

---

1 Van Hoesen. B...[38] p.239.
2 OTLET, Paul: Traité de documentation, &c. Bruxelles: Palais Mondial 1934. p.405.
3 IWINSKI, M.B: La statistique internationale des imprimés. (<u>Bull.Inst. bibliogr.intern</u>. 16:1-139, 1911)

[686] GRAESSE, Johann Georg Theodor: Trésor de livres rares et précieux. Dresden: R.Kuntze 1859-69. 7v. in 4.
Repr. Facsimile Paris: Welter 1900. 8v.
Berlin: Altmann 1922. 7v; Milano: Görlich [1951] 8v. Contains over 100,000 entries. On the same lines as Brunet but with more Central European material. Arranged alphabetically by author, & gives annotations. Last volume is a Suppl. Many of the entries are taken from other Bs and, therefore, are not quite reliable.

[687] EBERT, Friedrich Adolf: Allgemeines bibliographisches Lexikon.. Leipzig: Brockhaus 1821-30. 2v. in 1.
[English ed. by Arthur Browne]: A general bibliographical dictionary. Oxford Univ.Pr. 1837. 4v.
Contains 24,280 entries. Also based on Brunet, but gives more information on German literature (to 1819). Short title, a few valuable notes. No index. Arranged by author.

The catalogues of the world's great libraries come under this heading.

[688] BRITISH museum: Catalogue of the printed books...1881-1900. 393 Pts in 95v. Suppl. 1900-5.44 Pts in 13v.
Photolithoprinted. Ann Arbor: Edwards 1946. 58v.
– Suppl.1950. 10v.
Arranged alphabetically by authors or, for anonymous works, under the proper noun or adjective. Excludes maps & music. Some form & subject parts: Academies, the Bible, Place-names, Catalogues, Periodical Publications, etc. Indexes to the bigger parts.

[689] –General catalogue of printed books. 1,1931+
New ed. of the above. Suppl. to v.1–3 was published 1932. Others have been published in the Library's monthly 'List of accessions' s3, 1, 1932+

Unofficially supplementing the above is:

[690] PEDDIE, Rbt Alex: Subject index of books published before 1880. Grafton 1933–48. v.1–4.

200,000 titles. Arranged alphabetically by subjects, then chronologically.

[691]   BRITISH Museum: Subject index of the modern works added to the library of the British Museum. The Trustees 1, 1902+
v.1–3, 1902–3 (ed. by Fortescue) cover 1881–1900 (about 155,000 titles). Each of the following vols covers 5 years. Arranged alphabetically by subject-word, sub-divided systematically: an 'alphabetico-classed' catalogue. Does not include works that may be easily found in the General catalogue, e.g. Personal names, or Fiction. Whole of the second World war will be found in the 1941–5 vol. No indexes.

[692]   PARIS. Bibliothèque Nationale: Catalogue générale des livres imprimes. Paris 1, 1897+
In 3 Ser: 1: Authors known; 2: Pseudonyms & collected works; 3: Government publications, Academies, &c. Alphabetical arrangement under each.

[693]   LIBRARY of Congress: Catalog of the books represented by L.C. printed cards...to July 1942. Ann Arbor: Edwards 1942–6. 167v. Supplement. 1948. 42v.
Author list only provided with cross-references for change of name. The supplement covers Aug.1942-Dec. 1946. Restricted to Roman, Greek, Cyrillic, Hebrew, & Gaelic alphabets.

[693a] — Author Catalog. 1948+
1948: Cumulative catalog: published 9 times a year, cumulated quarterly & annually. (1948/52 in preparation); included a supplement of cards catalogued by the Army Medical Library, later published separately. The Author catalog includes all books catalogued by L.C. regardless of date of imprint.
For bibliographies of Anonyma see [768]
For bibliographies of Incunabula see [787-96]

[693b] — Subject catalog. 1950+
3 quarterly issues, cumulated annually. Arranged alphabetically by subject, includes all the information on the cards in the Author catalog except notes & tracings.[1] Only L.C. acquisitions with fairly recent imprints are included. See references in all issues, See also references in annual cumulations only.

---

1   GULL, C.D: The cumulative catalog technique at the Library of Congr. (Amer.Docum. 2(3) p.131–41,1951)

2. National Bibliographies.[1]

National or regional bibliographies are lists of materials published in, and/or about a given country or region. When the region is small, as a county or town, then the term Local bibliography is used. There are also what may be termed National subject bibliographies, i.e. lists of the publications in a given country on a given subject, e.g. Hall's South African Geology. These lists, however, fall outside our scope. There are also national, form bibliographies, e.g. Boyd [786] or the D.N.B. National bibliographies proper are divided into Trade bibliographies, compiled primarily to aid the book trade, and National bibliographies, compiled by professional cataloguers.

"A general national bibliography of all books and pamphlets published and on sale in each country, regardless of the language in which they are written, and preferably including published theses and academic publications and government publications of public interest...should enable items to be traced quickly by subject...author...and...title."[2]

For each of the following countries retrospective bibliographies are arranged chronologically by the latest year covered.

UNITED KINGDOM. Retrospective[3,4]

[694]   POLLARD, Alfred Wm, and Redgrave, Gilbert Richard, comp: Short-title catalogue of books printed in England, Scotland and Ireland, and of English books printed abroad 1475-1640. Bibliographical Soc. 1926. Repr. 1950.

---

1   WORLEY, Parker: Current national Bs. (Quart.J.curr.Acquisitions. Libr.Congr. 6(4)28- 33, 7(1)14–22, 7(2)11-13, 7(3)14-21, 8(2)15-26, 1949-
    Rev.Docum. [97] has had surveys of the bl resources of various countries in most numbers since 1950.
2   UNESCO. Conference on the Improvement of bl Services: General report. Paris: Unesco 1950. p.4-5.
3   COLE: Survey of the B. of English literature 1475-1640. (Pap.bibliogr. Soc.Amer. 23(2)1-95,1929)
4   BIBLIOGRAPHICAL aids to research. IV: General lists of books printed in England. (Bull.Inst.hist.Res. 12:164-74, 1934-5)

Called the <u>S.T.C.</u> A finding list of about 26,000 titles arranged according to B.M. Rules. Various libraries (Henry E. Huntington, Newberry, and others) have published supplements to it.

A subject index to the <u>S.T.C.</u> has been announced by A.A. White.

[694a] MORRISON, Paul G: Index of printers, publishers and booksellers in...<u>S.T.C.</u>... Charlottesville: Bibliographical Soc.of the Univ .of Va 1950.

[695] ARBER, Edw: A transcript of the registers of the Company of stationers of London, 1554-1640. London: Privately printed, 1875-94. 5v. Repr.[1]
v.1-4 reproduce the actual registers; v.5 lists the works in chronological order & alphabetically according to printers; 1571-6 were not published.

[695a] LONDON. <u>Stationers' Company</u>: A transcript of the registers of the Worshipful Company of stationers from 1640-1708; ed. for the Roxburghe club by G.E. Briscoe Eyre, etc. London; Privately printed 1913-4. 3v.

[696] WING, Donald Goddard: Short-title catalogue of books printed in England, Scotland, Ireland, Wales, and British America, and of English books printed in other countries, 1641-1700. N.Y: Index Soc. 1945-51. 3v.
Comprising about 90,000 titles, arranged alphabetically by author; anonymous works under first word, or under a few large headings: Bible, &c.

[697] WATT, Rbt: Bibliotheca Britannica... Edinburgh: Constable 1824. 4v.
Contains about 40,000 titles, including many periodicals & publications of societies. Includes also translations & some foreign titles. v.1-2: Alphabetical author list; 3-4: Subject index to all titles arranged alphabetically under subject words & subdivided chronologically. Anonymous titles are only mentioned in v.3-4.

[698] LOWNDES, Wm Thos: The bibliographer's manual of English literature: new ed...by Henry Geo. Bohn. Bell 1858-64. 11 Pts <u>in 6v</u>. Repr. 1890.

---

1   GREG: Entrance, licence & publication. (<u>Libr</u>. s4, 25(1/2) 1-22, 1944)

First ed. was published 1828-34 by Pickering. New ed. contains over 50,000 rare, curious, & useful books published in, or relating to Great Britain & Ireland. This is really the English "Brunet" with annotations & contemporary prices. Alphabetically arranged by authors, titles, or subject words. v.6: Societies & private presses. No indexes. Excludes theology.
— Supplement. See Marchmont [769]

UNITED KINGDOM. 2. Current.

[699] ENGLISH Catalogue of Books. Publishers' Circular 1801/36+
Published annually, arranged in one alphabet of authors & titles. Excludes periodicals. A supplement contains books in series & publications of societies. Comp. from [700]. Supersedes London catalogue, & British catalogue.

[700] PUBLISHERS' Circular and Booksellers' Record. ib. 1837+
Weekly. Contains the section "Books of the week" arranged as above. Cumulated in the last issue of each month.

[701] REFERENCE Catalogue of Current Literature. Whitaker 1951. 2v.
Has been published at intervals of a few years since 1874. Especially useful since 1936, when it was changed from a collection of publishers' lists of books in stock to one list of books in print arranged alphabetically by author, with an index to titles & some subject headings. 1952 ed. in preparation.

[702] WHITAKER's Cumulative Booklist. ib. 1924+
Quarterly, cumulated annually, & 4-or 5-yearly. Contains a classified section in 48 groups, which is a cumulation of the lists in Current literature [704] & an alphabetical section of authors & titles cumulated from The Bookseller [703] + a list of the more important government publications.

[703] BOOKSELLER. ib. 1858+
Weekly lists of publications, arranged alphabetically, cumulated monthly.

[704] CURRENT Literature, ib. 1858+
Small reviews & a classified list of publications. Published monthly.

[705]	BRITISH National Bibliography. Council of the B.N.B. 1950+
A weekly list based upon the copyright copies sent to British Museum. Excludes cheap novellettes, publications of the government of Eire, music, maps. Periodicals are only included for the first number, or when change of title occurs. Arranged by Dewey (15ed). Catalogued according to the 'Joint Code'. Weekly author index. Monthly cumulated author-title-subject index. Cumulated quarterly & annually. Index gives most of the information in the main entries in the classified part.

UNITED STATES.

[706]	EVANS, Chas: American bibliography...1639 to [1799]. Chicago: Blakely Pr. 1903-34. 12v. Offset Repr. N.Y: P.Smith 1942. 12v.
Chronological arrangement of books, pamphlets, & periodicals with locations. Each volume has 3 indexes: 1: Authors; 2: Classified (Dewey); 3: Typographers & editors. Should have gone to 1820, when [707] began.

[707]	ROORBACH, Orville Augustus: Bibliotheca americana... 1820– [61]. N.Y: Roorbach 1856– 61. 4v.

[708]	AMERICAN Catalogue of Books. N.Y: Publishers' Weekly 1866–71; 1880–1911. 2v. + 9v. Repr. N.Y: P. Smith 1938–40. 2v, + 9v.
First series covers 1861–71 & was ed. by James Kelly; 2.ser. 1876–910. Alphabetical sequence of authors, titles & subject-words. Excludes periodicals, music, maps, & almanacs.

[709]	UNITED States Catalog; 4ed. N.Y: Wilson 1928.
A list of publications in English published throughout the world & in print at the time of publication of the Catalog. Covers U.S. copyright entries & to some extent federal government publications. Arrangement as C.B.I. [710] of which the Catalog's 5-yearly supplements are cumulations.

[710]	CUMULATIVE Book Index. ib. 1898+
Published monthly, except August & October, cumulated quarterly, half-yearly, annually, & 5-yearly. Arranged in one alphabetical sequence of authors, titles, subjects, editors, translators, series, & illustrators.

[711] PUBLISHERS' Weekly. N.Y: Bowker 1872+
Author list of books, including pamphlets, with annotations. Cumulated title index monthly.

[712] PUBLISHERS' Trade List Annual. ib. 1873+
Annual lists from about 500 publishers. Indexed by <u>Books in print</u>. 1951+

AUSTRALIA.

[713] WHITE, H.L., <u>comp</u>: Australian books. Canberra: Commonwealth nat.Libr. 1949+

CANADA.

[714] CANADIANA. Ottawa: Canadian bl Centre 1923+
Published twice a month, with a monthly index, cumulated annually. Comprises books published in Canada, books about Canada or books published by Canadians in other countries. Includes government publications. 1923-50 published annually & called <u>Canadian Catalogue of books</u>.

UNION OF SOUTH AFRICA.

[715] MENDELSSOHN, Sidney: Mendelssohn's South African bibliography. Kegan Paul,Trench, Trübner 1910. 2v. Mainly an author list (but anonymous works are entered under subject or form word: S.Afr.War, almanacs, <u>&c</u>) of works published in or about South Africa mainly in the Mendelssohn Collection (now in the Library of Parliament) full title & very good notes. Appendixes: South African imperial blue-books (arranged chronologically under name of province); Magazines published in S.Afr. (arranged alphabetically by author's name under each title); Foreign periodical articles on South Africa (arranged alphabetically by author under each province); List of autograph letters; Chronological, topographical, & subject index; Cartography. Kept up-to-date by the Library of Parliament's <u>Annual List of Africana</u>.

LITERATURE: NATIONAL BIBLIOGRAPHIES

[716]   STATE Library. Publications acquired in terms of Act No.9 of 1916 (The Copyright Act). Pretoria: State Library 1933+
Monthly author list, cumulated annually, 5-year cumulation projected.
The other copyright libraries also publish lists of the acquisitions. - South African Public Library in its Quarterly Bulletin, & in Grey Bibliographies.

[717]   SOUTH African Catalogue of Books; 3ed. Johannesburg 1947. Suppl. ib. 1948+
Third ed. covers 1900–1947 & is arranged alphabetically by authors or titles. Suppl. published monthly (alphabetical author arrangement) cumulated into annual volumes, classified under about 30 headings, English for English titles, Afrikaans for Afrikaans titles.

[718]   SOUTH African Publisher and Bookseller. Johannesburg: South Afr. Publ. & Bksellers Ass. 1951+
Monthly. Each no. contains a list of new books published by the Ass's members.

GERMANY.

[719]   KAYSER, Chr. Gottlob: Vollständiges Bücher-Lexikon. Leipzig: Tauchnitz 1834–1912. 36v. + 6 indexes. Covers the publications of Germany (incl. translations) & the German publications of the surrounding countries (Austria, Switzerland, &c.) for 1750– 1910. Each section of about 2 vols covers about 3– 6 years. Arranged alphabetically by authors, indexes alphabetically by subject words (or form headings: Novels, Poems, &c.) Maps are included. (Index in 27–8)

[720]   HINRICHS Katalog. Leipzig: Hinrichs 1857–1913. 13v. Contents & arrangement as above. Each vol. covers about 3–5 years. Title varies. Superseded by Deutsches Bücherverzeichnis. [723] Covers 1851–1912. 1–2: Bücher-Katalog von A. Kirchhoff.

[721]   HINRICHS Halbjahrs–Katalog der im deutschen Buchhandel erschienenen Bücher, Zeitschriften, Landkarten, u.s.w. ib. 1797–1916. 235v.
Superseded by Halbjahrsverzeichnis der im deutschen Buchhandel erschienenen Bücher... later: Jahresverzeichnis des deutschen Schrifttums.[724]

[722] GESAMTKATALOG der deutschen Bibliotheken. Berlin: Preussische Staatsbibliothek 1931–9. 14v. A–Beethordung. Union list of books in German libraries. MS lost during war. v.1–8: <u>Gesamtkatalog der preussischen Bibliotheken.</u> The Library is now called Westdeutsche Bibliothek. About 18 libraries co-operated in v.1–8, about 100 in v.9–14.

[723] DEUTSCHES Bücherverzeichnis. Leipzig: Börsenverein der deutschen Buchhändler 1911/4–1936/40. 22v. Supersedes Kayser [719] & Hinrichs Katalog [720] 3–5-yearly list in 2 sections: one alphabetical, the other classified. 1941–50 to be published shortly in 48 pts.

[724] JAHRESVERZEICHNIS des deutschen Schrifttums. ib. 1917+ 1917–1944/5: <u>Halbjahrsverzeichnis der im deutschen Buchhandel erschienenen Bucher, Zeitschriften und Landkarten.</u> Supersedes <u>Hinrichs Halbjahrskatalog.</u> [721] In 2 sections, one alphabetical by author, the other classified. At present several years in arrear. Second half of 1944 not published, to be included in [723].

[725] DEUTSCHE Nationalbibliographie. ib. 1931+
A. A weekly list of publications in the German language available through the book trade. (Supersedes <u>Wöchentliches Verzeichnis</u>...published by the Börsenverein 1916–30). Classified under 24 headings with an index to authors & subjects, cumulated monthly & quarterly.
B. A monthly list arranged as A, including the publications not available through the regular book trade.
Postwar issues cover mainly the East zone.

[726] BIBLIOGRAPHIE der deutschen Bibliothek. Frankfurt a/M: Deutsche Bibliothek 1947+
A weekly list including books whether available through the booktrade, or not. Covers mainly the West zone. Cumulated every two months into [727] half-yearly as <u>Bibliographie der deutschen Bibliothek. Halbjahres Verzeichnis.</u> Annually & 6-yearly as: <u>Deutsche Bibliographie</u> in 2pts: I. Alphabetical title; II. Subject.

[727] Das DEUTSCHE Buch. ib. 1950+
Will eventually be published every two months.

AUSTRIA.

Before the collapse of Germany Austria participated in: Deutscher Gesamtkatalog [722]. Thereafter the Austrian National Library published:

[728] OESTERREICHISCHE Bibliographie. Wien: Oesterreichische Nationalbibliothek 1, 1945+
Quarterly or oftener. Classified with author & subject indexes.

SWITZERLAND.

[729] SCHWEIZER Bücherverzeichnis/Répertoire du livre suisse/ Elenco del libro suizzero: Zürich: Schweizerischer Buchhändler- und Verlegerverein 1948/50+
A cumulation of titles in "Schweizer Buch" which is published in two parts: A. fortnightly, containing books for sale, B. 6 times a year, containing books not in the trade. Partly a continuation of the National Library's Systematisches Verzeichnis der schweizerischen oder die in schweizbetreffenden Veröffentlichungen. (1901/20–1949?)

NETHERLANDS.

[730] BRINKMAN'S Cumulatieve Catalogus van Boeken. Leiden: Sijthoff 1846+
A monthly list in 2 parts, one alphabetical by authors, the other classified. Each no. is a cumulation of issues from the beginning of the year. The last issue forms the annual volume called Brinkman's catalogus..., which eventually is issued in 5-yearly cumulations. Includes maps & periodicals. Covers 1790 onwards.

DENMARK.

[731] DANSK BOGFORTEGNELSE. 1841/58- Köbenhavn: Gads 1861+ 18–20 times a year (only alphabetical) cumulated into monthly & annual volumes issued in two sections:
1. alphabetical author list, with full entry; 2. classified (Dewey) list. Eventually five-yearly. The 5-yearly catalogue contains a list for the Faroe Islands & for Greenland, & before 1940 included Iceland, too.

[732] Det DANSKE Bogmarked. Köbenhavn: Den danske Forlägger-
forening 1854+
Earlier called "Dansk Boghandlertidende." Weekly, contains a
list called "Dansk bogfortegnelse".

NORWAY.

[733] NORSK Bogfortegnelse. Oslo: Norsk Bokhandlerforening
1814/47+
Usually 5-yearly. Arranged alphabetically by authors, with subject index. Compiled from Arskatalog [734]

[734] ÅRSKATALOG over norsk Litteratur. Oslo: Cammermeyer
1893+
Annual list arranged alphabetically by author & title, & a systematic list. Includes a list of maps. 1893–1902: "Kuartalkatalog over norsk litteratur".

[735] KVARTALSFORTEGNELSE over norsk Litteratur. Oslo: Norsk Bokhandlerforening 1903+
A quarterly, classified list with an author index. Before its publication here appears as an alphabetical list in the weekly Norsk bokhandlertidende.

SWEDEN.

[736] SVENSK Bok-katalog. Stockholm: Svenska Bokförläggare-
föreningen 1878+
Usually every 5 years. Each vol. in 2 pts: 1. Alphabetical author & title list; 2. Classified subject list.

[737] ÅRSKATALOG för svenska Bokhandeln. ib. 1861+
An annual list arranged as "Dansk Bogfortegnelse"[731] includes a separate list of the year's musical compositions. Cumulated into [736]

[738] SVENSK Bokförteckning. ib. 1913+
A monthly classified list, with an author index. Cumulated from an alphabetical section in the weekly "Svensk bokhandelstidning".

FRANCE.

[739] QUÉRARD, Joseph Marie: La France littéraire, etc. Paris: Firmin-Didot 1827–64. 12v.
Period ca.1700–1826. A selective list of works of a certain literary value, including some books published in French by foreigners & translations into French. Arranged alphabetically by authors.

[740] – La littérature française contemporaine 1827–49. ib. Daquin 1842–57. 6v. Arranged as the above.

[741] CATALOGUE général de la Librairie française. Paris: Lorenz 1867+
A 4–10-yearly list of French publications (also some published in other countries) arranged alphabetically by authors or titles, excluding periodicals, university, or government publications. Annotated. Best for the humanities. Index to each section arranged alphabetically by subjects, fiction arranged under form (poetry, novels, etc.) Covers 1840+ Editors: 1–11: Lorenz; 12–28: Jordell; 28(3)–32: H. Stein; 33+: Service bl Hachette.e

[742] RÉPERTOIRE de Bibliographie française. Paris: Letoozey 1, 1935+
Will cover the literature of France & her colonies & French works published in other countries 1501–1930. Arranged alphabetically by author or title. Excludes official publications, maps, & music. Has only reached letter A.

[743] LIBRAIRIE française. Paris: Cercle de la Librairie 1930+
Annual & 3-yearly. Each vol. in 3 pts: 1. Classified by U.D.C; 2. Title index; 3. Author index. Annual vol. called Livres de l'année. Includes French books published in Switzerland & Belgium.

[744] BIBLIOGRAPHIE de la France. ib. 1811+
Weekly. The copyright list of France, arranged in classified order, including the press mark of the book in Bibliothèque Nationale. Irregular supplements of list of maps, music, theses, etc. Author & title index published at end of year, & alphabetical list of periodicals.

[745] "BIBLIO". Paris: Hachette 1933+
Monthly periodical, the greater part of which is taken up by an alphabetical list of authors, titles, & subjects. The annual, cumulated vols are similarly arranged.

SPAIN.

[746] PALAU, Ant: Bibliografia general espanola e hispano-americana... Baralme 1, 1948+
New ed. of his: "Manual del librero hispano-Americano". In one alphabetical arrangement of authors' names & pseudonyms, includes all books & pamphlets printed in Spain & the Latin Americas, as well as all translations into other languages since the invention of printing.

SECONDARY BIBLIOGRAPHIES

1. Eclectic.
2. Bibliography of Bibliographies.
3. Form Bibliographies.
4. Subject Bibliographies.
5. Author Bibliographies and 5a. Bio-Bibliographies.

1. Eclectic, or Educational Bibliographies.

The second kind of universal bibliographies, the eclectic, or educational bibliographies are much more numerous than universal bibliographies. They aim to be selective for the purpose of aiding reader or student. Such bibliographies are general in the sense that they need not be limited by time, place, or subject, but necessarily are not universal because they purposely omit many titles. When using secondary bibliographies one must realise that they are inevitably out-of-date when published.

[747] A.L.A. CATALOG. Chicago: American Libr.Ass. 1926.
The A.L.A. Catalog is a list of best books for public libraries. The first list was published 1904 & contained 8,000 titles. The latest, 1926, contained 10,000 titles & was supplemented in 1931, 1938, & 1943 by newer titles. The Catalog is arranged by Dewey. 11 per cent. is fiction & 9.2 per cent. childrens books. Largely based on:

LITERATURE: ECLECTIC BIBLIOGRAPHIES

[748]   BOOKLIST Books. ib. 1926+
An annual list of 300 books for the small library. Selected from [748a] May be considered as the annual supplement to [747]

[748a] A.L.A. BOOKLIST. ib. 1905+
Published monthly & contains lists of books for high schools, children's libraries, or lists of books in foreign languages, of topical interest, or of documents, new editions or pamphlets. Gives L.C. card no. & classification no. & Sept.1953+ '(W)' for H.W.Wilson cards.

[749]   STANDARD Catalog. N.Y: Wilson 1940.
The 1940 rev. ed. comprised 12,000 books for the medium-sized library; 1 suppl. 1941–5 added 3,908 titles; thereafter (annual) supplements. Arranged by Dewey. Annotated. Asterisks indicate suitable books for small libraries, or especially recommended books. The Wilson Co. publishes printed cards for most books in their Standard Catalog. Index to authors, titles, subjects, & analytical entries in one alphabetical sequence.

[750]   CHILDREN'S Catalog; 7ed.rev. ib. 1946.
First ed. 1909. Some early editions formed part of the 'Standard Catalog'. In 3 pts: 1. Arranged as a dictionary catalogue, full entries; 2. Classified catalogue; 3. Graded list. (Some other parts in the main ed: out-of-print books, &c.) 1947–9 + annual supplements.

[751]   BOOKS of the Month and Books to Come. Simpkin Marshall 1952+
Monthly. Supersedes Books of the month (1875) & Books to come (1944)

[752]   BRITISH Book News. National Bk Leag. for the Brit.Council. 1, 1940+
Monthly. Contains one or two subject Bs, & a classified, annotated select list of books published in the British Commonwealth. Cumulated annually. (1–14)1940–Apr.1941: Selection of recent Books published in Great Britain.

[753]   SONNENSCHEIN, Wm Swan: Best books; 3ed. Routledge 1910–35. 6v. 1–2,1910–2; 3–5,1923–31; 6 – Index. Still very useful. Brief annotations. First ed. 1887.

[754] MINTO, John: Reference books. Library Ass. 1929. Suppl. ib. 1931.
A classified list, arranged by the U.D.C. with an author & title index. No prices given. Best for U.K. books.

[755] WINCHELL, Constance M: Guide to reference books; 7ed. Chicago: American Libr.Ass. 1951.
An annotated list of reference books classified by Dewey. Has an international outlook, though mainly important for Anglo-American material. Includes prices. Supplements issued every 3 years. Editions 1–2 by Alice Bertha Kroeger; 3–6 by Isadore Gilbert Mudge.

2. Bibliography of Bibliographies. (a) Retrospective

[756] PETZHOLDT, Julius: Bibliotheca bibliographica. Leipzig: Engelmann 1866.
A list of 5,500 bibliographies arranged in 3 Sects: (i) Works on B. in general. B1 systems; (ii) Bs in several languages; (iii) National Bs. Subject Bs. Index to names of authors, titles of anonymous works. Best for German titles.

[757] VALLÉE, Léon Alex: Bibliographie des bibliographies. Paris: Terquem 1883. Suppl. ib. 1887. 2v.
Contains about 10,000 titles, including some Bs in periodicals. Arranged alphabetically by authors, followed by a painstaking subject index. Russian titles are only given in French translation.

[758] STEIN, Henri: Manuel de bibliographie générale. Paris: Picard 1897.
Contains about 5,500 entries arranged in classified order, sub-arranged chronologically. There is an index to subjects but none to authors. 3 appendixes: (i) Names of places where printing has been carried out, with their Latin equivalents; (ii) List of indexes to individual periodicals; (iii) Catalogues of the principal libraries of the world.

[759] COURTNEY, Wm Prideaux: A register of national bibliography. Constable 1905–12. 3v.
Contains Bs by Englishmen on other countries' literature, or by foreigners on English literature, including those published in books or periodicals. Arranged alphabetically by subjects with an index to subjects

& authors at the end of each vol. v.1–2 were published in 1905. v.3 is an appendix. Pagination is only given in cases where the B. forms part of an article or book.

[760] INDEX Bibliographicus; 3ed. Paris: Unesco 1952+ 2v. The 1st & 2nd ed. were published by the League of Nations. An international index to sources of current bl information in periodicals, or institutions; also to those periodicals which only publish material in certain fields. Arranged by U.D.C. classification, with an index by countries & another to titles. Notes whether coverage is comprehensive or selective. Comp. by Th. Besterman. Lists some 3,300 items.

[761] BOHATTA, Hanna, and Hodes, Frank: Internationale Bibliographie der Bibliographien. Frankfurt: Klostermann 1939–50. 8 pts.
In two parts: (i) National & general; (ii) Subject. Author & subject indexes. Includes mostly separately published Bs, many foreign Bs included. A few annotations. W.Funke was co-editor for the first parts.

[762] BESTERMANN, Theodore: A world bibliography of bibliographies...2ed. Privately printed 1947–9. 3v.
Includes only separately published Bs, but incl. abstracts, digests, abstracts of patent specifications, catalogues of special libraries, calendars, indexes, &c. Contains 63,776 entries. International in scope, excl. works in the oriental languages. Number of items in each B. is indicated after the entry. Arranged by subjects, sub-arranged by countries, & again chronologically.

[763] MALCLES, Louise Noëlle: Les sources du travail bibliographique. Genève: Droz 1950–
v.1–2 published so far. Planned in 3v: 1. Bs générales, &c; 2. Humanistic; 3. Scientific, subject Bs; superb annotation.

2. Bibliography of Bibliographies. (b) Current

[764] BULLETIN of Bibliography and Dramatic Index. Boston: Faxon 1897+
Regular features: Magazine notes & Births & deaths in the periodical world; Principal contents of the library press; Index to library reference lists. Dramatic index see [779].

[765] INTERNATIONALER Jahresbericht der Bibliographie (Joris Vorstius). Leipzig: Harrassowitz 1,1930+
A periodical supplement to Schneider's Handbuch...[130] Arranged in 3 Sects: (i) Theoretical B. & int. lists; (ii) Ordinary, national Bs; (iii) Subject B. Annotated, & contains an alphabetical subject & title index in each vol. None published since 11,1940.

[766] BULLETIN de Documentation bibliographique. Paris: Bibliothèque Nat. 1934+
10 times a year. Incl. current Bs of Bs on all subjects, published in books & periodicals. Classified arrangement. Annual index.

[767] BIBLIOGRAPHIC Index. N.Y: Wilson 1938+
Quarterly. Cumulated annually, & eventually, in 4-yearly vols. Includes Bs from periodicals. International in scope, but best for American & English periodicals. Dec.1948+ incl. notes of new Bs & Bs in preparation. (cf. also News Sheet bibliogr.Soc. Amer. [49])

3. Form Bibliographies.

Lists of materials limited as to types of material included.

ABSTRACTS

See under Reviews, Theses.

ANONYMA AND PSEUDONYMA

[768] HALKETT, Samuel, and Laing, John: Dictionary of the anonymous and pseudonymous English literature; new & enl. ed. by James Kennedy [and others] Edinburgh: Oliver & Boyd 1926–34. 7v.
Arranged alphabetically by first word of title not an article. v.7 = Index & second suppl. First ed. was published 1882–8.

[769] MARCHMONT, Fredk: Concise handbook of...literature issued anonymously, etc. The Author 1896. Supplement to Lowndes [698]

BANNED BOOKS

[770] GILLETT, Chas R: Burned books. N.Y: Columbia Univ.Pr. 1932. 2v.

[771]   INDEX Librorum prohibitorum. Vatican 1948.
Started by bull of Pope Alexander VI in 1501. Issued at irregular intervals. A mixed alphabet of authors & titles.

BELLES-LETTRES

See Cambridge B...[143]

BIOGRAPHY

[772]   RICHES, Phyllis M: Analytical bibliography of universal collected biography. Library Ass. 1934. 55,000 entries.

[773]   ARNIM, Max: Internationale Personalbibliographie 1800–1943; 2Aufl. Leipzig: Hiersemann 1952. 2v.
Supersedes the personal Bs in Petzholdt [756] & Vallée [757]. Includes Bs of the writings about some 25,000 writers of all nationalities. Incl. material in periodicals & serials.

[774]   BIOGRAPHY Index. N.Y: Wilson 1947.
Best for American material. Portraits indicated. Subject index of professions & occupations. Indexes some 1,500 periodicals.

See also Portraits, [817] & Bio-Bibliography p.108 here.

CONGRESSES

[775]   GREGORY, Winifred: International congresses & conferences 1840–1937. N.Y: Wilson 1938.
Arranged alphabetically by congresses, thereunder chronologically. Lists all publications by the congresses, but includes only international congresses. Locates copies in American libraries. Subject index.

DIARIES

[776]   MATTHEWS, Wm: American diaries...prior to 1861. Berkeley: University of Calif.Pr. 1945.

[777]   – British diaries...between 1442 & 1942. ib. 1950. Includes MS diaries. A B. of British autobiographies & a B. of Commonwealth diaries are <u>in preparation</u>.

DRAMA

[778]   BRITISH Drama League: The player's library and Bibliography of the theatre. Faber & Faber 1950. – 1st Suppl. ib. 1951.
A catalogue of the League's library. An alphabetical, annotated author list, index of titles & subjects. Critical section with author index.

[779]   DRAMATIC Index. Boston: Faxon 1909+ Annual.

[780]   FIRKINS, Ina Ten Eyck: Index of plays, 1800–1926. N.Y: Wilson 1927. Suppl. 1927–34. ib. 1935.
Only plays in English (also translations). Main author list with title & subject index.

[780a] LOGASA, Hannah, and Ver Nooy, Winifred: Index to one-act plays. Boston: Faxon 1924. 1–3 Suppl. ib. 1932–40. Plays in English (also translations into English) published separately or in collections. Author, title & subject indexes.

ESSAYS

[781]   ESSAY and general Literature Index. N.Y: Wilson 1900/33+
Published half-yearly, cumulated annually, & every 7th year. In one alphabet gives entries under author, title & subject; full entry under each, unless the work appears in several collections.

FICTION

[782]   FICTION Catalog; [4ed.] N.Y: Wilson 1941.
Formed part of Standard catalog [749]. In dictionary form. 1st Suppl. 1942/6, thereafter published annually.

[783]   SADLEIR, Michael: XIX century fiction. Cambridge Univ. Pr. (1951) 2v.
(I) Alphabet of authors, describing their first (& certain subsequent) editions, with a sub-section "comparative scarcities".
(II) The yellow-back coll., arranged in a mixed alphabet of author, series-titles & a few group-headings.
(III) "Novelists Libraries", "Standard Novel" Series & Collections of tales, alphabetically listed under key-word. A selective list of the author's own library. Index of titles in each vol. Index of authors in v.2.

GOVERNMENT PUBLICATIONS

[784] GREGORY, Winifred: List of the serial publications of foreign governments 1815–1931. N.Y: Wilson 1932. Arranged by countries, sub-arranged by departments. Finding list for American university libraries.

[785] GREAT Britain. Stationery Office: Government publications. H.M.S.O. 1922+
Monthly list arranged in 3 pts: (i) Parliamentary; (ii) Classified list (by Dept.); (iii) Periodicals. Index. Cumulated annually into the Consolidated list.

[785a] – – Sectional List.
Separate lists each covering a department incl. all relevant material in print.

[786] BOYD, Anne Morris: United States government publications; 3ed.rev. by R.A. Rips. N.Y: Wilson 1949. Does not include all federal publications & gives no bl details of those superseded. Arranged by departments. Good annotations.

[786a] UNITED States. Library of Congress. Guides to the official publications of the other American republics are also very useful. One list published for each country. Arrangement: General publications; Legislative branch; Executive Branch; Judicial Branch; Other agencies.

ILLUSTRATIONS

See Biography, & Portraits.

INCUNABULA

[787] HAIN, Ludwig Fried. Theodor: Repertorium bibliographicum... Stuttgart: Cotta 1826–38. 4v.
Repr. Berlin: Altmann 1925. 4v. in 2; Milano: Görlich [1948] 4v. 16,299 titles of 15th century books arranged alphabetically by authors, each entered under the assigned heading consisting of name of author & brief title, followed by: transcript of incipit, important caption headings, colophon, collation, & bl characteristics. Entries are numbered.

[788] COPINGER, Walter A: Supplement to Hain... Sotheran 1895–1902. 2v. in 3.
Repr. Leipzig: Lorentz 1926; Milano: Görlich [1950] 1 follows Hain's notation & constitutes 7,000 additions & corrections. v.2 consists of 6,000 new titles & has its own notation. Contains also a list of printers & publishers of the 15th century with lists of their works arranged chronologically under each printer or publisher (works with no printer's or publisher's name under latinized place-name) by Konrad Burger.

[789] REICHLING, Dietrich: Appendices ad Hainii-Copingeri. [München]: Iac.Rosenthal 1905–11. 7 fasc. Supplement. [Munster]: Thessingian 1905–14.
All 7 parts are divided into 2: (i) containing new titles (2,143 for 1–7) & (ii) additions to Hain & Copinger. Pt 7 contains indexes to both sections in all parts. The Suppl, is an index in one alphabet to the whole work.

[790] PROCTOR, Rbt Geo. Collier: Index to the early printed books in the British Museum...with notes of them in the Bodleian library. I–II. K. Paul 1898–1903. 2v. Arranged according to 'Natural history' method.
See p.113–4. German types of 1501–20 are reproduced in pt II.

[790a] – Supplements for 1898–1903. Chiswick Pr. 1900–3. 4v. Register by Konrad Burger 1906.

[791] ISAAC, Frank: Index to the early printed books in the British Museum, Pt II(2–3) The Museum 1939. Continues [790] covers Italy, Switzerland & Eastern Europe. A second volume covering the rest of Europe may appear later.

[792] BRITISH Museum: Catalogue of books printed in the 15th century now in the British museum. The Museum 1908+ 8v. have been published. A new ed. of the above & arranged in a like manner. For size, mentions a specific page & gives the number of lines & size of type-block in mm. Each vol. has an introduction by A.W. Pollard; later ones by Victor Scholderer who, together with Dr Esdaile & L.A. Sheppard, are or were responsible for the Catalogue. Gives history & type descriptions for each press.

[793] GESAMTKATALOG der Wiegendrucke. Leipzig: Hiersemann 1925+
An international catalogue & finding list which, when completed, will contain about 35,000 titles. By 1940 it had reached 8(1) Fradericis, & the copy is still intact. Entries are numbered, arranged alphabetically by authors, sub-arranged chronologically, bl details give the Hain no. & references to other Bs. For size, mentions lines from several places in the book. Gives also references to Haebler's Typenrepertorium [128]

[794] STILLWELL, Margaret Bingham: Incunabula in American libraries. N.Y: Bibliographical Soc. of Amer. 1940.
11,132 entries. 2ed. of Winship's Census of 15. century books. (1919)

[795] POLAIN, Louis: Catalogue des livres imprimés au 15ème siècle des bibliothèques de Belgique. Bruxelles: Société des Bibliophiles 1932. 4v.
Lists about 4,100 incunabula.

[796] BRUNET, Pierre Gustave: La France littéraire au 15ème siècle. Paris: Franck 1865.
Rather incomplete.

INDEXES

[797] HASKELL, Daniel Carl: Check list of cumulative indexes to individual periodicals in the New York Public Library. N.Y: The Library 1942.

LIBRARY CATALOGUES

See under Universal Bs, p.80–1.

MICRO-REPRODUCED MATERIAL

See also under Theses.

[798] MICROCARD Bulletin. Middleton,Conn: Microcard Fdn 1949+ Lists all material reproduced by the Fdn. Cumulates every 3–4 nos.

[799] UNION List of Microfilms; 2nd enl.ed. Ann Arbor: Edwards Bros. 1951.
Lists about 25,000 works, by author or title, in 197 libraries in the U.S. & Canada. Annual supplements.

NEWSPAPERS

[800] GREGORY, Winifred: American newspapers, 1821–1936. N.Y: Wilson 1937.
Arranged by states & cities. A union list of newspapers available in the U.S. & Canada.

[801] The TIMES: Tercentenary handlist of English & Welsh newspapers, magazines, & reviews, 1620–1920. The Times 1920. (i) London & suburban, chronologically arranged by first year of publication, finding list for libraries other than the B.M; (ii) Provincial, 1701–99, in alphabetical order, thereafter as above. Index to titles follows each section.

[802] AYER: Directory of newspapers and periodicals. Philadelphia: Ayer 1880+
Includes publications from the U.S. & Canada, arranged by state & city, with several indexes. Gives much useful information (mainly for advertisers) as to size of town, range of types, circulation, &c. Absorbed (1910) Rowell, which ran from 1869–1908.

OUT-OF-PRINT BOOKS

See also under Prices.

[803] ADAMS, Scott: The O.P. market. N.Y: Bowker 1944.

PERIODICALS

[804] WORLD-List of Scientific Periodicals 1900–1950; 3ed. Butterworth 1952.
A list of 24,029 titles in Dewey's 500–600. Periodicals that ceased publication before 1900 are excluded. Arranged by title, e.g: Report, R.Acad..., under R; is a finding list but includes titles then not available in Britain. Important for its abbreviations, by far the most comprehensive system ever made.

[805] UNION Catalogue of the Periodicals in the University Libraries of the British Isles...excluding titles in the World List 1934; comp. by M.G. Roupell, etc. National Cent.Libr. 1937.
Same arrangement as [804] but gives cross-references from the names of institutions & omits abbreviations of titles. A new ed. with a wider scope is in preparation & will be called British Union Catalogue of Periodicals.

[806] GREGORY, Winifred: Union List of Serials in the U.S; 2ed. N.Y: Wilson 1941. Suppl. ib. 1943.
Entries arranged alphabetically by titles or, for society publications, under name of the society. Annual reports, governments publications other than periodicals, and all American newspapers & foreign newspapers after 1820 are excluded. Gives more bl information than the above. A 2nd Suppl. is in preparation.

[807] FREER, Percy, ed: Catalogue of Union Periodicals.
I. Science & technology. Jhb: National Res.Bd 1943. Suppl. Pretoria: South Afr. Council for sci. & ind. Res.1949–53. 2.The Humanities. Pretoria: National Coun. for Soc.Res. 1952.
A Union list of periodicals, serials, & government serial publications in libraries of the Union of South Africa. Arranged by subject catchword, & includes World List abbreviations.

[808] ULRICH'S Periodicals Directory; 7ed. by Eileen C, Graves. N.Y: Bowker 1953.
A list of 14,000 current periodicals of international scope, but especially useful for South America. Arranged under broad subject-headings. Index.

[809] WILLING'S Press Guide. Willing's 1874+
Alphabetical list of English newspapers & periodicals, supplemented by the most important periodical publications of the Commonwealth & foreign countries, arranged by country & city. Includes a classified index to trade publications, & county newspapers arranged by place of publication. List of changes in title during the last 10 years.

PERIODICALS INDEXES

[810] POOLE'S Index to Periodical Literature; rev.ed. by Wm Fletcher. Boston: Houghton 1891. 2v.
Repr. N.Y: Peter Smith 1949. 6v. in 7.
Covers 1802–1907, for 470 American & English periodicals. Non-fiction arranged under subject headings in one alphabet, with the fiction which is entered under first word not an article (authors' names only used as headings for biographical articles or reviews of books with no definite subject). Volume is given, year must be worked out from the chronological conspectus in each vol.

[811] READERS' Guide to Periodical Literature. N.Y: Wilson 1877+
For the first 25 years published by the Amer.Libr. Ass. Issued 22 times a year, cumulated at intervals during the year, annually, & 2-yearly. Scope: General periodicals in the English language, & a few in other languages (about 125 in all). Arranged as a dictionary catalogue under subject & author (& sometimes title)

[812] INTERNATIONALE Bibliographie der Zeitschriftenliteratur. Osnabrück: Dietrich 1891+
Annual. In 2 pts: (i) indexes German periodicals, serials, & society serial publications; (ii) indexes non-German periodicals. Arranged alphabetically by subject-word, with numerical reference to periodical. Author index at end of vol.

[813] INTERNATIONAL Index to Periodicals. N.Y: Wilson 1907+
Originally a supplement to [811] but is more scholarly & indexes more foreign periodicals (about 250 in all). Issued quarterly, cumulated annually, & every 3 years.

[814] LIBRARY Association: Subject index to Periodicals. 1915+
Indexes about 600 periodicals & transactions, chiefly British & American. 1925+ issued annually. Arranged as the above. 1917/9–1922 published as class lists. 1923–5 not published.

[815] INDEX to South African Periodicals. Johannesburg Publ. Libr. 1940+
1940–2 published by the South Afr.Libr.Ass. Divided into an Afrikaans & an English section; arranged alphabetically under subjects, with an author index. Issues for 1941–2 are printed, the rest are roneod. 1940/9 cumulation in preparation.

POETRY

[816] GRANGER'S Index to Poetry & Recitations; 3ed. Chicago: McClurg 1940. Supplement. N.Y: Columbia Univ.Pr. 1938/44+
Indexes collections by titles, author, & first lines.

PORTRAITS

[817] AMERICAN Library Association Portrait Index. Washington: Library of Congr. 1906.
An index to portraits contained in 6,216 printed books & periodical vols, arranged alphabetically by name of person portrayed.
See also under Biography.

PRICES

[818] BOOK-Prices Current. Witherby 1888+
An annual, author list of books sold for at least £1.1.0 at auction in London, giving name of sale, price & buyer. 3 10-yearly indexes, covering 1887–1916, have been printed.

[819] AMERICAN Book-Prices Current. N.Y: Bowker 1895+
Annual list of books, autographs, or MSS, broadsides, maps, & charts (arranged separately) selling for more than $5.00. 5-yearly indexes.

[820] UNITED States Cumulative Book Auction Records...ed. by S.R. Shapiro. N.Y: Want.list...1940/5+
Annual list of literary property selling at more than $3.00. Cumulated 5-yearly.

PRIVATELY PRINTED BOOKS

See Bibliography. Chapter XIII, p.65–6 here.

REPRINTS

[821] ORTON, Rbt Merritt: Catalog of reprints in series; 12ed. N.Y: Wilson 1951. Supplement. ib. 1952.
An author & title list of reprints in 80 American & Canadian series, giving foreign title for translations (when known) date of first publication; editions arranged alphabetically by name of series. Anthologies classified by subject; 1ed. 1940.

REVIEWS

[822] BOOK Review Digest. N.Y: Wilson 1906+
Published 9 times a year, cumulated half-yearly & annually. Arranged alphabetically by author's name. Abstracts of several reviews for each title. Symbols indicate whether favourable(+) or not(-)

SEQUELS

[823] GARDNER, Frank M: Sequels; 3ed. Association of Assistant Libr. 1947.
First ed.(1922) by Th.Alfred; 2ed.(1928) by W.A.Parker. Mainly fiction but includes also autobiography & some other non-fiction, arranged by author's name. Gives title only.

[824] KERR, Elizabeth Margaret: Bibliography of the sequence novel. Minneapolis: University of Minn.Pr. 1950. Includes novels originally published as separate, complete novels but which, as a series, form an artistic whole, excluding ephemeral literature, unfinished works. Includes French, Spanish, Portuguese, German, Italian, Scandinavian, Polish, Russian, &c. novels, each language separately.

SOCIETY PUBLICATIONS

[825] OFFICIAL Yearbook of the Scientific & Learned Societies of Great Britain & Ireland. Griffin 1884+ Societies are arranged in groups. Under each society are given the publications of the preceding year.

SUBSCRIPTION BOOKS

[826] SUBSCRIPTION Books Bulletin. Chicago: American Libr. Ass. 1930+
Quarterly. Each issue contains 8–10 long reviews. Index in 4th issue of each year.

THESES

[827] AMERICAN Doctoral Dissertations. Washington: Library of Congr. 1912+
Annual. Lists the printed, copyright copies of theses received by L.C.;alphabetical arrangement, & a classified list, subject index, & list of authors arranged by universities.

[828] DOCTORAL Dissertations accepted by American Universities. N.Y: Wilson 1933/4+
Annual. Includes also unpublished theses. Arranged under subject-headings. Author index. List of universities, indicating whether copies may be borrowed.

LITERATURE: FORM BIBLIOGRAPHIES

[829] JAHRESVERZEICHNIS der deutschen Hochschulschriften. Leipzig: Deutsche Bücherei 1885–1942. 58v. 1–51: JVerz.d.an dtsch.Univ.(u.tech.Hochschulen) erschienenen Schr. arranged by kind of institution; 52–8 by place-names. Alphabetical author & subject index to each vol. Not published since 1942. Vols for 1943/4 & 1945/8 in preparation.

[830] DISSERTATION Abstracts. Ann Arbor: University Microfilms 1938+
A list of abstracts of doctoral dissertations & monographs available in complete form on microfilm. Cumulative title-index at end of each vol. v.1–11: Microfilm Abstr. Issued 6 times a year.

TRANSLATIONS

[831] INDEX Translationum. Répertoire international des traductions/ International Bibliography of Translations. Paris: Unesco 1, 1932+
Annual. v.1–31, 1932–1940 published by the International Institute of Intellectual Co-operation. Arranged alphabetically by name (in French) of country, sub-arranged by main U.D.C. classification. Includes works published in pamphlet or book form under translated title with a note of original title. Index to authors & translators, & publishers. Not published 1941–51. Cumulated from the quarterly I.T. published by the International Institute of Intellectual Co-operation.

UNFINISHED BOOKS

[832] CORNS, Albert Reginald, and Sparke, Archibald: Bibliography of unfinished books in the English language, etc. Quaritch 1915.
Arranged alphabetically by names of authors.

[832a] MEHR nicht erschienen. (Bibliotheca bibliographica 2) Announced. To contain 14,000 titles.

UNION LISTS

See under Periodicals.

VERTICAL FILE MATERIAL

[833] VERTICAL File Service Catalog. N.Y: Wilson 1932+ Monthly, cumulated annually.

4. Subject Bibliographies.

Subject bibliographies are included here only if they are concerned with the subject of The Book, e.g: Bibliography (including the history of printing) e.g: Appleton: Guide to the literature of the pulp & paper industry.[223] Other subject bibliographies are excluded.

5. Author Bibliographies.

Author bibliographies are lists of books by, or by and about an author; also called Individual Bibliographies[1] e.g: Keynes's Jane Austen. 1929. A bibliography dealing with a single title is known as a Unit Bibliography, e.g: Robinson, Geo.W: Bibliography of Thomas Pringle's "Afar in the desert" (In: Pap.bibliogr.Soc.Amer. 17(1)21-54,1923)

Some author bibliographies are referred to as Topical, or Analytical Bibliographies. In these the MSS and editions are analysed as well as classified. Thus each poem occurring in either will be recorded in the section devoted to that particular poem, and the same with critical works, e.g: Carpenter's Spenser; Hammond's Chaucer; and Thompson's Milton.

5a. Bio-Bibliography.

Bio-Bibliography is related to Author Bibliography, being a combination of Bibliography and Biography, e.g: Chevalier, U.J: Repertoire des sources historiques du moyen-âge et bio-bibliographie, 1905-7. 2v; Manley, J.M., and Rickert, E: CContemporary British literature [1929]; Millet, F.B: Contemporary American authors: a critical survey and 219 bio-bibliographies. 1940. "Frequently an encyclopedic article on an author, followed by a fairly comprehensive list of materials by and about that author, may be considered a bio-bibliography.[2]

Students must realise that the bibliographies described above constitute only a small section of the published bibliographies and that, in spite of their number, bibliographies record only part of the published literature.[3]

---

1 GRAHAM: Bookman's...[5] p.16-34.
2 SHORES: Basic...[108] p.211.
3 EVANS, Luther H: Bibliography by coöperation. (Bull.med.Libr.Ass. 37(3) p.201, 1949)

> "...the ideal of bibliographical exposition is that which supplies the greatest number of wants with the least expense of time and effort on the part of the user."[1]

IV

COMPILATION AND ARRANGEMENT

Before embarking on bibliographical work the compiler must define his purpose and make up his mind whether his objective is[2]

1. the determination of <u>authentic</u> texts and their place in the stream of published documents, e.g. the publication of a literary form;
2. the study of the <u>methods of publication</u>, e.g. the output of a certain locality or person[3,4]
3. the <u>evaluation</u> of some of the material of study, e.g. the best books on a subject.

---

1 FEIPEL: Elements of B. (<u>Pap.bibliogr.Soc.Amer</u>. 10(4)p.187, 1916)
2 COWLEY: B1...[126] p.9.
3 HYETT: County Bs. (<u>Trans.bibliogr.Soc</u>. 3:27–40, 1895)
4 – Suggestions as to the limits and arrangement of county B. (ib. p.167–70,1895)

Having determined his objective the compiler must consider the steps to be taken to reach it. The processes involved, as described by Gaselee[1] are

1. Collection, i.e. the gathering (or at least locating) of the material to be studied;
2. Enumeration, or placing the items side by side, physically if possible, but if not, on paper;
3. Description of each separate item;
4. Analysis, or the elucidation of the points brought to light by the description;
5. Conclusion, or the determination of the significance, literary or historical, of the results reached by the preceding steps.

The sources of information for a compiler are: Bibliographies of bibliographies; General bibliographies; Library catalogues; National catalogues; Sale catalogues; Special bibliographies, e.g. forms of national literature: plays, romances, etc; Indexes to periodicals; Reference works; Periodicals and their indexes; Year's works, etc; Bibliographies in treatises on the subject. Consult the catalogues of local libraries; correspond with private owners and booksellers, and finally, advertise.

---

1   GASELEE: The aims of B. (Libr. s4,13(3)p.247–50,1932)

List the items on slips 3" × 5", 20 × 25cm(Cole), arrange them temporarily in author order and note their locations, or the book from which reference is taken, on your working list. The completion of the working list and the determination of the material which is to form the subject matter of the bibliography constitute together the "Enumeration" or the second stage in bibliographical compilation. It will often be found useful to use punched cards.

The third stage, <u>Description</u>, will be found in Chapter V.

The fourth and fifth stages, <u>Analysis</u> and <u>Conclusion</u>, Cowley takes in the course of Description, Annotation, and Arrangement.

<u>Annotations</u> may be: (a) Contents note (Chapter headings); (b) Descriptive note; (c) Evaluating note; (d) Historical and bibliographical note; (e) Location of a copy or copies.[1]

<u>Arranging</u> factors are: Author; Title; Subject; Form; Place; Date; Size; Bookbinding; Price; Edition; Numbers printed; Printer; Publisher; Owner of copyright.

---

1 BROWN: Manual...[113] p.92–4.

Pollard[1] has indicated certain criteria for selecting the best arrangement, as follows: 1. For detailed information about individual books, alphabetical arrangement by author, and under authors alphabetically by title; 2. To illustrate the history and development of a subject, or the author's literary biography, chronological; 3. For direction in reading, subject–index, alphabetical by subject and under subject chronological; 4. To show how far the whole field has been covered and what gaps remain to be filled, a class catalogue, arranged by subject, logical divisions.

Arrangement is, or ought to be determined by the purpose of the bibliography[2], that purpose being to afford guidance in some branch of literature or record of knowledge. The compiler is not bound to any conventional rules of arrangement. Since the most important function of bibliography is to tell a story, it is only natural that an historical or chronological basis is very often the most satisfactory for author bibliographies. Varieties: by order of publication, the "annalistic" method; dividing the bibliography first into groups according to form or composition; e.g. poetry, plays, essays, etc. with a distinct group for collected writings. It is most suitable for a bibliography intended for the use of collectors and for the identification of editions.

---

1   (1) POLLARD: Bibliography. (In Encycl.Brit. lled. 3:910,1910)
2   EVANS: B. by co-operation. (Bull.med.Libr.Ass. 37(3)p.197–212,1949)

Arrangement by date of publication must be disregarded in planning the main divisions of a work intended as a guide to the literature of a subject. The contents of the material described and not the publication dates determine the place that each item occupies. In subject bibliography, therefore, the arrangement can only be decided after all the material available has been examined and described. An alphabetical order of authors' names is of no use to a reader who seeks direction as to what to read on a subject. In a bibliography in which the object is to give the reader guidance in the most up-to-date literature of a subject, the chronological order may well be reversed, beginning with the latest publications. A peculiarly useful form for a trade, or national bibliography is one based on the alphabetical order of subject headings.[1,2]

The 'natural history' method in bibliography, used by Bradshaw in "A classified index of the 15.century books in the M.de Meyer collection sold at Ghent, Nov.1869"[3] has an arrangement by places, subdivided by printers, and thereunder arranged chronologically. Bradshaw was influenced by Panzer, and by his contemporaries Blades, Campbell, and Holtrop. His principle

---

1 AUSTIN: The printed catalogue of a local collection. (Libr. s3,8:315–38,1917)
2 ESDAILE: Student's...[34] p.249–65.
3 BRADSHAW: Collected papers... Cambr.Univ.Pr. 1889. p.206–36.

became definitely established in 1898 when Proctor applied it in his Index...[790]. The present British Museum Catalogue...[792] the work of Pollard, Scholderer, and others, is also based upon the "Proctor order". Haebler, with Crous and Husing in the Gesamtkatalog...[793] bring to bear comparable methods and standards. "The principle which Bradshaw first clearly enunciated in his 'De Meyer' list was that if we will understand old books we must study them as the research workers in natural history study the plants and birds and beasts with which they have to deal, by classifying them according to their characteristics. We must study old books in a series of groups of books issued in the same country, in the same town, from the same press; for only in this way can we assign to their printers those which bear no printer's name, and arrange in chronological sequence those which bear no date. This principle has won permanent recognition in bibliography".[1,2]

Note the value of contents lists, chapters, and section headings, analytical tables and appendixes as guides to arrangement. Division of primary and secondary material. Useful to distinguish between elementary works and advanced treatises.

---

1 POLLARD: Human factor in B. (Publ.Edinb.bibliogr.Soc. 12(2) p.69–77, 1925)

2 JENKINSON: List of the incunabula collected by George Dunn, arranged to illustrate the history of printing. (Trans.bibliogr.Soc. Suppl. no.3, 1923)

Cowley says that "division by form of publication" must be avoided.[1]

The editing of the completed work differs only in a few particulars from that of any scholarly work, and most of the details will be found under Chapter XII. The problems peculiar to the preparation of bibliographies are headings[2] and citation. The student must form a habit of adopting standard forma of entry and using them consistently for 1. a whole book or set of books; 2. part of a book; 3. for periodical articles, by (i) author or (ii) title; 4. for references to society publications and other series; 5. title entry; 6. for reference to an anonymous article in an encyclopaedia; 7. to a signed article in ditto; 8. for a government publication; 9. a periodical; 10. a thesis.[3,4,5,6]

Criteria for a good bibliography are: 1. Accuracy; 2. Completeness; 3. Absence of repetition; 4. Arrangement and form; 5. Critical value.

Standards of bibliographical work. Consider: 1. The authority of the compiler; 2. The arrangement; 3. Definition and scope; 4. Fullness of the information given; 5. Fullness of annotation.

---

1 COWLEY: B1...[126] p.179–87.
2 ib. p.188–94.
3 BARNARD: B1 citation. (Librarian Bk world. 34:105–10,171–5, 125–9 [sic] (should be 194–9) &c. 1950)
4 COLE: Compiling a B. (Libr.J. 26:791–5,859–63,1901)
5 FULTON: Principles of bl citation. (Bull.med.Libr.Ass. 22 (4)p.183–97, 1933/4)
6 WORDS...[478] p.33–5.

"...full titles with collations and descriptions... tidy, exact, compact and comprehensive, showing in a nut-shell all the reader wishes to know or see, short of the books themselves"[1]

V

COLLATION AND DESCRIPTION OF BOOKS (OLD AND NEW) THEIR STRUCTURE AND PARTS

I. MODERN BOOKS.

The normal "make-up" of a present-day printed book, according to Simon[2] is (a) Half-title, Title-page (recto and verso), Dedication, Acknowledgments, Contents, List of illustrations, etc., List of abbreviations, Preface, Introduction, Corrigend(a)um or Errat(a)um, constituting the Preliminaries or "Prelims"[3]; (b) The Text, or Body of the Book; (c) Subsidiaries: Appendixes, Author's notes, Glossary, Bibliography, Index(es).

Esdaile[4] varies the order and adds the following to (a) Imprimatur, Number of copies printed; to (c) Imprint or Colophon, "Finis", Blank leaves, Plates, End-papers, Dust-jacket.

---

1 STEVENS: Photo-bibliography. Stevens 1878. p.46.
2 SIMON, Oliver: Introduction...[173] ...p.7.
3 The first signature of a book is called the Title sheet or Title signature.
4 ESDAILE, A: Student's...[34] p.83–92.

Actually the inside of the book may have, in addition to all the above (a) On the verso of the half-title, also called bastard-, false-, or fly-title: Publisher's advertisement, "By the same author", Series note (which sometimes appears at the top of the title-page, or may even have a title-page of its own, facing the title-page of the specific volume in the series); and Frontispiece; Foreword (before contents only if short), Addenda slip, or Postscript, a half-, or caption-title repeated between the "Prelims", and (b) the Text; the illustrations often appear amid (b); (c) Sometimes a duplicate, printed title-label is pasted in between the last page and the end-paper[1]. Advertisements (especially...19th century).

Then outside the book proper as part of the binding, we have the fly-leaves (back and front), trimmed, stained, sprinkled, marbled, or gilded edges, the covers (casing) and finally the lettering.

Some of the "Parts" call for further comment. The title-page proper (recto) may carry a printer's, or a publisher's device and, of course, the latter's Imprint. The verso may state the edition and year of publication (which we prefer to find on the recto, or title-page proper). On this verso we often find

---

1 Discussion in T.L.S. 16.Mar.–6.Apr.1922.

a bibliographical "history" of the book, i.e. a note on reprintings, revised editions, etc., and a copyright date (always in U.S.A. titles) and frequently the printer's imprint, which may, however, occur at the end. Other features, too, appear sometimes on this verso and sometimes at the end, e.g. the modern "Colophon", with information about the book's typography, number of copies printed, etc.etc. Many publishers (Cape in England) give here the Dewey number, or the pre-assigned L.C. card number (Duell, Sloane & Pearce in America).

Edition:	All copies of a book printed from one setting of type.
Impression:	Forms part of an edition, and consists of all copies of a book printed from one setting of type at one time.
Issue:	Caused by some change in the physical make-up of a book after some copies have already been circulated.
State:	Caused by a similar kind of change before any copies of the book have been circulated.[1,2,3,4]

---

1 MUIR: Book-collecting...[522] p.38.
2 ESDAILE: Student's...[34] p.76–82, 370.
3 Defined for <u>older books</u> in BOWERS: Principles...[724] p.39: Edition: The whole number of copies of a book printed at any time or times from substantially the same setting of type-pages.
Issue: The whole number of copies of a form of an edition put on sale at any time or times as a consciously planned printed unit & varying only in relation to the form of an "ideal copy".
Later issue or re-issue: Either a re-impression: some special form of the original issue of an edition, removed in point of time from the original form, which has left the printing shop to be sold...& in which for the most part the original printed sheets are substantially present

L.P. or F.P. Copies printed on a larger and finer paper (never to be cut by the binder)

Extra illustrated books may be a form of an édition de luxe having more illustrations, or with the illustrations in several states. Grangerized copies are furnished by their owner with relevant material (illustrations, etc.) taken from other books.

Difficulties in collating modern books are caused by: (a) careless paging of the "Prelims"; (b) Omission of (list of and) actual frontispiece, plates, maps, etc; (c) Inclusion of some plates in pagination and not others; (d) Putting titles of plates on tissues and not numbering plates; (e) Pasting in of single leaves of matter at the beginning or end of the book. The title of the book as running-title on the verso of all pages makes identification of loose leaves easier.

Modern books should carry their own bibliographical collation.

---

but with a different title-leaf...or as re-imposed: a form of the edition where the original type-pages have undergone re-imposition or a minor substitution.

State or Variant: Any part of a book exhibiting variation in type-setting including the addition or deletion of material in some copies, caused by alteration executed in the course of the original printing before public sale; in its broadest sense also covers alterations made after sale has begun where no change is made to the original title-page by cancellation.

4   WOLF: Press-correction in 16th & 17th century quartos. (Pap.bibliogr. Soc.Amer. 36(3)p.187–98,1942)

II. OLDER BOOKS.

"Again and again it will be found that careful collation, checking of pagination or foliation, reading of prefaces, dedicatory epistles, imprimaturs and advertisements, and all the processes that are required for full description lead to the discovery of important evidence concerning the authorship, composition, date of writing, and method of production of the work in question"[1].

Examination should follow the order to be taken in writing the description, which is generally:

1. Title-page[2,3], Ornaments and borders[4]; 2. Imprint and Colophon[5,6]; 3. Incipit and Explicit; 4. Binding and Casing, Wrappers; 5. Preliminaries (Imprimaturs, etc.); 6. Advertisements; 7. Text and collation[7,8,9] "examination of the interior of the book is taken in conjunction with the collation, i.e. the determination of the number and size of the quires that constitute a perfect copy and their order, together with their pagination

---

1   COWLEY: Bl...[126] p.21.
2   MCKERROW: Introduction...[36] p.88–95.
3   COWLEY: Bl...[126] p.46–76.
4   MCKERROW: Introduction...[36] p.109–20.
5   SHAABER: Meaning of the imprint in early printed books. (Libr. s4, 24(3/4)p.120–41,1943/4)
6   GRANNISS: History of the colophon. (Colophon 1:1–16,1930) Also in Bennett: Books...[158]
7   ESDAILE: Student's...[34] p.229–43.
8   MCKERROW: Introduction...[36] p.153–63.
9   GREG: A formulary of collation (Libr. s4 14:365–82,1934)

or foliation...To make a thorough examination the gatherings should be taken separately in the order in which they occur... and notes should be made...for each quire: 1. The signature (or absence of signature); 2. The number of leaves; 3, Cancels; 4. The pagination or foliation, noting any discrepancies; 5. The nature of the printed matter contained in it checking the continuation of the text by means of the catchwords". "...No attempt should be made to write a description at the first sight of a title-page"[1,2]; 8. Prefaces, Dedications, etc...

"It is not wisdom...to compel all scholars to employ the same set of rules[3]... One set is required for a check-list [e.g. S.T.C.] another for the catalogue of a particular collection [e.g. The English Bibles in the John Rylands Library, 1899] and still another for an exhaustive, analytical, definitive bibliography whether of an author, a press, or a genre[4]... For the analytical bibliographer...it would be...desirable to supplement the (general) heading by a collational heading, and a list of the literary contents of the volume... The collational heading... would include...the format, the number of leaves, the quires, signatures, foliation or pagination the "make-up" (i.e. types, initials, illustration, etc.) and the particulars as to the general appearance of the printed page... The measurements of the type-page[5]. This ought to be followed by a section of notes...to explain technical problems; accounts of printing practice...a detailed study of the illustrations, as well as particulars connected with the transmission of the text... This section...promises...to play a progressively important role in the future bibliographies and catalogues of incunabula.[6] The bibliographers approach to the description of a book should be in terms of the printing craft... Equipped with

---

1 COWLEY: Bl...[726] p.40–1,45.
2 STEVENSON: Watermarks are twins. (Stud.in Bibliogr. 4:59–91, 1951.
3 BÜHLER: Standards...[125] p.24.
4 ib. p.65.
5 ib. p.8 & 35. (6) ib. p.12.

a thorough knowledge of...methods of investigating books as the "physical vehicle of transmitting literary texts" [Greg] a scholar is prepared to undertake the enumeration and description that are the foundations of bibliography[1]. Textual editors long ago adopted the maxim that the unit of study is the form[e]...but...bibliographers must adopt as their unit, or comparison the letterpress of each individual page, and... of units even smaller...[2] Requisites for Standards...of bibliographical description: 1. The general agreement that the purpose of a bibliography is to describe the _ideal_ copy; i.e. the book in the precise state in which the publisher intended it to be put on sale as complete and perfect... 2. The establishment of a sound, uniform terminology and the precise definition of terms, particularly of original and variant states, issues, and editions, mixed copies, etc. 3. A generally accepted formulary of collation...to describe concisely the physical make-up of a book"[3]

There have been several attempts to formulate rules, or at least recommendations for the systematic description of books. Madan, Duff, and Gibson's scheme[4] "endeavour to afford standard examples of ordinary book description, the books being divided on the one hand into Early (to 1557), Middle (1558–1800) and Modern books (1801+); and from another point of view into (A) Important, (B) Interesting, and (C) Ordinary". They are applied to 12 parts of a book: 1. Heading; 2. Title; 3. Imprint; 4. Date; 5. Size; 6. Collation; 7. Chief type (1–7 give the technical details); 8. Contents; 9. Notes;

---

1   BÜHLER: Standards...[125] p.67,69–70.
2   ib. p.78–9.
3   ib. p.70–3.
4   MADAN, Falconer, Duff,E.G., & Gibson,S: Standard descriptions of printed books with examples. (Proc.Oxf.bibliogr.Soc. 1(1)p.13–4, 55–64,1922/6)

10. Supplements; 11. Appendixes; 12. Index; further they give examples of Minima and the "one-line system".

Another system was introduced by Pollard, Greg [129] and Madan[1] divided into Full description, Description, Short description, and Minimum description. Most of the later systems by McKerrow[2], Esdaile[3], Greg[4], Cowley[5] are derived from Pollard, Greg, and Madan's. Another is Williams'[6].

The student would be well advised to study in addition the rules laid down by the compilers of some of the best descriptive works, e.g. British Museum [92], Gesamtkatalog...[793], Polain's Catalogue...[795], Stillwell [794] (Miss Stillwell's suggestions for bibliographical analysis are applicable in general to books printed up to the end of 16th century. For books of 17th and 18th centuries, a consideration of her points 1–3,6–7 is presumably sufficient), and Guppy[7] for incunabula; also Edmond[8],

---

1 MADAN, Falconer: Degressive B. (Trans.bibliogr.Soc. 9:53–65, 1909)
2 MCKERROW: Introduction... [36] p.145–63.
3 ESDAILE: Student's...[34] p.248–71.
4 GREG, W.W: A formulary of collation. (Libr. s4 14:365–82, 1934)
5 COWLEY: Bl...[126] p.46–142.
6 WILLIAMS: Elements...[528] p.74–93.
7 GUPPY: Suggestions for the cataloguing of incunabula. (Bull.John Rylands Libr. 8:444–55,1924) (2ed. as Rules for the cataloguing of incunabula. Library Ass. 1947)
8 EDMOND: Suggestions for the description of books printed between 1501 & 1640. (Libr.Ass.Rec. 3:133–142,1901) Repr.1902.

Klebs[1] and Madan[2]. Methods for rare books in general have been described by Cole[3].

Except in Short description, entries consist of (A) Heading, (B) Title, (C) Imprint[4], (D) Technical, or Collation note, (E) Analysis of contents, (F) Notes.

(D). The technical description, or note on the physical makeup of the book, is designed to tell the reader something about its size, arrangement of its physical parts (collation, foliation or pagination), style of printing, typographical peculiarities, etc. The technical description in full consists of 1. Format or folding, and number of volumes; 2. Signatures; 3. Foliation or pagination, and number of plates; 4. Number of columns and lines of an ordinary page; 5. Measurement of the space occupied by the letterpress on an ordinary page (the type-block); 6. Kind and size of type generally used. Give the measurement in mm. of 20 lines of the text set solid, and describe the text; 7. Typographical peculiarities, such as printing

---

1. KLEBS: Desiderata in the cataloguing of incunabula. (Pap.bibliogr.Soc.Amer. 10(3)p.43-6,1916)
2. MADAN: Oxford books to 1680. Oxford: Clarendon Pr. 1895–1931. 3v. By Cowley called "One of the best models for the full description of English books...with its adaptation of method to books of different periods".
3. COLE: Cataloguing of rare books in the Henry E. Huntington Library. (Bull.Amer.Libr.Ass. 16:247–57,1922) Repr.1922; also in Arnett, L.D. & E.I: Readings in library methods. N.Y: Stechert 1931. p.22–6.
4. Date may be given as a chronogram. WHITE: Chronograms. (Libr. s4,4:59–74,1923)

in colours, rubrication, woodcut capitals, etc. Description of type may be omitted in later printed books. For modern works, unless format and signatures are significant, use a short collation note consisting of pagination, illustrations, maps, etc; and the measurement in cm. of an uncut copy, following the A.A. Code.[1]

In collation[2,3,4] the tabulated record should comprise:

1. Size of the book according to make-up: (a) by format: fol, 4°, 8°, etc; (b) in linear measurements: inches, cm., or mm. Format assists to assign the date of printing, to distinguish between editions, to detect forgeries, variants, and cancels.
   Recognition of format is made possible by signatures, watermarks, chain-lines, register, pagination, and foliation, catchwords, and gatherings.
2. Analysis of the book by signatures. Signatures were originally intended, and still are, for the use of the binder; each sheet in the quired MSS being numbered, and the numbers cut away by the binder; early printers wrote them in by hand or stamped them; when they were eventually printed, they had to be placed near the type-page, where they could not be cut away.[5]

---

1 COWLEY: Bl...[126] p.89,207.
2 POLLARD: Objects & methods of bl collations & descriptions. (Libr. s2,8:193–217,1907)
3 PRACTICAL B: Collation & description of books. (Libr.Assistant. 17:33–4,57–8,83–4,1924)
4 THOMAS: Bl collation. (ib. 22:9–15,24–7,1929)
5 BLADES: The use & development of signatures in books. (In his Books in chains. E.Stock 1892. p.85–122)

3. Total number of leaves, or of pages.
   The "signature equation" is mostly used to denote the entire gathering; its total number of single leaves being given as an exponent, or superior number, e.g. A-B^8, C^4. Some bibliographers prefer to keep the equation on a single line, as: A-B in 8, C in 4.

Terms[1]	Gathering		Single leaves	Pages
Unionem	1	Folded sheet[2]	Folio in twos[3]	4
Duernio	2	A quire or G. of (original)	fours	8
Ternion	3	sheets; conjugate, paired	sixes[4]	12
Quaternio[5]	4	or double leaves folded together	eights[6]	16
Quinternio	5		tens[7]	20
Sextern	6		twelves	24

4. Number of columns to the page, if the text is so printed; (number of lines to the average page, number of lines on a definite page, with the size in mm. of the type-page of that page in incunabula)
5. Identification of the type: Gothic, Roman (and Italic 1501+)

---

1 Mostly from classical or medieval Latin (or Italian)
2 The word is derived from quaternum: a book of 4 leaves. (Hall: Companion to classical texts. Oxford: Clarendon Pr. 1913)
3 Common in the 18th century.
4 MCKERROW: Introduction...[36] p.31-2, figs.7 & 8.
5 From old French quaer now cahier (Latin quaterni)
6 A favorite gathering in Elizabethan times.
7 A common gathering in early folios.

6. Presence of a printer's device[1], also of illustrations, maps, diagrams, etc. (In incunabula, note presence of woodcut initials, printed marginal notes[2], etc.)
7. Notes:, (a) Bibliographical reference numbers with which the collation of the copy has been found to agree; (b) statement of edition, or issue, if necessary; (c) imperfections in the copy; (d) note on the binding, if of importance; (e) statement of provenance. (N.B. 7a-b relate to the work as such; 7c-e to the circumstances of the copy in hand. The distinction must be kept clearly in mind between variations in printing or in make-up, which constitute another issue, and the so-called accidents of condition, which affect merely the given copy)

"The concern of the descriptive bibliographer...is to examine every available copy of an edition of a book in order to describe in bibliographical terms the characteristics of an ideal copy of this edition, to distinguish between issues and variants of the edition, to explain and describe the printing and textual history of the edition, and finally to arrange it in a correct and logical relationship to other editions"[3]

"Bibliographical analysis...and the fine points in the technique of the game should not be mistaken for bibliography itself. Behind the physical make-up and the questions involved in determining the physical origin of a book are an understanding and evaluation of its subject matter. Behind these is the personality of its author. Behind that is the relation of the book and its writer to the thought of the times. Technical analysis

---

1 MCKERROW: Printers' & publishers' devices in England & Scotland,1485–1640. (Illus.Monogr.bibliogr.Soc. 16,1913)
2 BÜHLER: Margins in mediaeval books. (Pap.bibliogr.Soc. Amer. 40(1)32–42,1946)
3 BOWERS: Principles...[124] p.6.

is but a means to an end. It is the chemical analysis through which...in its accurate identification of author, place, date, printer, edition, etc...each printed work is given its rightful place among the records of the past. It is in this final aspect that bibliography appears in its true light, and it is through sources and methods as these herein indicated that...bibliographical study... may be undertaken."[1]

Tests for determining whether two copies of an early book are of the same edition compare: (a) Catchwords on certain pages (but not the final page of sections); (b) Last words of some dozen lines on random pages in different parts of the book; (c) Positions of signatures - what letter they appear under; (d) Size, etc. of ornamental initials; (e) Wrong fount punctuations; (f) Swash letters; (g) Broken letters; (h) Measure diagonally across the page from a letter in one line to a letter in a line 7 or 8 lines higher up the page; (i) Press figures.[2,3,4,5,6,7,8,9]

---

1 STILLWELL: Incunabula...[132] p.ix.
2 BOWERS: Bl evidence from printer's measure. (Pap.bibliogr.Soc.Univ.Va. 2:1-53-67,1949/50)
3 - The headline in early books. (Engl.Inst.Annu. 1941:185-222) HINMAN: New uses for headlines as bl evidence. Headlines provide evidence as to 1. Order of formes through the press; 2. Help to determine the priority of variant states; 3. May enable us to show the existence of cancels; 4. May furnish proof of unusual procedures, such as page-by-page printing,etc.
4 MORGAN: On the difficulty of correct description of books. (Libr.Ass.Rec. 4:247-73,1902) Originally in Companion to the Almoner 1853.
5 CHAPMAN: Elementary exercises in B. (Libr. s4,9:197-201, 1928/9)

Difficulties in collating old books are caused by: 1. Lack of title-page; 2. Lack of detail in the colophon as to author, printer, place, and date of printing, etc., or the giving of fictitious details; 3. No paging, catchwords, or signatures, and errors in these items when given; 4. No watermark; 5. Rebinding, resulting in signatures, catchwords, or watermarks being cut away; 6. Blank leaves arising from faulty estimation of "copy" - either too little or too much; 7. Textual variations in the same edition, due to (a) "Farming out", (b) Pieing and reprinting; 8. Cancels; 9. Photographic facsimile pages inserted; 10. Insertion of pages from other copies.

---

6 COLE: Bl problems with some solutions. (Pap.bibliogr.Soc.Amer. 10(3)119–42,1916)

7 MADAN: On method in B. (Trans.bibliogr.Soc. 1:91–106,1893)

8 HINMAN: Mechanized collation. (Pap.bibliogr.Soc.Amer. 41(2) 99–106,1947)
   Reflections of the same page in different copies are flashlighted on a screen with intervals of split-seconds; any difference shows as a wobble, & the particular page can be further examined in the orthodox way.

9 TODD: Observations on the incidence & interpretation of press figures. (Pap.bibliogr.Soc.Univ.Va. 3:171–200, 1950/1)
   Press figures appear at the foot of the page, in books printed between 1680 & 1823, to certify the identity of the pressman at work on the formes. Useful for discovering impressions & editions.

PART 2

MODERN
BOOK PRODUCTION

'With the art of writing, the age of miracles began.'

'Are we not driven to the conclusion that of the things which man can do or make here below, by far the most momentous, wonderful, and worthy are the things called books?'

Carlyle

"They mowed and babbled till some tongue struck speech and patient fingers framed the lettered sound"[1]

VI

HISTORICAL INTRODUCTION

I. THE HISTORY OF WRITING.

'The history of writing is the history of variations and their causes'. Stanley Morison[2] suggests as the chief causes of variation: (a) Necessity for speed; (b) Reservation of special hands for certain purposes; (c) Change in the nature of the materials and tools of writing, and in the manner of their employment.

The earliest method of communication and transmission of thought was by means of words: story-telling. Memory aids followed as the "Knot-writing" of the Peruvians and various drawings and picture writings, e.g. the one the American Indians used until fairly recent times (Pictographs). The Egyptians

---

1   LIGHT of Asia. Bk 4.
2   HEAL: English writing-masters, &c. Cambridge Univ.Pr. 1931. With an introd. On the development of hand-writing, by Stanley Morison. p.xxiii.

used Hieroglyphics which were of five kinds:

1. Thing-pictures = Pictograms.
2. Idea-pictures = Ideograms.
3. Word-sound pictures = Phonograms.
4. Syllable-sound pictures.
5. Letter-sound pictures.

The Chinese still use hieroglyphics and write in the same way as the Egyptians used to, i.e. from the top of the page to the bottom. Chinese ink is very quick-drying, but Egyptian not, and when they found that they smeared the first line when writing the second they changed to writing horizontally, and since the scribe kept the roll in his left hand while writing, he wrote from left to right.

The Hieroglyphics changed gradually to Hieratic (Greek: hieratikos = priestly) writing, a sort of speeded-up form of their writing.[1]

The Phoenicians brought writing another step forward. They probably got most of their characters from the sound-symbols of the Egyptian hieratic writing about 1,200 B.C., but may also have been influenced by the cuneiform (wedge-shaped) characters of the Assyrians, Babylonians, and the Hittites, all of which were Ideograms. The Phoenician alphabet had no vowels and was written from right to left.

---

1 A third form was the ordinary writing of the Egyptians, the Demotic, the opposite of Hieratic.

From the Phoenician alphabet derives three groups of alphabets:

1. Aramean, which includes Georgian, Arabic, Hebrew (which still has no vowels) and others.
2. Sabaean: Indian, and Ethiopic.
3. Hellenic, from which is derived Russian, Coptic, and Greek.

The Greeks got 19 consonants from the Phoenicians about 900 B.C. (including some unused Phoenician characters that they changed into vowels); they added some of their own until they had 24 characters. In the beginning the Greeks wrote in both directions (boustrophedon = as the ox turns) but later changed from left to right.

While the Greek alphabet was still developing, about 700 B.C., the Romans borrowed 13 letters: A,B,E,F,H,I,K,M,N,O,T,X,Z direct, and through the Etruscans got, altered, and added 10 others, making 23 letters in all.[1,2,3] All these letters were capitals. As the Egyptian Hieroglyphics had as their informal companion the Hieratic writings, so the original Roman letters (seen at their best on the Trajan column 114 A.D.) developed on

---

1 ATKINSON: Alphabet. (In Encycl.Brit. 14ed.)
2 HUNT: Origin & development of the printed alphabet. (Libr. Assist. 21:5–11, 30–3, 52–61, 1928)
3 ULIMAN: The origin & development of the ABC. (Amer.J. Archaeol. 31:311–28, 1927)

vellum (see next section) first into square Roman, to Rustic Roman (more flourishing) then to uncials, and later half-uncials. This, added to certain cursive, private handwritings used in ancient Rome, together formed the semi-uncials. At the end of the 8th century the emperor Charlemagne established the Carolingian school in the abbey of St Martin, near Tours, with Alcuin of York (735–804) as head, and here was developed the first alphabet of good, small letters, the Carolingian minus-cules, that later became the models for the Roman printing types of the 15th century. Capitals were only used for the initial letter at the beginning of a section.

In Germany the Carolingian minuscules developed into Gothic, which existed in three forms:

1. Formal: Lettre de forme; or Pointed missal; or, Texture, and also in a round variety: round missal; or Italian rotunda.
2. Semi-formal: Lettre de somme (the regular book hand)
3. Cursive; Lettre bâtarde (cursive book hand)

The handwritings were transformed into types in the order here given.[1,2,3,4]

---

1 DE ROOVER: The scriptorium. (In Thompson: The medieval library. Chicago Univ.Pr. 1939. P.594–612)
2 LEHMANN-Haupt: Heritage of the MS. (Dolphin. 3:3-23, 1938).
3 LOWE: Handwriting. (In Crump, & Jacob: Legacy of the middle ages. Oxford Univ.Pr. 1932. p.197-226)
4 MADAN: Books in MS. [205] contains a chart showing the development of handwriting in Europe in the Middle Ages.

HISTORICAL INTRODUCTION

As a reaction against the "Gothic" script the Renaissance scribes early in the 15th century developed the humanistic, "Roman" script, mostly used for the classics ("antique let–ters": German "Antiqua").

Figures also have their origin in Hieroglyphics.

Roman numerals:

I, II, III = 1, 2, and 3 fingers.
V = Hand with thumb held out at an angle.
X = Two hands so held out.

Arabic numerals:

II. <u>TOOLS.</u>

We must realize that the forms of letters are to a great extent dependent on the materials on which they are written. On stone they were stiff and straight; on clay they took the form of wedges, and on wax they bent over like commas.

Writing-materials of the Past:

<u>Stone</u>: Lasts for a long time but is difficult to "write" on, or transport. Used by the Egyptians, Assyrians, and central American Mayas, and others.

<u>Clay</u>: Used in Babylonia about 2,400 B.C. for very minute cuneiform writing impressed on tiles, while they were still soft, with a sharp pointed bone or metal stylus. Some are in the form of cylinders with an outer shell of the same shape to protect them.

Papyrus: Made (about 3,500 B.C.–1,000 A.D.) from a Nile reed which was glued, laid in two layers at right angles, soaked, dried, and polished; 20 pages glued together formed a strip. Written on in many columns, rolled up round a little rod. Ink made of soot and water and gum arable, and pens made of a sharpened reed were used for writing on papyrus which began to supersede the clay about the 14th century B.C. Papyri rolls were sometimes provided with wrappers of parchment. Papyrus has very little resistance to humidity and was only written on that side where the strips lay horizontally.

Parchment: and Vellum: Skins of goats, sheep, lambs, and calves. Washed and scraped to remove hairs, then rubbed with pumice and dressed with chalk to produce a smooth surface. Had the advantage that it could be folded and made into folios and then sewn together. Dearness of parchment and vellum compelled scribes to abbreviate freely. A less valuable text could be erased and another written instead (Palimpsest). Jewish sacred books are still on parchment.

Wax tablets: Invented by the Romans and in use up to the French Revolution for notes or ephemeral news. Two tied together formed a Diptych; three a Tryptych; written on with a metal stylus.

Other materials: Leaves (the Greek word for which developed into Leaf (<u>Liber</u>) and <u>folio</u>; Bark; Silk; Board; Palm leaves (India, Ceylon, Bali, etc.); Bone; Silk textures; Metal.

Paper: Invented in China 103 A.D.[1] and guarded as a close secret until it reached Samarkand in 751 and Europe in 1050, but as late as 1231 it still encountered resistance because of its perishability.[2] See further in next chapter.

---

1 CAIN: Encyclopédie française. Gives 75 as the date, & the inventor as Ts'ai Loon.
2 GUPPY: Human records. (<u>Bull.John Rylands Libr.</u> 27(1)182–222, 1942) Repr. by Manchester Univ.Pr. 1942.

III. FORM OF THE BOOK.

The modern book form was evolved from the hinged wax tablets, which were found to be handier than rolls. Sheets of vellum or papyrus were folded once and placed inside one another -from 3-6 sheets in a quire. (See note p.127). This codex-form was invented 2,300 A.D.[1,2,3]

IV. ILLUMINATED MSS.

Scribes left blank spaces (or put in 'guide' letters) at the beginning of chapters and sections where the rubrisher (ruber = red) was to fill in the initials in colours and gold. This practice was followed by the early printers even when they possessed wood initials for printing or stamping in. The colours were gold (first powder, later gold leaf) red, and blue. The illustrations proper were illuminated miniatures, pen and ink drawings, water-colours or wood-blocks or metal cuts that were printed in and scroll-work surrounding the page of text. They preceded the blockbook (xylographic printing), which appeared in larger numbers about 1450, first in Latin and, about 10 years later, in German and Dutch. So, in actual fact, the blockbooks did not

---

1 JAMES: Books & writing [in Greece]. (In Whibley: Companion to Greek studies; 4ed. Cambridge Univ.Pr. 1931.p.606-10)

2 – Books & writing [in Rome]. (In Sandys: Companion to Latin studies; 3ed. Cambridge Univ.Pr. 1943.p.237-42)

3 HALL: Companion to classical texts. Oxford: Clarendon Pr. 1913.p.1-21.

precede the books printed fromx movable type, but developed parallel with, and independent of them. Their popularity waned about 1480.

V. THE INVENTION OF PRINTING IN EUROPE.

Incunabula represent the bridge between the MSS and the printed books as we know them to-day. One of the first steps was the making of a separate title-page, including the information given in the first two lines of the MS (the incipit) and in the colophon at the end of the MS., and the substitution of printed initials, borders, and illustrations for hand decoration. However, the influence of the MS was so strong in the first years of printing from movable type that it may be difficult to tell at first glance whether one has a MS, or an incunable in hand. And the first printers closely copied the national, MS. styles in their types. Morison[1] calls it "imitation calligraphy", and mentions Fraktur as a horrifying example. He has pointed out that the early typecutters owed much to the metal engravers in their type-design, which is only proper because printing is "a department of engraving". This is particularly evident in Francesco Griffo, typecutter to Aldus Manutius.

---

1 MORISON: Art of printing. (Proc.Brit.Acad. 23:373–400, 1937)

It is believed that printing from movable type was first invented by Johan Gutenberg about 1440, but several rival claims have been, and are still being upheld. Printing by means of movable type was "in the air" about that time. Firstly there was a need for more and cheaper books; secondly most of the material for printing was already in existence. Block printing had already been practised on textiles and playing cards; as woodcuts and metal cuts for illustrations, and as binders' stamps; the press too, already existed and was used by paper-makers; and casting in moulds, too, was known and practised by bellfounders and other artisans.[1,2,3,4]

Gutenberg was financed by Johann Fust but was later sued by Fust who, then, together with a lay brother, Peter Schoeffer brought out the 42-line Bible (1455) while one believes that Gutenberg himself kept the type for, and printed the 36-line Bible (1458–61) (the type of the 42-line Bible closely resembles the pointed missal, MS-hand in use in Mains). Fust and Schoeffer in 1457 brought out their Psalter, which is famous as being the

---

1 AUDIN: Mystery of the origins of typography. (Libr.Ass.Rec. s3, 1:153–62, 1931)
2 SCHMIDT: Ein Rückblick auf das Gutenberg-Jahr 1940. (Zbl.f. Biblwesen 59(9/10)412–41, 1942)
3 SMITH: Initial letters in the printed book... (Fleuron 1:61–4, 1923)
4 BORHARDT: Some aspects of the history of early printing & the advancement of learning. (N.Z.Libr. 14(3)61–71, 1951)

first printed book with a colophon.

From Mainz the art of printing spread rapidly, first to Strasbourg where the first printer, Johann Methelin's son-in-law Rusch (known as the R-printer) printed what was for a long time believed to be the first Roman type, but in later years it has been proved that the first Roman types were cut by the German printers Sweynheim and Pannartz, in the cloister of Subiaco in 1467.[1,2]

Printing in Paris (1470+) was connected with the Sorbonne, and the titles were edited by the professors. They used Roman type.

In the later years of the century Italy took the lead in printing. Many German printers went back home, but in Venice Nicolas Jenson developed a gothic type that became much used in Germany, a Roman type, which is one of the most beautiful ever cut, and a good Greek type which, unfortunately, was ousted for many years by that of Aldus Manutius. Aldus Manutius[3] cut (1501) the first italic type, derived from the cursive hand of

---

1 MORISON: Early humanistic script & the first Roman type. (Libr. s4, 24(1/2) 1–29, 1943)

2 SCHOLDERER: Adolf Rusch & the earliest Roman types. (Libr. s4, 20(1) 43–50, 1939)

3 ROBERTSON: Aldus Manutius. (Bull.John Rylands Libr. 33(1) 57–73, 1950)

HISTORICAL INTRODUCTION

the medieval scribes for his Virgil.[1,2,3]

Henceforth the cutting of new printing types is not modelled on manuscript hands, but on older types. (See Chapter VIII)

The history of printing in South Africa, as far as it is known, began with the arrival in 1784 in Cape Town of Johan Christian Ritter, who printed some handbills. It is known that an almanac was printed for each of the years 1795–6–7, but a fragment of the one for 1796 is the only part of them which has survived.[4]

In January 1799 Harry Harwood Smith arrived in Cape, where he printed government proclamations, and in the same year the first pamphlet printed in South Africa: "Brief van het zendelings genootschap te London"[5] printed by V.A. Schoonberg, sen., probably on Ritter's old press.

A commercial firm, Messrs Walker and Robertson, had meanwhile got printing materials out and set up their press in 1800.

---

1 GUPPY: Evolution of the art of printing. (Bull.John Rylands Libr. 24(2) 198–233, 1940)
2 SCHOLDERER: Invention of printing. (Libr. s4,21(1)1–25, 1940)
3 UHLENDORF: Invention of printing & its spread till 1470. (Libr. Quart. 2(3)179–231, 1932)
4 LLOYD: The birth of printing in South Africa. (Libr. s3, 5: 31–43, 1914)
   (Also Common room magazine, Winter 1924, p.6–9; S.Afr.Libr. 1(1)11–8, 1933)
5 VARLEY: An early Cape printing discovery. (Bull.S.Afr.Libr. 1(1)7–12, 1946)

The next year they were appointed sole printers to the Government and given the right to all commercial printing. On the 16 August 1801 they issued the first number of the "Cape Town Gazette and African Advertiser", but from October all printing was taken over by the Government and was to be done for them by H.H. Smith. In 1823 Georg Greig arrived at the Cape.

As far as can be ascertained printing in other parts of South Africa began in the following order: Graaff-Reinet (1801) Betheledorp (1804?) Natal (1838)[1,2]

---

1 SMITH: Chronological list of the more important places in South Africa where printing was introduced during the early years. (S.Afr. Libr. 6(2) 67–71 & map 1938)

2 TOUSSAINT: Early European printing in the Indian Ocean. (Int.Bull. Print.allied Tr. (45)13–7, 1948)

"Sweet ladies pray be not offended,
Nor mind the jest of sneering wags;
No harm, believe us, is intended,
When humbly, we request your rags"[1]

VII

PAPER

Paper Chronology[1,2,3,4]

Invented in China 103 A.D. (see foot-note (1) on p.138) After the Mohammedan victory over the Chinese 655 paper was manufactured in Samarkand, Damascus, and towns in North Africa, whence it followed the Moors' conquest of Spain about 1050.
1150. First paper-mill in Europe, Xativa, Spain, started. The Stamping mill was invented here.
In 1221 the use of paper for public documents was already resisted because of its perishability.
After the fall of the Moors paper was manufactured primarily in Italy.
1270 Paper-mill in Fabriano.
The oldest paper manufacturers used starch for sizing but from about 1270 the Italian mills used animal glue.
1282. The first watermark was made in Italy.
1389. Paper was fabricated by Stromer in Nuremberg.
1490 by John Tate, Hertfordshire.
1495 Wynkyn de Worde, successor to Caxton, printed <u>De Proprietatibus Rerum</u>, the first book printed on English-made paper.
1700 (?) The "Hollander" displaced the stampers formerly used.
1719 Wood and the Wasp. (Réaumur).
1750(?) Baskerville invented "wove" paper and 1758 used it for an edition of Virgil.

---

1 A papermaker in Northern New York.
2 AITKEN: Some notes on the history of paper. (Trans.bibliogr. Soc. 13:201–17, 1914)
3 JAHANS: Brief history of paper. (Book-Coll.Quart. 15:42-58, 1934)
4 JENKINS: Paper-making in England 1495–1788. (Libr.Ass.Rec. 2:479–88, 577–88; 3:239–51; 4:128–39, 1900–2)

1765 Common vegetables, weeds, and woods were used by J.C. Schäffer in papermaking.

1774 Bleaching (following the discovery by Scheele of chloride).

1798 Louis Robert invented the paper machine later called the Fourdrinier.

1806 Engine sizing (with resin) invented by Illig.

1826 Dandy roll used first (in London). Invented between 1825–30 at the firm of T.A. & C.D. Marshall.

1844 Mechanized pulp method invented.

1851 Esparto paper fabricated and shown at the Great Exhibition. Commercialized 1857.

1854 Chemical wood pulp invented.

1890 Coated papers first made.

Manufacture[1,2,3,4]

Basic Raw Materials.

I. Rag Fibre.

(a) Seed hair fibres

	Percentage of Cellulose Content	
Cotton	92–7	Cotton is the purest form of cellulose, the basis of papermaking. The fibres (about 1" long) have a very long and very wide central canal attracting a large amount of moisture, thus leading to stretching and shrinking. Used for producing blotting paper.
Kapok		

---

1 CRAIG: Practical paper making. (Paper & Print 22:245–7, 389–92; 23:72–8, 186–92, 274–81, 408–13; 24:58–64, 188–94, 303–10, 420–6; 25:61–70, 175–9, 1949–52)

2 HUNTER: Papermaking. (Dolphin 3:345–70, 1938)

3 CUNANE: Printing paper. (Stationers' Co's Craft Lectures 4(3)53–76, 1925/6)

4 SINDALL: Paper for books. ib. 1(2)14–24, 1922/3)

	Percentage of Cellulose Content	
(b) Bast fibres. Flax (Linen)	82	Fibres are long, cylindrical, bamboo-like. Resulting paper hard and strong (used for bank-notes) Fibres stretch.
Hemp	±75	Fibres similar to linen but thinner at ends and ends rounder.
Jute	±60	Thick, medium length. For wrappings.
Manila hemp	65	Long and strong fibres, for envelopes.

Ramie (China-grass) 60–80 paper mulberry (used for papermaking in Japan from earliest times) mitsumata, gampi, sisal, hemp, <u>Adansonia digitata</u> (West African monkey-bread tree)

II. <u>Rag Substitutes.</u>

(c) From whole cells or leaves:

Straw:[1]

Barley	48.6	Short, thick fibres. Waste during process gives only 33 per cent. of the weight of straw recovered.
Oats	43.8	
Rye	36.3	
Wheat	56.7	
		Esparto processing plant is used.

---

1   GRANT: From straw...to paper. (<u>Int.Print</u>. 1:54–9, 1947)

	Percentage of Cellulose Content	
Esparto	42–8	Central canal of fibre is very fine; cell-diametre 1/20 of that of cotton, no stretching and shrinking, but fibre weak.
Norfolk reed, Bagasse (Sugar cane)		
Bamboo, Papyrus, etc.		
(d) Woods.		
either Coniferous: Spruce	60.9	Long-fibred, sheet may be transparent.
White pine, Fir, Cypress, Larch		
or Deciduous:		
Aspen	62	Short-fibred
Poplar, Chestnut, Eucalyptus, Beech, Birch, etc.		

Non-fibrous Ingredients:

1. Mineral   (a)   mixed into the pulp-"Fillers": Chalk, Kaolin (China clay, usually from Cornwall), Soapstone 8–25 per cent., Calcium, or Barium sulphate, Gypsum, Satin white, etc.
              (b)   applied to the surface-"Coatings".
2. Sizing   (a)   mixed with the pulp-"Engine-sized", usually vegetable, or
              (b)   applied to the surface-"Tub-sized": Starch, Casein, Silicate of soda (Water glass), Resin(+ Alum) and Animal size, usually.

Without sizing paper would be like blotting paper. Sizing does not, however, affect the printability.
3. Pigments and Dyes (Aniline) used for "whitening", or colouring.
   Pigments - India tint. Also act as fine "filler".
   Aniline dyes: 1. Direct colours; 2. Basic colours; 3. Acid (Alkali resistant) colours.

III. <u>Water.</u>

The <u>first stage</u> converts the raw-materials into "half- stuff". Rags are sorted and cut into 2-3 inch squares, dusted, boiled with alkaline containing caustic soda, sodium carbonate, lime, sometimes under pressure. Then it goes into the "breaker", is washed and bleached.

The mass at this stage is called pulp, and is classified as follows:

1. <u>Wood pulp</u>:
   A. Mechanical wood pulp (M.W.P.)
      Usually made from spruce by purely mechanical means (grinder). M.W.P. is really ground wood-sawdust. High opacity.
   B. Chemical wood pulp (C.W.P.)
      Obtained by boiling, or "digestion" of wood with solutions of various chemicals. The principal chemical processes are 1, 3–4 mentioned below.
      1. Sulphite (bi-sulphite of lime). From coniferous trees.
      2. Neutral: Sulphite (Monosulphite).
      3. Sulphate. (Kraft) (Mixture of caustic soda and sulphate of soda) Coniferous.

4. Soda. (Caustic soda solution). Poplar.
   5. Semi-chemical.
   6. Screenings.
   7. Miscellaneous, e.g. Soda-chlorine process of Pomilio.
2. <u>Rag Pulps, old and new</u>.
3. <u>Reclaimed papers</u>.
4. <u>Pulp from other fibres</u>: Rope, Jute, Esparto, Straw. Bagasse, Cotton linters, Bracken, Hop-vines, Nettles(Ramie), Reeds, etc.

The most common pulps for printing papers are Rag, Sulphite, Soda, and pulps prepared from reclaiming waste paper, magazines and books. In 1928 there were more than 2,000 of these.

During the <u>second stage</u> the pulp (0.5–3 per cent. pulp, 99.5–97 per cent. water) passes through the beater (Hollander) and becomes 'stuff'. The fibres are here disintegrated and fibrillated. For machine-made paper the pulp is "loaded" (i.e. "fillers" are added) which gives paper a more uniform colour and a more even surface; it absorbs ink better and the friction of paper in contact with type is lessened (but it chokes the type). Loading helps to bind the paper fibres together and the cost is reduced, but overloaded paper will, in contact with damp, become a clayey mass. Engine size, which renders the paper partially resistent to humidity, inks, and grease, and colouring matter is also added at this stage.

Hand-made paper, usually made from cotton, linen or hemp goes, thirdly, to the vat, where the vat-man takes the stuff up on his mould, framed by a deckle. The coucher takes the sheet from the vat and lays it between felt; whole layers of paper and felt are repeatedly pressed, then dried in a loft and fin-ally tub-sized.[1]

The fourth stage – Finishing - for hand-made paper consists in glazing or hot-pressing (H/P), if it is not treated it has a "rough finish".

Machine-made paper in its third stage passes through a paper machine, which usually consists of an endless, woven wire gauze, various suction boxes and steamheated, hollow cylinders to dry it, and a dandy (or water-marking) roll. The formation of the paper may be either laid or wove, depending on the nature of wiring or face of the mould or cover of the dandy-roll used. Laid papers, when held up to the light, show a ribbed, or lined appearance, due to the paper being thinned by the wires of the mould in hand-made papers; by the wires of the dandy-roll in machine-mades, or by the felt in machine-glazed. A laid paper has its roughness in tiny furrows across the paper, running with the closely laid lines. The "chain" lines (about 1" apart) run

---

1 See Evelyn's Diary 1641–1706.
    Quoted in Cockerell: Bookbinding...[427] p.282–3.

at right angles, i.e. down the printed page. This obtains the best impression from the type. A wove paper has no direction in its roughness. Most machine-made papers are wove.

Coating is done at this stage. Some machine-coated, art papers are spray-coated on their way through the paper machine, while real art paper is coated, dried, and calendered on a separate machine. Machine-coated art papers are superior to Imitation art papers. Coating helps to retain a paper in a state of stability.

There are six major (surface) <u>finishes</u>:

(i) Uncoated: Antique, Eggshell, Vellum, "M.F." (Machine Finish, which is good for type and perhaps a few line blocks) English Super-calendered (S/C)

(ii) Coated: Matt(Dull) or Glossy.

Machine-made papers are finally cut. The machine-direction will, if the paper has been correctly cut, run along the spine of the book when the sheet is folded.

<u>Differences between Hand-Made and Machine-Made Paper.</u>

1. "Machine direction". In machine-made paper the strength is much greater in one direction than in the other. This is less noticeable in hand-made paper because the vat-man's shake of the pulp felts the fibres more in every direction than does the shake of the wire of the machine.
2. Hand-made paper is thicker towards the edge of the sheet than at the centre.
3. The water-mark in hand-made paper is said by some to be more clearly defined.

4. The "look-through" of hand-made paper has a wilder and more cloudy formation - mottled.
5. A crease made in a hand-made paper is less prominent than one made in machine-made paper.
6. If a circular disc of hand-made paper is put on water it should curl up saucer-shape. A disc of machine-made paper should roll up like a cigar.
7. A deckle edge is found on all four sides of a full sheet of hand-made paper, but the imitation of mould-made paper is usually deckled only on the two opposite edges, formed by the deckle-strap.
8. As a rule the "wire" (under-, sieve, German: <u>Sieb</u>- or <u>Unterseite</u>) side is the right side in hand-made papers, and the wrong in machine-mades. (The right side is the side from which one reads the water-mark; in hand-made papers the side which touches the wire-cover of the mould; in machine-made papers the upperside where the couch roll, and not the wire acts. Felt side is that side of the web of paper which has not been in contact with the wire during manufacture; it is, therefore, the smooth side of the paper as distinguished from the wire side)

Watermarks.

Purposes: Historical - Religious symbolism.
             Collation.
             Modern - Trade mark.

<u>Requirements of Modern Book-Papers.</u>[1,2,3,4]
Lightness, strength, flexibility, opacity, durability (and

---

1 PARLEY: Durability of printed papers & MSS. (<u>Libr.Ass.Rec</u>. ns 6(23) 161-72 Sep.1928)
2 - Enduring paper. (<u>Book-Coll.Quart</u>. 3:29–38, 1931)
3 REICHARDT: Durability of paper. (<u>Libr.Quart</u>. 8(4)510–20 Oct.1938)
4 SCRIBNER: Preservation of records in libraries. (<u>Libr. Quart</u>. 4(3)371–83 Jul.1934)

permanence for some) good, printing qualities; capacity of paper for reflecting light, and a suitable colour.

Durability.

"The degree to which a paper retains its original qualities under continual usage, this is not to be confused with permanence, which is the degree to which a paper resists chemical action which may result from impurities in the paper itself or agents from the surrounding air" (Amer.Paper and Pulp Ass: Dictionary... [227])

The essential thing in a paper for permanence is that it should be close-textured and well compacted. The above mentioned Dictionary defines texture-formation:

"A property which is determined by the degree of uniformity of distribution of the solid components of the sheet with special reference to the fibers. It is usually judged by the visual appearance of the sheet when viewed by transmitted light. This property is very important, not only because of its influence on the appearance of the sheet but because it influences the values and uniformity of values of nearly all other properties".

Factors making for <u>permanence</u> in papers are: 1. Quality of the materials used; 2. Length of the individual fibres; 3. Way in which they are knitted together; 4. Chemical purity. All-rag paper should not contain any resin size at all, as it is a very unstable compound and oxidizes very easily in the presence of light and air. No paper should be classed as permanent if it contains resin. Flax and cotton, from experience, are known to be absolutely durable, other materials are at best presumed to be.

A good modern book-paper should have a close, firm texture, not overbleached, nor excessively calendered. The thickness depends largely upon the size of the paper. A thin, strong paper is preferable to a thick one, but a very fine paper is not recommended for library books.

It should contain not less than 70 per cent. cotton, flax, or hemp fibre. A "Standard" paper should be made from normal paper-making materials: rag, Esparto and "C.W.P."; should be sized with not more than 2 per cent. resin size. (Resin size is acted on by sunlight, and gelatine by micro-organisms); should not contain more than 10 per cent. mineral matter, i.e. loading. Note result in art papers and their objectionable smell. (Mineral content seems to be lessening: from 15 per cent. in 1913, 10 per cent. in 1930, 5–6 per cent. in 1931)

Printability of paper involves the following factors: 1. Receptivity of the paper surface to printer's ink; 2. Nature of the paper surface; 3. Nature & viscosity of the printing ink; 4. Levelness of paper surface.

Testing of papers(1)[1] includes tests of the quality, length of fibre, elasticity, anti-creasing (folding) potential, bulk

---

1   DAY: Paper testing for the paper user. (Paper & Print 23(1) 44–8, 1950) See also his: Paper...[236] p.100–17.

(thickness v. function), finish, surface (half-tones), and grain direction.

The process in printing of "work and turn" requires, for a satisfactory job, a paper without a pronounced underside. And it is essential that the printer recognize the difference between the top- and undersides of a sheet, so that where choice is possible, illustrations and single-sided jobs may be confined to the more printable top-side of the paper. Art papers and "twinwire" papers are always equal on both sides. There has been some success in removing wire-marks from the underside of Imitation art papers. Esparto papers, because of the finer fibres, are always much easier to make reasonably equal-sided compared with wood papers.

Classes of Modern Book Papers, with some Titles exemplifying them.

ALL-RAG.   Used for certain editions of The Times (1917+) New York Times (1926+) Sydney Morning Herald (1928+) and for some years of the New York Public Library: Bulletin. [88]

ANTIQUE.   This term is applied to any printing paper of a rough surface. (It should be noted that nearly all but expensive hand-made papers have a "right" and a "wrong" side. Care should be taken that the right side is used for any single-sided job. This is also important for Litho work). In modern usage the term "Antique", whether laid, wove, or book, is generally used to indicate a surface which is "unfinished", i.e. not calendered, in the papers of the 'Featherweight' class. Sindall writes of "incredible antique", and "Featherweight": 'A paper made from a soufflé of pulp -

all puff, fluff and bluff"! As the word suggests, the term is applied to papers of extreme lightness in proportion to their bulk, made chiefly from Esparto, held together so loosely that 2/3rds or even 3/4ths of their body is air-space. The bulkiest are entirely unloaded and have very little sizing. They go to pieces in a few months, will not lie open flat, and easily absorb dirt. The defects arise from the conditions of manufacture, only 11–12 hours "beating".

ANTIQUE DE LUXE. Hardy, Thos: Famous tragedy of the Queen of Cornwall, etc. Macmillan 1923.

ANTIQUE WOVE. Gill, Eric: Essays; illus. with woodcuts by the author. Cape (1947); Mackley, Geo. E: Wood engraving. National Mag. Co. 1948.

ARCHES: Called after the town in France where this paper is fabricated; used also for bank-notes. Flaubert, G: Bibliomania; a tale, etc. Evanston, Ill. [1929] Winterich: Grolier....[604]

ART PAPER. Also called 'body' paper, is paper that has been coated on one or both side(s) with mineral substances such as china-clay, which produces a smooth surface (like bath-room tiles) taking, if desired, a very high polish, and used for printing from fine screen, half-tone blocks.
Read, Herbert Edw: Practice of design. Lund Humphries 1946.

ART (COATED) PAPER. Up to 50 per cent. good Kaolin. Hackleman, Chas W: Commercial engraving and printing, etc. Indianapolis: Commercial Engr.Publ. Co. 1924. [162]

ART. WHITE ART PAPER. Richards, Jas Maunde: Edward Bawden. Penguin Books 1946.

BATCHELOR'S KELMSCOTT. The Phoenix nest 1593; repr. Etchell & McDonald 1926. Some copies on Kentish "All-rag".

CARTRIDGE. MELLOTEX CARTRIDGE. Cowell: Handbook... [296]

CHINA PAPER. Ritson, Jos: Robin Hood...with 80 wood-engravings by Bewick... Nimmo 1887. 2v.

DURABILITY PAPER. Grade 1(a) Library Ass: Durability of paper...[249]
1(b) same
2 Esdaile: Student's...[34]; Library Ass. Book...[35]; Library Ass. Subject...[814] 1929–30; Libr.Ass.Rec. 1930–3 [81]; Minto: Reference...[754]; S.Afr. Libr.[99]; Year's work...[16].

ESPARTO. Used for its bulk and opacity for "Featherweight" papers. Surface is smooth, texture close, gives clear watermarking. Further, Esparto papers when wet, expand rather less than other papers, thus tending to make esparto particularly suitable for good register in multi-colour printing. Association of Makers of Esparto Papers: Esparto papers. [256].

"EVENSYDE" (Dickinson) or "TWINWIRE" PAPER is a machine-made paper, made on two separate wires of a paper-making machine and then joined at an early stage with the two undersides together, forming a paper with two top sides structurally identical. The two sides are "welded" together because the two sheets are brought together before felting. The production from 1935 of this paper is one of the most important paper-making developments of the century. Curwen, Harold: Printing. Penguin Books 1948.

FEATHERWEIGHT. See under ANTIQUE.

HAND-MADE PAPERS. Sawyer, Chas Jas: Dickens v. Barabbas, etc. Sawyer 1930. 10 copies on Japanese vellum, 100 on Abbey Mill Antique.

IMITATION ART PAPER. Is a highly finished "printing", prepared by the addition of a heavy percentage (up to 35 per cent.) of china-clay to the pulp, plus a water-finish giving it a surface, opacity, and absorbency suitable for printing half-tones. (The water-finish may be substituted by dampening & super-calendering). The distinction between Art paper and Imitation Art paper is that Art paper is coated, i.e. the mineral is spread on the surface, while in Imitation art

PAPER: MODERN BOOK PAPERS

paper it is <u>mixed with</u> the fibre. Coating with mineral matters renders the paper brittle, so that the process of binding is very difficult. Usually Esparto base. With matt finish: Hunter, Dard: Papermaking... [238].

INDIA, OR BIBLE PAPER. (Made from rags; generally imported from China(!) More suitable for the "personal" library than the institutional. It is light, permanent, thin, strong, and opaque. Also used for pocket editions, and sometimes reference books. Made opaque by the addition of a "filler' such as calcium carbonate. <u>Encycl.Brit</u>.; and pocket editions.

JAPANESE VELLUM. Hand-made, with a vellum surface. Its manufacture is no longer confined to Japan, nor is it made from calf skins. Its "look-through" is very "cloudy". It is tough and durable. Its colour is creamy, ivory, or "natural". The thinnest variety is used for repairing broken sections, covering newspapers, and for printing etchings and engravings. Bodoni, G.B: Preface to the <u>Manuale tipo-grafico</u>. E. Mathews 1925.

KENTISH ALL-RAG. See under BATCHELOR.

MOULD-MADE. Albert Spicer...1847–1934. Simpkin Marshall 1938.

NEWSPRINT. Paper made from "stock" (furnish) varying from 70 per cent. "M.W.P." and the remainder unbleached sulphite ("C.W.P.") to 100 per cent. "M.W.P." Constitutes about 75 per cent. of all printing papers.

PHOTOX OFFSET. Smith, Percy T. Delft: Civic and memorial lettering. A. & C. Black 1946. White Art for half-tones.

STRAW. <u>Endeavour</u>. 3(12)1944, made from pulp of straw and waste wood from England itself for 85 per cent. of the fibrous material. Coating for paper used for illustrations in <u>Endeavour</u> is normally made from China-clay from Cornwall.

> "With twenty-six soldiers of lead I
> will conquer the world".[1]

VIII

PRINTING

Printing Chronology

Printing developed early in China; from stone rubbings, through seals and wood-blocks (Diamond Sutra 868 A.D.) till ±1050, when printing from movable, earthenware type was practised by Pi-Sheng.
±1400 Movable metal types cast from a mould used in Korea.
1423 The St Christopher block-print (now in the John Rylands Library, Manchester)
±1440 Gutenberg invents type-founding.
1454 The first dated publication (an Indulgence, printed by Gutenberg)
1457 The first time a book carries the name of the printer (Peter Schoeffer's Psalter)
1461 The first illustrated printed book, published by Albert Pfister of Bamberg (common about 1470)
1463 The first book with a title-page (a bull of Pius II, printed by Fuat and Schoeffer at Mainz)
1465 Printing introduced into Italy.
1470 Printing introduced into France.
– The first book with printed leaf-numbers, and head-lines, and a second title-page published by Arnold Ther Hoernen of Cologne.
1472 The first book with printed signatures, by Johann Koelhoff of Cologne.
1474 Caxton prints in Brughes.
1476 – Introduces sprinting into England.
– First complete title-page (Ratdolt's <u>Calendarium</u>).
1501 Aldine <u>italic</u>.
1705 Experiments with stereotype.
1720 Caslon cuts his first fount, in London.
1727 William Ged improves the stereotype process, and prints his <u>Sallust</u> (1739) from plates.

---

1 Author unknown.

1798–1800 Charles, 3rd Earl Stanhope, perfects the iron press.
1812 Bensley invents the cylinder press.
1814 Koenig's cylinder, flat-bed printing machine driven by steam operates in The Times printing office. His is the first automatically inked press. Patented 1811.
1834 David Bruce invents the first commercially successful typecasting machine.
1837–9 Electrotype perfected.
1846 Hoe invents the Rotary press; constructed by Applegarth.
1884–6 L.B. Benton invents and perfects the punch-cutting machine.
1886–90 Linotype comes into use. (Invented 1876–86 by Otto Mergenthaler)
1887–99 Monotype machine perfected and brought on the market.
1946 Photographic type-composing perfected. Principle patented as early as 1921.

Printing in its broadest sense includes three distinct, major methods of reproduction, classified according to the nature of the printing surface:

RELIEF, or letterpress printing, as its name implies, is that in which the printing surface stands in relief, i.e. above the surrounding, non-printing area. Examples are: letterpress from type, halftone, and line-blocks, and wood cuts.

INTAGLIO. The design to be printed is below the surface. Examples are: Photogravure, steel, and copper engravings, the artist's aquatints, line etchings, and dry points.

PLANOGRAPHIC is the term used to describe a printing surface on the same level as the plate which, by special treatment based on the antipathy of grease and water, accepts ink, while the area around resists it. Examples are: Lithography, photo-litho-offset, and collotype.

There are other means of putting ink on paper, e.g. Silk screen stencil printing (Serigraphy) and printing by electrical abstraction ("onset", or Xerography).

PRINTING: TYPE METAL

Type metal is an alloy of lead, tin and antimony[1]. Antimony helps to keep the outline of type sharp, tin makes the alloy flow freely when molten and makes it hard when cold. In the old times type was cast by hand, one letter at a time, in foundries. Since the advent of monotype, "sorts" can be obtained from any printer who has a Monotype caster. The Lino-type caster makes lines ('slugs') of type. For Monotype casting the composition formulas of the type metal vary, but representative proportions are: lead 72 per cent., tin 9 per cent., antimony 19 per cent; Linotype: 84 per cent., 10 per cent., and 12 per cent; Foundrytype: 50 per cent., 25 per cent., and 25 per cent. When type is cast for hand-setting more antimony is added for greater hardness. Plastic type has lately come into use, also for Monotype casting.

A type has three dimensions: I. "Height to paper" which, in English type, is 0.918 of an inch or, roughly, the height of a shilling standing on its edge; II. Width, i.e. "set", the size of the widest letter, usually M or W; III. Gauge or body-wise dimension, or 'point' size, a point being 0.013837" or about 1/72 of an inch. Founts of type are divided by printers into two classes: body, and display types. The first is again divided into book, which we are mostly concerned with, and news,

---

1 ELLIOTT: Type metal. (Monotype Rec. 32(3)25–9,1933)

i.e. newspaper types. A good book type must be readable and unobtrusive, largely of literary appeal; while a news type must have largely advertising appeal. The largest display types are called poster types, usually cut in wood, and their size designated by "lines", e.g. a 20-pica wood type would be called 20- line. Wood types are available in sizes beginning at 48-pt and running up to 10".

The point size of the body is fixed by the mould; the size of the face by the matrix. Thus "10-on-12" means types cast from 10-pt matrices in a 12-pt mould. This gives the effect of slightly spaced lines and saves leading".

The length of a line of a certain type is usually given by printers in "ems", or "ens" (half an "em"). The "em" (also called Mutton so as not to be mistaken for "en") in hand-setting days, was always the square of the body and the "en" ("Nut") half the square, e.g. an 8-pt "em" = 8×8-pts, and its "en" = 4×8-pts. Monotype "ems" are not always exactly square, a 12-pt "em" may vary from 10½ to about 13-pts width.

The making of type begins with the cutting of punches (and counter-punches for the white spaces within letters); the making of the matrix from the punches (now done by a punch-cutting machine, which pantographically traces the punch from an enlarged master pattern); and finally the casting of type.

The setting up of copy is the next step: by hand, then from type-cases, of which there are two, the top one containing the capitals which, therefore, get the name "Upper-case"; and the small letters in the lower one ("lower-case"-letters). Type must be packed closely together before printing, therefore the spaces which do not print on the page must be filled out by <u>spacing materials</u> which (between lines) are called "leads" (up to 6-pt and as long as the line is wide); slugs (an American term for leads larger than 6-pt); clumps, or reglets (the English term for slugs, usually made in 6-8-pt); spaces between words (also ½-spaces and hair-spaces) (measured in parts of "ems" in foundry type) and quads (also called "rats"). Large quads are called 'quotations', and are hollow. Spacing material above 12-pt size is called "furniture" (because it is usually made of wood) and is measured in 12-pt ems = 'Pica'.

The assembling of letters and spaces is called <u>composition</u>. In hand-setting the compositor holds the composing stick in his left hand and takes the letters from the type-cases with his right. 'In order to produce the proper impression the type has to be set upside down and backwards...'. When he has set several lines he transfers them to the galley which, when full, contains about 3 pages of text. Type-setting by machine is usually done on Linotype, Monotype, or Intertype-machines, of which only the first two are used for book-work. The <u>Linotype</u> operator works on a kind of typewriter keyboard. When he presses one of the keys, the corresponding matrix is brought along beside the matrices already "called"; at the end of the line he can see from a calculator how much space he has to distribute between words, which he does by pressing a button. Molten type metal is then poured into the matrices and the finished type comes out as slugs. The <u>Monotype</u> is really two machines. The first one consists of a keyboard. When a key is pressed holes are cut in a roll of paper; spacing is also indicated by holes. When finished the roll is taken to the second machine and the caster fastened to it; a stream of air is directed against the unwinding paper roll and, when the holes pass the air-stream, it slips through and "calls" the corresponding matrices. Monotype means one type for each letter. In the <u>Intertype</u> machine the matrices are fed to it by hand. It is mostly used for display work.

The latest development in printing is leadless type composition, of which there are several processes. The three most common photo-type-setters are: Intertype Fotosetter, Rotofoto (Westover), and Hadego which, in their construction, resemble the Lino-caster, Monotype, and Ludlow machines respectively.[1,2,3,4,5]

---

1 KING: Intertype fotosetter machine. (<u>Sh.Yr Knowledge Rev</u>. 32(1)35–9, 1950)

2 A newspaper without compositors: facts about the Leesburg experiment. (<u>Brit.Print</u>. 60(357)21,48,Nov./Dec.1947)

PRINTING: PHOTO-COMPOSING

The advantages of photo-composing are several: greater speed; no ink squash (but that may mean that new type-faces to suit their softer impression will have to be designed); the product may be reproduced by offset, gravure, or letterpress plates; no outlay in type metal; one can used kerned letters; the same matrix is used for various sizes of the same letter, etc.

If the compositor were to leave the spaces between words equal, the printed page would look like a typed one does. The art of the compositor consists in distributing evenly the space left at the end of the line between words in the line, and in regulating the spaces in the line, so that there will be no "rivers" of white meandering down the page. Although the justification mechanism on composing machines is highly developed, good hand composing is still superior.

The first proofs are pulled from the galley, also called slip-, or "stone-proof". Next the printing matter is divided up into pages, and the pages locked up in the "chase", and "quoins" are inserted to keep "sorts" from falling out. If

---

3   PATRA Information Leaflet. 32,Oct.1948.
4   SILCOCK: "Monotype" photo, typographical composing machines. (Penrose Annu. 43:114,1949; 44:102,1950.
5   Type composition without type. (Bookb.Bk Prod. 46(4)46–7, Oct.1947)

sorts fall out and become mixed, they are said to have "pied". The process of arranging the pages for printing is called imposition, and the pages assembled in the chase constitute the forme[1]. In half-sheet imposition the same forme is printed on both sides of the sheet ("work and turn"); this of course, can only be used when a half-sheet is required at the end of a book, or for "prelims". When different formes are printed on the two sides of the sheet it is called sheet imposition. The number of proofs the author gets depends upon the corrections made, but the minimum is: the galley proofs, and the second, or revised page-proofs. If a book is printed from electrotype the author may get a "foundry-proof".

Types of printing presses:

A. Both paper and printing surface flat.
    1. The original, primitive hand-press of wood, with screw, dates from before the invention of movable type[2].
    2. The hand-press with lever, piston, and toggle, still used for proofs, and by private presses.
    3. The machine, platen-press used for jobbing: (a) both paper and forme flat; (b) forme vertical, platen at an angle; (c) open - neither vertical; or closed -

---

1   "Outer forme" printed first, contains p.1; "Inner forme" printed last, contains p.2.
2   MADAN: Early representations of the printing press. (Bibliographica. 1:223-48,499-502, 1895)

both vertical, since both are on a common pivot.

B. With printing surface flat and paper applied by a revolving cylinder, called flat-bed cylinder, or cylinder flat-bed press, or machine.

C. Rotary, with both paper and printing surface cylindrical. The printing surface may be either (a) Plates cast (stereotyped) in semi-cylindrical form; or (b) Aluminium, or zinc lithographic plates; or (c) the rubber cylinder of the "offset" machine; or (d) the etched, curved cylinder in use for mechanical, rotary photogravure.

The so-called perfecting press is in reality two presses united, one printing one side of the sheet, which is turned over and printed on the opposite side. (Perfecting = to print the second side of the sheet).

Making-ready. Before the actual printing begins the press-man has to ensure that the printing surface will print evenly on the sheet, and in order to achieve that, he will patch-up the roller where the impression is weak and take some away where the impression is too strong. It should be possible to reduce make-ready in the future when stereos of soft, elastic materials (rubber or thermo-plastics) come to be used.

Printing inks consist of varnishes and pigments. The base of the varnish is usually linseed oil freed from fats, and boiled; plus resin and soap. Pigments are usually prepared from lamp black with, or without added indigo, Prussian blue, etc. Inks for special purposes may vary. (See following chapter).

Rollers are made from gelatine, from calf-skins, glycerine, treacle, or they may have a plastic covering.[1]

The machining, or printing-off is usually, and always for long runs, done not from the type, but from "duplicate plates" which are of two kinds: (a) those for the reproduction of original copy, e.g. half-tones, and line-blocks - zinco(graph)s. (See later under Illustration): (b) those for the duplication of cuts, or type formes already made up. The processes under (b) are either Electrotypes ("Electros") made from impressions moulded in wax or lead (mostly for illustrations); Nickel types, which are Electros faced with nickel for extra long life; or Stereos, where the copy is made from a mould made of dry flong, plaster of Paris, or plastics.

There are many advantages in duplicating: speedier production, because the printer can prepare multiple formes. (Even from dry flong it is possible to prepare as many as six satisfactory plates). It is possible to produce the same subject matter in identical form, at the same time, in a number of different places. Duplicating saves wear and tear on expensive type and on original blocks. It makes it possible to 'dis'(tribute) type immediately, instead of keeping it standing for a future impression.

---

1 HUGHES: Printing ink rollers. (Paper & Print. 23(1)34–43, 1950)

Its disadvantages are: it is difficult to make corrections; the impression is not so sharp as an impression from original matter and, for stereos and electros, they soon wear out.

Type Faces.

'The beauty of letter, like that of faces, is as people opine'.[1]

The basic styles, or classes of type, are Gothic (black letter), Roman, and Italic, originally inspired by the hand-writings in use at the time of the invention of printing, as told in Chapter VI. Italics are now very seldom used for book-work except for poetry, and the use of Gothic, as Fraktur, is practically confined to Germany, where many new founts have appeared. It is in Roman that the greatest development has taken place within the 500 years since the invention of printing. Roman type can be divided into Venetian, e.g. Centaur, Cloister: Old Face, e.g. French O.S: Granjon; English-Dutch O.S: Caslon; Transitional, e.g. Baskerville; Old Style = a modernized Old Face, e.g. Goudy Imprint; and Modern, e.g. Bodoni.[2,3,4]

---

1 Thos James (1710) in McKerrow: Introduction...[36] p.305.
2 SCHMOLLER: Who's who among type-faces. (S.Afr.Libr. 10(3) 49–62, 1943). Also as S.A.L.A.Repr. 13.
3 MONOTYPE Corporation: How & why type-faces differ. (Newslett. Monotype Corp. 44, 1952)
4 RILEY's bookbinding advertisements in Libr.Ass.Rec. Feb.– Dec.1947 & in Brit.Print. Mar./Apr.1947 contain a series illustrating the history of type-design.

Biggs [280] uses the division: I. Sans serif (e.g. Gill Sans); II. Serif, and sub-divides II into (a) those with diagonal stress, (e.g. Old-Face); (b) Vertical stress, (e.g. Modern Face); (c) Slab serif, (e.g. Egyptian).

"The study of type faces is concerned with the identification, criticism, and comparison of the design of type impressions. It is essentially a morphological study".[1]

"It is even now possible for the bibliographer to add to his description of a printed book the name of the type face used... recognition of special characteristics, common to whole groups of faces, brings the student directly to the point where he can verify the face in question as of a given origin".[2]

Most of the following type-faces are available in Monotype.[3]

Face:	ARRIGHI italic. See: Centaur.
Face: Class:	BASKERVILLE. Old-Face, but transitional, foreshadowing the "Modern" face. Cut in 1751 by John Baskerville. "Monotype" first sizes cut in 1923. There is a modified form equipped with its special, long ascending, and descending sorts: "New" Baskerville 169. Goes well with nearly every form of illustration. ..."It is pleasant to report that M.Charles Peignot has just made a magnificent gift to Cambridge University of the original B.punches which he purchased from the Fonderie Bertrand. Thus are returned to England the typographic treasures it failed adequately to appreciate during B's own day."...[4]

---

1   WARDE: Type faces, old & new. (Libr. s4,16(2)121)
2   ib. p.125.
3   50 years of type-cutting 1900–1950. (Monotype Rec. 39(2)1–30, 1950)
4   PATTBERG, Eugene P: The Caslon story. (Print 8(2)40 Aug. 1953)

Leading:	To advantage.
Set:	Wide, but close-fitting letters.
Colour:	Each fount varies.
Paper:	Wove, of calendered, but not coated surface.
Earmarks:	Roman caps: W, J, E (distinctive); l.c: j, g (distinctive); Italic l.c: j, g (distinctive).
Examples:	Jennett: Making...[164]; Morison: Typographic...[272] Britain to-day 1941+; The King Penguins. Richards, J.M: Edward Bawden. Penguin Books 1946. Smith, P.J.D: Civic and memorial lettering. Black 1946; Tarr: How...[544]; Proust, Marcel: Pleasures and regrets. Dobson (1950+) is in Baskerville Linotype, which is more old-face than the Monotype Baskerville.
Face:	BELL.
Class:	Earliest English "Modern" face. John Bell was the first to abolish the long "s" from English printing. Engraver of the punches: Richard Austin in 1788. Rescued by Bruce Rogers. Monotype version 1931.
Leading:	Quite a lot.
Set:	Medium.
Colour:	Light.
Paper:	Varying surfaces.
Earmarks:	K, Q, R; h, k, (but all have alternatives)
Examples:	Aldis: Printed...[156]; World's classics; Exhibition of books 1951 Festival of Britain. N.B.L. 1951; Morison: John Bell.[576].
Face:	Aldine BEMBO.
Class:	Venetian, "loveliest of all old-face designs". Designed in 1495 by Francesco Griffo for Aldus Manutius, who used it in a tract De Aetna, by cardinal Pietro Bembo. The face was imitated in 1531 by Garamond. Monotype cut in 1929. Lovely even in small sizes.
Italic:	"Bembo italic" in the 'chancery' style first used 1520; reminiscent of calligraphy; or "Narrow Bembo".
Leading:	Not essential.
Set:	Narrow, or condensed.
Colour:	Light.
Paper:	Adaptable. Not good on surfaced papers.
Earmarks:	B, E, J, K; c, f, g, j, o, r; italic: A, G, O, P; s, y; Fi, fi distinctive; not ligatured, small x-height; ascenders taller than the caps.
Examples:	Berry and Johnson: Catalogue...[295]; Carter: Taste...[654]; British book news; Biggs: Approach...[280]; A portrait of Logan Pearsall Smith. Dropmore Pr. (1950)

Face:	BLADO italic. See: Poliphilus.

Face:	BODONI.
Class:	Types cut by Giambattista Bodoni of Parma, ca 1800. "Bodoni" is the classic example of the so-called "Modern" style, that owes nothing to calligraphy; axis vertical, geometric outlines, mechanically precise; serifs horizontal, finely pointed; thick stems contrasting with thin hairlines. Shows the influence of Baskerville, Didot, and Fournier. Monotype.
Leading:	Demanded.
Set:	Medium to wide.
Colour:	Weighty.
Capacity:	Durable for long runs.
Paper:	Calendered, but not coated; tends to dazzle on art papers, except when generously leaded.
Earmarks:	A, B, D, G, N, O, R, T, W, l.c. g, r, e, d, s.
Examples:	Bodoni, G.B: Preface to the Manuals tipografico of 1818. Elkin Mathews 1925; Douglas, M.T: Teacher-librarian's handbook, Chicago: American Libr.Ass. 1941.

Face:	CASLON.
Class:	Old-face. First cut 1722. Revived by Pickering. Monotype 1915.
Italic:	An accessory merely.
Leading:	Not essential.
Set:	Medium.
Colour:	Light.
Paper:	Types cut to be used on damp paper ("antique") Earmarks: A(distinctive) C, M(heavy) T(distinctive); g, r, e, d, s; ital: S, A, W, E; h, k, x.
Examples:	Esdaile: Student's...[34]; McKerrow: Introduction... [36]; The Countryman.

Face:	CENTAUR.
Class:	Venetian; prototype: Jenson's Eusebius 1470; 1914 Bruce Rogers cut for private use, first used in 1916; Monotype reproduction 1929. Good for large sizes and for display.
Italic:	Arrighi (Vicentino); drawn by Frederic Warde from a script developed by the 15th century calligrapher, Ludovico degli Arrighi.

PRINTING: TYPE FACES

Leading:	Obviated by long descenders.
Set:	Narrow.
Colour:	Light.
Paper:	Antique.
Earmarks:	J, T; d, j, y; ital: g.
Examples:	Dent lectures [659–67], though point-size too small to display face to best advantage. Centaur is best over 12-pt. Best seen in magnificent 'Lectern Bible'. Oxford Univ.Pr. 1935.
Face:	FOURNIER.[1]
Class:	French old-face, tending to "Transitional". First cut by P.S. Fournier 1745. Recut by Monotype in 1925. Good for small books.
Italic:	"Transitional" style.
Leading:	Preferably set solid.
Set:	Condensed.
Colour:	Light.
Paper:	Off white, featherweight.
Earmarks:	B, A, R; b, a, t, j; ital: g, z.
Examples:	Shaw, G.B: Works; standard ed. Constable 1931. The Adelphi.
Face:	GARAMOND.[2]
Class:	Old-face. Originally cut by Jean Jannon, Sedan, 1621, and later (17th century) incorrectly ascribed to Claude Garamond. Monotype 1922.
Italic:	There is an alternative italic, with regularized caps.
Leading:	Not essential.
Set:	Medium.
Colour:	Light. (Garamond "Heavy" for catalogues and textbooks, appeared in 1925)
Paper:	Antique.
Earmarks:	D, G, T(distinetive); m, r(scooped-out serifs), a, c, d, e(distinctive) g, q, z; ital: Q; c, g, p, k, w, z.
Examples:	Library Ass: Book...[35]; Library Ass: Yearbook. The Association 1947+; Bibliographical studies. Bibliographical Soc.Univ.Va. v.2–3; Greig, J.Y.T: Language at work; repr. Johannesburg: Witwatersrand Univ.Pr. 1948.

---

1 'BEAUJON': Pierre Simon Fournier. (Monotype Recorder. 25 (212/3) Mar./June 1926)

2 – The Garamond types. (Fleuron. 1926:131–79)

Face:	GILL SANS [Serif]
Class:	Sans serif. Designed by Eric Gill. Monotype 1928.
Set:	Many variations.
Colour:	" "
Paper:	Art or coated.
Earmarks:	No serifs.
Examples:	Nelson's Basis and essentials series (Duff, C., ed.) Gardner: Sequels.[823]
Face:	IMPRINT.
Class:	Old-face. Cut in 1912 as a modernized re-cutting of Caslon's old-face. First used as the text face of the Imprint.[73]. Imprint 101 has many special sorts.[1]
Italic:	Normal.
Leading:	Usually leaded.
Set:	Wide.
Colour:	"Weighty".
Paper:	Any kind, except hard-surfaced, "Antique laid".
Earmarks:	C, K, Q; k, q.
Examples:	Curwen: Processes...[386] 1934 ed; S.Afr.Libr. [99] 1933+; [New] "Home University Library". Oxford Univ. Pr; Proc.R.Instn.; Mon.Notices.R.astr.Soc.; Proc.phys.Soc.; Quart.J.micro.Sci; J.Inst.Actu.
Face:	PERPETUA.
Class:	Modern, with modifications. Designed by Eric Gill, 1925, first used for his 'Art nonsense'. Cassell 1929. Caps inspired by Trajan column. Monotype 1932.
Italic:	Slanting roman.
Leading:	Unnecessary, because of the long ascenders.
Set:	Narrow.
Colour:	Light.
Paper:	Both coated and antique.
Earmarks:	J, A, R, E; c, a, f, d, u, g, y; ital; B, D, P, R; g, o, q. Caps range lower than l.c. ascenders.
Examples:	The Bible designed to be read as literature. Heine-mann 1937; Lewis: Story.[329]; Albert Spicer...1847–1934. Simpkin Marshall 1938.

---

[1] Imprint Ser.101; Modern Ser.7; Times New Roman Ser.327 (Monotype) are especially recommended for scientific periodicals in R.Society Consultative Committee for Co-operation with printing Organizations: Notes on the choice of type face for scientific periodicals. 1950.

PRINTING: TYPE FACES

Face: PLANTIN.
Class: An old-style deliberately based on a fount cut originally either by Garamond or Granjon. Monotype sizes first cut in 1913 after prints supplied by the Museé Plantin, Antwerp, of types used by Christopher Plantin 1561.
Leading: Desirable, except for the alternative long extruder sorts of "Bible" Plantin.
Set: Wide.
Colour: Plantin 110 is weighty.
Capacity: Monotype Plantin 113 is the more suitable for normal book composition. It has special advantages for offset, and gravure reproduction, having no hairlines to crumble away under these processes.
Paper: Plantin 110 is the first design ever cut for use on coated paper. Plant in 113 looks best on non-coated paper.
Earmarks: P(distinctive) A, C; a, f; ital: Q, N(distinctive), P; f, j, v, y; short descenders.
Examples: Plantin 110; Manchester Guardian: Printing supplement. 1922; Bunyan, J: Pilgrim's progress. Faber & Faber 1947; Hogben, L: Science for the citizen. Allen & Unwin 1938; Shakespeare, W: Works. Oxford: Shakespeare Head 1934.

Face: POLIPHILUS.[1]
Class: Venetian, old-face. The Monotype recutting in 1923 of the roman is a facsimile of that cut by Francesco Griffo for the Hypnerotomachia Poliphili of Colonna, published 1499 by Aldus Manutius, one of the most famous of illustrated books.
Italic: BLADO(Chancery); recut 1923 from the type used by Antonia Blado, Rome, 1520, might have been cut by Arrighi. Has had an influence on contemporary handwriting. Has been successfully used for entire books, e.g. the Nonesuch Divina Commedia 1928.
Set: Narrow, and close-fitting.
Colour: Weighty.
Paper: Antique; legible, but not looking right on coated paper.
Earmarks: G; a, b, e, s, q(distinctive); ital: K, R; h; wide caps, but not full height of ascenders.
Examples: Libr.Assistant. [80] 25 1932- ; Hadfield, M: Everyman's wild flowers and trees. Dent (1938); Marshall, K: David goes to Zululand. Nelson 1936.

---

1 WARDE, Beatriće: Poliphilus & Blado. (Libr.Assistant. 25(1) 4–6, 1932)

Face:	SCOTCH ROMAN.
Class:	Modern, but less rigidly geometric than its French (Didot) and Italian (Bodoni) counterparts. There are many versions. "Monotype 137" was cut on the model of Miller and Richard's O.S.
Leading:	Usually leaded.
Set:	Wide.
Colour:	Light.
Paper:	Designed for use on smooth-surfaced, but not coated paper.
Earmarks:	Italic: v, w.
Examples:	Fowler: Dictionary...[471] 3ed. 1937; Shaw, G.B: Complete plays. Constable 1931 (but cf. Fournier)
Face:	THE TIMES NEW ROMAN.
Class:	Cut by the Monotype Corporation in 1932 after designs by Stanley Morison for The Times. Designed "to give greatest legibility, offer resistance to high pressure, and remain unaffected by high-speed printing" (Schmoller). 'Times New Roman' was soon used for all kinds of work. Series 327 has many special sorts. Available in many small sizes, and also with long descenders.
Leading:	Beneficial, unless "measure" narrow.
Set:	Wide.
Colour:	Weighty.
Capacity:	Reproduces well by offset.
Paper:	Coated, rather than antique.
Earmarks:	Kerned, f and y, and italic f; shortened ascenders and descenders, large x-height.
Examples:	The Times 3 Oct.1932+; T.L.S. 8 Oct.1932+; Libr. Ass. Rec. [81]; Alph.Image.[39]; Meynell: Nonesuch century...[586]; Penguin and Pelican books; Updike, D.B:
	Some aspects of printing. New Haven: Rudge 1941, Colsen, K: Fractures...2ed.rev. Jhb: Witwatersrand Univ.Pr. 1944; Associated...Information...[479]; Sci. Abstr.; Proc.Instn elect.Engrs; Brit.J.appl. Phys.; Quart.Trans.Instn naval Archit.

The Monotype Corporation [300] also describes the following in this publication: Ehrhardt; Emerson; Goudy Modern; Lutetia,

Romulus; Van Dyck; Walbaum. Mr Schmoller discusses[1] in addition: Caledonia; Cloister; Electra; Estienne; Fairfield; Granjon; Janson; Old Style No.2; Pastonchi.

The student should examine as many books as possible in order to become acquainted with the most used type faces. Among publishers Allen & Unwin, Denis Dobson, Harrap, Readers Union and, in U.S.A: Chase Thomas of Springfield, frequently state the faces they use.

---

1 See footnote on p.171.

"Remember that there are parts of what it most concerns you to know which I cannot describe to you; you must come with me and see for yourselves. The vision is for him who will see it".[1]

IX

ILLUSTRATION

Illustrations accompanying books have been known since the Egyptian "Book of the dead". The medieval manuscripts were illustrated, and had borders in colour. The initials are a chapter in themselves. In early printed books the outlines were stamped in and then coloured by hand. Illustrations fall into the same three groups as ordinary printing: Relief, Intaglio, and Planographic (and were invented in this order). They may be either by the artist's own hand: autographic, or by one of the photo-mechanical processes.[2,3]

A. AUTOGRAPHIC.

I. Relief.
1. Woodcut. The oldest method used for reproducing illustrations. Used in China. In Europe used for printing patterns on textiles and playing cards before the

---

1 PLOTINUS.
2 FIGENBAUM: Graphic arts processes. (More Bks. Dec. 1946–May 1947)
3 HOFER: The illustration of books. (Dolphin. 3:389–446, 1938)

invention of printing with movable types. The first wood-cuts printed white lines and the craftsman got the impressions by rubbing the back of the paper. But as the first printing presses could not print the large, black areas, the cutters began to make two cuts for each line and to cut away the areas between the lines. Pfister did this for book-illustration for the first time, in 1461, but in 1471 Zainer got into difficulties with the cutters' guilds and was not allowed to cut his own blocks. 1486 Cross-hatching begins.

2. Wood-engraving. Began about the end of 17th century in an effort to imitate copper-engravings. Reached perfection in the hands of Bewick, but sank quickly to a spiritless reproduction by craftsmen of artists' drawings. Modern revival began about 1920 with the foundation of the Society of Wood-engravers.
3. Lino-cut. 1934(?) Potato. Rubber.

II. <u>Intaglio.</u>

In Line.
1. Line engraving or copper-plate printing. Began 1446 ("Berlin Passion") used first for book-illustration in Boccaccio's <u>De la ruyne des nobles hommes et femmes</u> published by Colard Mansions in 1476. Great period: 18th century.
2. Steel-engraving. Very popular about 1823–35.
3. Drypoint. 1480(?)
4. Etchings. About 1513. (Graf: "Girl bathing her feet")

In Tone.
5. Mezzotint. About 1640. Has gone entirely out of use.
6. Soft-ground etching. 1800.
7. Aquatint. Invented by Le Prince 1768.
8. Stipple. 1750. No longer used for book-illustration.

III. Planographic.

Direct or drawn lithography. 1798, invented by Alois Senefelder. Introduced into England by Ackermann 1817.

IV. Special methods.
1. Relief etching. William Blake, 1797.
2. Metal cuts. Late 15th century.
3. Wood-engraving as an intaglio process.

B PHOTOMECHANICAL.

1826 Niepce invents heliogravure.
1839 Daguerreotype patented.
1841 W.H. Fox Talbot patents the first negative-positive process and calls it the Calotype process.
1844 The first book illustrated by photography: Talbot's "Pencil of nature". The photographs were pasted in.
1851 Wet collodion process by Frederick Scott Archer.

I. Relief.
1. Line blocks or Zincos. 1859, Chas Gillot in Paris.
2. Half-tones. Talbot had an idea in 1855. But screen first invented 1880. 1882, Meisenbach uses ruled screen, turned during exposure; 1888, perfected by Max and Louis Levy; Daily Graphic publishes the first half-tone illustration 4 Nov. 1891.

II. Intaglio.
1. Photogravure. 1852 basic process found by Fox Talbot. Worked out finally by Karl Klic in 1879, common about 1894.
2. Rotogravure 1895.
3. Woodburytype. 1864. Obsolete.

III. Planographic.
1. Photo-lithography 1852 in Paris. 1859, zinc substituted for stone. Photo-litho-offset, 1905. Goes under different trade-names, e.g. "Adprint" (Collins), "Replika" (Lund, Humphries) etc.
2. Collotype. 1865, Du Motay and Maréshal, or 1867, Joseph Albert of Germany.
3. Aquatone.
4. "Deep etch".
5. Pantone.
6. Bi-metallic. 1935.

IV. Special methods.
1. Xerography. 1948.

COLOUR-PRINTING.
A. I. Chiaroscuro 1506.
1482, Ratdolt in Venice printed a book by Sacro Bosco illustrated with woodcuts in brown, red, and black.
II. Coloured aquatint. Le Blon 1756. Good from 1808.
III. 1. Lithotint. 1825.
2. Chromolithography. Owen Jones began "Plans, sections, and details of the Alhambra" in 1836.
B. I. Line-blocks in colour.
2. Half-tones in 3–4 colours. 1890.
IV. Special.
1. Baxter colour process. 1835.
2. Lumiprinting. 1942(?)
3. Silk screen 1938 (but started in Japan 1,000 years ago)
4. Stencils. Used 1493 for book-illustration (were used for playing cards till colour lithography took over. Pochoir, 1929.

A.I.I. WOODCUT.

<u>Making of plates</u>. In white-line woodcuts the artist cuts v-shaped grooves in the wood withhis knife. In black-line woodcuts two cuts are laid along each line and the larger areas in between are cut away with gouges. Blocks of standard height (0.918") from side-wood of pear, birch, or poplar are used. The blocks are ground smooth before being drawn upon.

<u>Tools</u>. Knife, or blade, and gouges; V-tool or scrive for whiteline cuts.

<u>Paper</u>. Antique.

<u>Ink</u>. Before the invention of printing from movable types began, ordinary writing ink was used, later printed with text, and ordinary printer's ink used.

<u>Impressions</u>. Limited, but plate may be metal-faced, or stereos may be taken.

<u>Examples</u>. Works by Dürer and Holbein, but one must remember that at least the latter did not cut the blocks himself. The prints from the German school of wood-cutters were rather stiff, while the Italians were freer in their execution. Many think that perfection was reached by the unknown artist who illustrated Francesco Colonna's <u>Hypneroto-machia di Poliphilo</u>. Also very beautiful, but relatively unknown until the Pre-Raphaelite revival in England, are a succession of illustrated books produced in Florence between 1490–1510. The blocks made during the period when woodcuts were mostly in use, were use, were used for more than one book and travelled widely, often for such long periods that wormholes appeared in them. The wormholes, which print as white spots, can sometimes help bibliographers date a certain book, if they know when a pull from the same block, but without the holes, was made.

SHAW,H: Dresses and decorations of the Middle Ages. Pickering 1843.

> Illustrated with woodcuts, over-printed with colour from other blocks.

E. BURNE-JONES designed the cuts, but did not cut the blocks for Morris, Wm: The wood beyond the world. Kelmscott Pr. 1894.

> Chaucer: Works, ib. 1894.

RICKETTS, Chas. Both the following books were "deliberatedly evolved from the <u>Hypnerotomachia di Poliphilo</u>": Daphnis and Chloe, <u>etc</u>. Elkin Mathews & Lane 1893. Marlowe, C: Hero and Leander. ib. 1894.

PISSARRO, Lucien.

Coleridge, S.T: Christabel, <u>etc</u>. Eragny Pr. 1904.

Gautier, J.,<u>comp</u>: Poèmes tires du Livre de jade. ib. 1911. Both in colours, the second also with gold.

CRAIG, E.H. Gordon.
The mask; a journal of...the theatre. Florence 1908–(?)

A.I.2. WOOD-ENGRAVING. [1,2,3]

Making of plates. The end-wood of boxwood, or pear, or maple, when dried for a long time splits into sections which are glued together to form blocks, carefully ground smooth and engraved upon with a burin. The artist can work freely on the wood or make a drawing on the plate, but as the print will be reversed some artists make their design on trans parent paper, turn it upside down on to the plate and transfer it. From about 1850 dates the photographing of the motive on to the plate. For some years wood-engraving was a purely reproductive process, to-day it is a flourishing artistic medium. Wood-engravings are usually white-line engravings.

Tools. Graver or burin, spit stick, tinter (for fine lines), scorper (for removing large areas).

Paper. Any, but preferably antique finish. Bewick used Chinese, ribless paper.

Ink. Ordinary printers' ink.

Impressions. Eric Gill says that up to 50 are perfect, but coarser woodcuts are very strong; Bewick reports that one has been used for 300,000 impressions. Electros from blocks can be made.

Press. Wood-engraving goes well with type and can be printed in any printing press, but some artists get their prints by just burnishing the back of the paper with a spoon.

Examples.
  BEWICK, Thos: A general history of quadrupeds. Newcastle; Bewick & Hodgson 1790.
  – History of British birds. Newcastle: Beilby & Bewick, 1797–1804. 2v.
  Ritson, Jos: Robin Hood, etc. Nimmo 1887. 2v.
  BLAKE, Wm. Thornton, R.J: The pastorals of Vergil...3ed. Rivington 1821.
    The blocks were severely cut, 8 of them uncut, were published by the Nonesuch Pr. 1937.

---

1 BALSTON: English wood engraving, 1900–1950. (Image.5,1950)
2 FUST: Wood-engraving in modern illustration. (Penrose Annu. 41:77–80,1939)
3 SANDFORD: Progress of wood-engraving in current book-illustration. (Book Handb. 1947(4)255–62)

DALZIEL[1] brothers engraved the designs by J.E. Millais for "The Parables"... Routledge 1864, and A. Boyd Houghton for "Arabian Nights' entertainments". Ward, Lock & Tyler 1865.
TENNIEL, Sir John. Engraved the plates for the 1865 "Alice".
GILL, Eric: The four Gospels. Golden Cockerel Pr. 1931.
– Devil's devices. Hampshire Hse Workshops 1915.
The Gospels is the masterpiece of the master of woodengraving.
GIBBINGS, Rbt: Sweet Thames, run softly. Dent 1940.
– Coming down the Wye. ib. 1947.
– Lovely is the Lee. ib. 1944.
NASH, Paul: Places. Heinemann 1922.
WHITE, Ethelbert. Jefferies, R: The story of my heart. Duckworth 1923.
RAVILIOUS, Eric: Fifty-four conceits. Cresset Pr. 1933.
BLISS, D.P. Johnson, Samuel: Rasselas. Dent 1926.
FARLEIGH, John. Shaw, G.B: The adventures of the black girl... Constable 1932.
PARKER, Agnes Miller, Fables of Aesope. Gregynog Pr. 1932.
HASSALL, Joan. Gaskell, E.C: Cranford. Harrap 1940.
LEIGHTON, Clare. Country matters. Gollancz 1937.
O'CONNOR, John: The golfer's manual. Dropmore Pr. 1947.
STONE, A. Reynolds: The Farmer's year. Collins 1933.
– Apostate. Faber 1948.

A.I.3. LINO CUT.

Making of plates. As for above. But owing to its softness the lines in a lino cut are coarser than those in a wood-cut. Elastic, so less make-ready.

Tools. Penknife, gouge, a divider (makes a v-shaped groove in one operation)

Paper. Any.

Ink. Block-printers' ink or water-colours.

Impressions. Depends on the design, if it consists of a few white lines, with a fair amount of black in between, one may expect up to 100,000.

Examples.
DARLOW, Biddy: Fifteen old nursery rhymes. Bristol: Perpetua Pr. 1935.
FARRAR, Mildred R.H. Milton, John: The mask of Comus. Nonesuch Pr. 1937.
Coloured.
Potato and rubber provide fun for the amateur too.

---

1   Pronounced: dee-el.

The following intaglio processes are very often combined with each other:

A.II.1. LINE-ENGRAVING.[1]

Making of plates. A copper plate is highly polished. The graver is pushed in the same direction all the time and the plate turned when necessary for the making of curves. A minute burr is made which the early engravers left, but now usually cut away. The ink is worked down into the furrows and the surface wiped with muslin and the hand. At one time, when many artists might be working on one plate which had to be finished before a certain time (e.g. before photography was used for plate-making for magazines) a certain style, called "Lozenge and dot" was adopted to give a uniform impression. Still used for music.

Tools. Gravers, spit sticks, and scorpers, burnishers for corrections and high lights.

Paper. Antique, usually dampened.

Ink. A nearly solid bstance, worked down into the heated plate.

Press. The plate covered with paper and several blankets, is passed through a press resembling a clothes wringer.

Impressions. Rather few; if steel-faced up to 3,000.

Examples. Work by Raphael, Dürer, Mantegna, and Rembrandt was often reproduced by copper engravings.

Curtis's Botanical magazine. 1787–?

KIRK, T: Outlines from the figures and compositions upon the Greek, Roman, and Etruscan vases of the late Sir William Hamilton. W. Miller 1804.

BLAKE: Illustrations of the Book of Job. The Author 1826.

GOODEN, Stephen. Anacreon. Nonesuch Pr. 1923.

La Fontaine, Jean de: Fables. Heinemann 1933.

WADSWORTH. Windeler, B: Sailing ships, etc. Etchells & MacDonald 1926.

JONES, David. Coleridge, S.T: The rime of the ancient mariner. Bristol: Cleverdon 1929.

---

[1] WOODBINE: Methods of book illustration. (Libr.Assistant. 23:21–6, 1930)

A.II.2. STEEL-ENGRAVING.
Making of the plates. As above. Steel is harder and, therefore, more durable than copper; the lines are also finer.
Tools, etc. As above
Examples. TOMBLESON, W. Fearnside, Wm Gray: Thames & Medway, etc. Holmes [1834]
The Literary souvenir. 1832.

A.II.3. DRYPOINT.
Making of plates. The design is cut into the metal with a steel needle or diamond. A heavy burr is thrown up at one side and holds the ink. Very heavy burr may leave thin, white lines in the impression.
Tool. A handle with a sharp needle, diamond, or ruby.
Impressions. 12–20 with a good impression of the burr. After the burr has worn down the plate prints with thin lines. If the plate is steel-faced by electrolysis 200 prints can be obtained.
Examples. Rembrandt, and middle of 19th century.

A.II.4. ETCHING.[1]
Making of plates. The agent in etching is not an instrument, but acid. The plate is first covered with an acid-resisting ground, e.g. wax and asphaltum, which is then blackened over a lighted taper. When the design is cut the lines stand out light against the darkened ground. But some artists prefer to see the plate as it will print (although, of course, in reverse) and use zinc-white as a background. When the artist is satisfied the whole plate is bitten by acid until the finest lines are satisfactory, then the lines which are not to print strongly are covered with acid-resist ('stopped out'); the plate is bitten again, stopped out, and so on until the darkest lines are etched to a sufficient depth. Ground now cleaned off. The plate may be retouched by means of drypoint, in which case the burr is removed. Some artists, such as Rembrandt, and Whistler, left a film of ink on the plate before printing it.

---

1   BRADSHAW: Methods   of   book-illustration.   (Libr.Assistant. 23:48–53,1930)

Tool.. Needle (Acid) and a polished copper-plate. (Early plates were of iron)

Ink, Paper, and Press. As for other intaglio processes.

Impressions. About 1,500.

Examples. COTMAN, John Sell: A series of etchings illustrative of the architectural antiquities of Norfolk. Longmans 1818.
BROWNE, H.K. Dickens, Chas: Pickwick papers. Chapman & Hall 1837.
CRUIKSHANK, George. Dickens, Chas: Oliver Twist. Bentley 1838.
LEECH, John. Surtees, R: Mr. Sponge's sporting tour. Bradbury 1853.
JUNIOR etching club: Passages from modern English poets. Day 1861.
Two of the plates are by Whistler.
Other artists in etching are Meryon, Griggs, John Dodd, Haden, & Cameron.

A.II.5. MEZZOTINT.[1]

Making of plates. We saw under line-engraving and drypoint that corrections could be made with the burnisher which flattened the area concerned which then would print white. In mezzotint the whole plate is covered with a burr, that the artist then scrapes down in varying degrees, and burnishes the high lights.

Tools. Rocker, or roulette to lay the ground; scraper for taking the burr away from medium tones; burnisher for high lights.

Ink, Paper, and Press. As other intaglio processes.

Impressions. 130, burr wears down quickly, but plate may be steel-faced by electrolysis.

Reproduces. Its rich black, and lovely high lights reproduce oil paintings, portraits, and landscapes.

Examples. MARTIN, J. Milton: Paradise lost. Prowett 1827.
TURNER, J.M.W: River scenery of England, etc. Cook 1827.

---

1 HAMMELMANN: English 18th century book illustration. (Book Handb. 2(3)127–35, 1951)

A.II.6. SOFT-GROUND ETCHING.

<u>Making of plates</u>. The plate is covered with a ground of wax, asphaltum, and tallow, and covered with a thin piece of paper. The artist draws on this paper with pencil or chalk and the soft ground adheres to the paper where it was touched by the writing tool and is lifted off from the plate when the paper is lifted. The plate is then bitten in the usual way.

<u>Paper, Ink and Press</u>. As for other intaglio processes.

<u>Raproduces</u>. Pencil, and chalk drawings.

<u>Impressions</u>. About 1,500.

<u>Examples</u>. WILSON, Richard: Studies...at Rome...1752. Oxford 1811.
RUSKIN: Seven lamps of architecture. Smith, Elder & Co. 1849.
COX, David: Young artist's companion. Fuller 1825.
40 soft-ground etchings, 24 aquatints.
PENNANT, Thos: Account of London, <u>etc</u>. 1795.
ATKINSON, John Augustus: Picturesque representation...of the Russians. Bulmer 1803–4. 3v.

A.II.7. AQUATINT.

<u>Making of plates</u>. The ground prepared for aquatint is not solid but porous. Either the plate is left in a box where minute grains of resin are suspended and allowed to settle on the plate - they are fixed by heating; or the ground is diluted with spirit and fixed on the plate when the spirit evaporates. If a print were to be taken from the plate when the ground was first put on, and lightly bitten, we should get an area of uniform, light tint. The artist works the plate as the etched plate was worked, i.e. by stopping outeach time certain areas have reached the desired darkness, and etching again until the darkest areas are bitten far enough down into the plate. The ground is then cleaned off.

<u>Tool</u>. Acid.

<u>Paper, Ink, and Press</u>. As other intaglio processes.

<u>Impressions</u>. About 1,500.

<u>Reproduces</u>. Water colours and caricatures.

<u>Examples</u>. SANDBY, Paul: XII Views...in South Wales, <u>etc</u>. Boydell 1775.
First time aquatint was used for book illustration in England whence it came from France. AUDUBON, J.J: Birds of America. The Author 1827–38. 4v.
"The most sumptuous work to which aquatint was ever applied". (Prideaux [373] p.296)

BURCHELL, W.J: Travels in the interior of Southern Africa. Longmans 1822–4. 2v.

See also under Colour Collotype.

PUGIN, A., and ROWLANDSON, T. Pyne, W.H., and Combe, W: Microcosm of London. Ackermann 1808. 3v. Hand-coloured. The revival came with:

PIPER, John: Brighton aquatints. Duckworth 1939.

CAASTEL, Roger. Eluard, Paul: Bestiaire. Paris: Galerie Maeght 1948.

Other artists: Goya and Picasso.

A.II.8. STIPPLE.

Making of plates. The plate is covered with a solid ground and a roulette is run over it in all directions, making groups of dots which, when bitten by acid, give a dark background to the main design that was put in with an etching needle.

Tools. Roulette, needle (acid).

Paper, Ink, Press, and Impressions. As other intaglio processes.

Reproduces. Chalk drawings.

Examples. Bartolozzi, Thos Cheesman.

A.III.1. LITHOGRAPHY.[1,2]

Making of plates. The proper lithographic stone is now seldom used because of its weight, price, and the work involved in preparing it for taking a new image after use. The grain of the stone can be imitated in zinc, aluminium, or plastic[3,4,5]. Lithography can be adapted to almost any technique. The artist can write on the material with a greasy

---

1 DALLISON: Methods of book-illustration. (Libr.Assistant. 23:45–8, 1930)

2 JACKSON: Lithography. (Imprint. 1:18–23, 125–7, 171–4, 319–20, 1913)

3 CARRINGTON: Autolithography on plastic plates. (Penrose Annu. 1950:64–6)

4 Advertisement in Alph.Image 8:90,1948)

5 Also in Print.Rev. 15:50, Summer 1949)

ILLUSTRATION: LITHOGRAPHY

pencil or pen; apply the grease with a brush; or cover the whole surface with grease and scratch the high lights out with a point; or use a transfer paper, and if the transfer paper is placed on a coarse piece of textile the image will have its texture in addition to the grain of the stone. If the artist has drawn on a lithographic stone (which consists of carbonate of lime) the stone will be covered with gum arabic and nitric acid which transform the surface of the stone into nitrate of lime, and the ink that the image was drawn with into an acid (insoluble in water). The rest of the process is the same, irrespective of the material the image is drawn upon. The plate is first covered with water which cannot remain on the parts where the image is drawn, then the plate is inked; water and ink will not mix, so the ink is confined to the parts of the plate where the image occurs. When the lithographic image has been fixed on a zinc plate this plate can be bent round a cylinder and printed on a rotary printing machine. Most lithographic printing to-day is done by the "offset" method, where the image is first transferred on to a rubber roller, and from the roller on to the paper. This method has the added advantage that the artist need not draw in reverse on the plate. Also the rubber cylinder (it is actually not solid rubber, but a blanket round a cylinder) being elastic, can print on all kinds of paper.

Tools. Chalk stick, or lithographic ink, sponge, brush, or needle.

Paper. "Litho".

Ink. Litho inks contain lard, soap, wax, shellac, Venetian turpentine, carbonate of soda, and Paris black for colouring, if the ink is to be black.

Press. A special press, where pressure is brought by a scraper, unless offset is used.

Impressions. 20 for a wash drawing on stone; 50,000–80,000 from a zinc plate.

Examples.
    RAVILIOUS, Eric. Richards, J.M: High Street. Country Life 1938.
    FREEDMAN, Barnett. Tolstoy: War and peace. Limited Ed.Cl. 1938.
    BADMIN, S.R: Trees in Britain. Penguin Books 1943.
    All the above artists were inspired by the lithographic revival from 1923 onwards. Other artists in this medium are John Piper, C. Hutton, and Spencer Pryse. Daumier was the artist who first used lithography successfully as a medium in its own right.

A.IV. SPECIAL METHODS.
1. RELIEF ETCHING.[1]

Making of plates. William Blake claimed that his method was revealed to him in a dream. He painted text and picture (in reverse) on the plate in a resisting medium and etched the rest of the plate down. Printed as a relief cut.

Examples.
  BLAKE: Jerusalem. The Author 1820.
  – Songs of innocence. ib. 1789.

A.IV.2. METAL CUTS.

Making of plates. A reversed engraving.
Tools. Punches (for dots) and engraving tools (for lines)

A.IV.3. WOODCUTS PRINTED IN INTAGLIO.[2]

Making of plates. As ordinary woodcuts, but printed from the recesses.

B. PHOTOMECHANICAL.[3,4]

It has been known since antiquity that a picture of the landscape would be shown on the wall of a dark room if light were allowed in through a small hole. It was, however, first in the 19th century that means to fix this true image was found. Niepce's invention, based on the hardening of the emulsion and the washing off of the unhardened parts, is still in use in printing works. The first exposures were a matter of hours, but the use of more powerful lenses and more sensitive layers to receive the image have reduced the time to fractions of a second. The next

---

1 KEYNES: Blake's copper plates. (T.L.S. 24 Jan. p.48,1942)
2 GILL: Intaglio printing from wood blocks. (Woodcut. 1:27–9, 1927)
3 HILL: Methods of book illustration. (Libr.Assistant. 23: 100–4, 1930)
4 BLOCK: The centenary of photo-mechanical reproduction. (Repr. from Engng in Brit.Print. Sep./Oct. p.50–1, 1952)

problem which arose was to fix this image, and then, later on, to multiply the image. Fox Talbot's negative-positive process was improved on in Archer's wet collodion process, also still in use. Collodion is a solution of gun-cotton in ether. This is placed on a glass-plate (to avoid grains in paper) and sensitized with silver nitrate (silver salts are sensitive to light, i.e. turn black or grey where the light strikes them); the plate is exposed when still wet. (But this, which is a nuisance for an amateur photographer, is very easy in a printing establishment, and that is why this process which was abandoned years ago for other forms of photography, is still in use there). The next step in ordinary photography is to print on paper a positive from the fixed negative. In printing work, however, this positive must be printed from a raised (relief) surface; from a recessed surface (intaglio) or from a planographic surface. The printing surface is a positive in so far as the dark parts of the picture show dark on the plate when inked, but turned from left to right in relation to the printed picture.

B.I.1. LINE BLOCKS OR ZINCOS.
Making of plates. We want on the plate a reversed - left to right - image of the original standing up from the surrounding area. In order to obtain that the original is photographed by the wet collodion process with a prism in front of the camera's lens (to reverse the image on the negative). The resulting negative is a reversed image in white lines. This negative is placed on top of a zinc or copper plate (copper for fine line engravings) or magnesium (still in experimental stage) which has previously been covered with bichromated albumen and both are exposed to the light of a powerful arc lamp, where the light penetrates the white lines in the negative & the albumen underneath is hardened. The plate is then inked and washed. The image now shows up on the plate in black lines, which are powdered with bitumen and heated slightly. This turns them into an acid-resisting enamel, and it is now possible to etch the rest of the plate down, only stopping now and again to powder the sides of the lines as they emerge, to prevent "undercutting" by the acid. When the etching has gone far enough the enamel is removed, large white areas are routed out, the plate mounted type-high on wood, and is now ready for printing, with text, if so required.

Reproduces. Ink, or sepia drawings on white paper, scraper board, woodcuts, and wood-engravings. Anything in line, but one must remember that the colour of the lines has the same intensity although the widths can be varied.

Points of recognition. A slight ink-squash at the edges, shows slightly on the reverse side of the paper.

Ink. Letterpress.

Paper. Any, especially antique.

Impressions. Original line blocks: 200,000; Electrotypes: 175,000; Stereotypes: 125,000.

Examples.
> CARROLL, Lewis: Alice's adventures underground; being a facsimile of the original MS...with 37 illustrations by the Author. Macmillan [1886]
>
> The artists most talented in this medium are: Hugh Thomson, Aubrey Beardsley, C. Lovat Fraser, Albert Rutherston, John Nash, E. McKnight Kauffer, Wyndham Lewis, and Edward Bawden.

Line blocks are the cheapest for reproduction and are extensively used in advertising. Their one drawback, that they cannot reproduce tone, is partly overcome by combining them with Ben Day screens that may be had in various patterns and are usually printed directly down on the plate. Line blocks are also combined with half-tones, in which case two separate negatives are made and arranged together on a glass plate before being printed down on the plate. Ben Day screens are rather coarse and print well on almost any paper, but in case of fine half-tones being used, the paper will have to suit their requirements.

B.I.2. HALF-TONE.

Making of plates. Half-tone corresponds closely to the above except that this process seems to give tonal values. The original is photographed by the wet collodion process, but a screen is imposed between the camera and the original. This screen is of glass with 45–225 lines to the square inch, running horizontally, and the same number running vertically on another glass plate which is cemented on to the first. The negative is thus cut up into white dots of varying sizes, largest where they represent the shadiest parts of the original. The negative is brought is contact with a sensitized plate of zinc or copper, but more often copper, since half-tone work is of necessity fine work. The plate is inked and washed after exposure. If the plate, as most often happens, is covered with fish glue, then the burning-in process takes place as for line blocks. But heating to high temperatures is dangerous for zinc plates and, therefore, the dots may be covered with a cold-top enamel which only requires a little heating to turn it into an acid-resist. After etching the plate consists of dots 0.002" high. Only the cheapest kinds of half-tones are finished when they have been etched to a sufficient depth all over the plate. For finer effects they are fine-etched by hand, and the high lights are etched until the dots disappear completely.

Reproduces. Original photographs and wash drawings. Half-tone reproductions of collotypes or photogravure illustrations have also a chance of coming out well because the screen in the one is irregular and in the other does not show up much. It is difficult to make half-tones from half-tone illustrations because the two screen patterns may fall together in such a way that they form a kind of pattern on the finished picture (moire), if it has to be done the original must be tilted at an angle while photographing.

Points of recognition. Varying size of dots; sudden change from grey to white.

Ink. Letterpress, containing linseed oil; rotary inks dry by absorption and contain mineral oils.

Paper. M/F, S, and S/C or coated "Art" papers.

Impressions. 50,000–100,000; Electrotypes; 75,000; Stereo-types: 60,000.

Examples.
READ, H: Art and industry. Faber 1934. DAVENPORT, Cyril Jas Humphries: Cameos. Seeley & Co. 1900. Colour added from wood-blocks.
ASHTON, Leigh, and GRAY, Basil: Chinese art. Faber [1935]

A new kind of half-tone, made without the use of any etching fluid, is now produced by the Fairchild "Scan-a-graving".[1] One part of this machine measures the tone value of minute parts of the original and controls a stylus which cuts into a plastic plate at varying depths. It is made in four different models corresponding to 65–, 85–, 100– and 120–screens. The plastic plate will stand up to 100,000 impressions.

---

1 Fairchild plastic half-tones. (Brit.Print. 53(377–8)22,49; 54(381) 54–5,1951)

B.II.1. PHOTOGRAVURE (often used for B.II.2 also; here only for the hand-process).

Making of plates. Photogravure may be called the intaglio half-tone, but instead of dots we have holes. As it is the actual image we are etching into the plate, we have to use a photographic <u>positive</u> for the contact printing. The positive is not printed down on to a sensitized plate as its corresponding negative in the relief process, but on to a piece of sensitized carbon tissue, which is squeegeed on to the plate that has previously been dust-grained, and the grains fixed by heating. The placing of the tissue on the plate is the most difficult job in photogravure as the printer must avoid, at all costs, stretching the tissue. After the tissue has been placed on the plate it is washed in warm water which removes the non-hardened parts of the gelatine. (Remember, these parts will eventually print, just the opposite of the relief processes). The plate is then etched, the depth of the etching depending on the degree of hardening of the gelatine, e.g. a dark shade on the original would be dark on the transparent, photographic positive, too. The gelatine of the tissue underneath will not be hardened, but be washed away afterwards, the acid bites deeply, and it prints dark. The dust grain is necessary to hold the ink.

Reproduces. Photographs, paintings, etc.

Ink, Printing, Paper. See all intaglio, autographic processes.

Impressions. 1,000 if steel-faced; the steel-facing can be cleaned off and another put on. Chromium plating also used sometimes.

Examples.
    COLVIN, Sidney: Early engraving...in England (1545–1695) 41 fasc. in photogravure. British Mus. 1905.
    REID, <u>Sir</u> Geo: Twelve sketches of...Great N. of Scotland railway. Edinburgh: Douglas 1883.
    ETRUSCAN sculpture. Phaidon ed. Allen & Unwin 1941.

B.II.2. ROTOGRAVURE.

Making of plates. The machine-fed equivalent of Photogravure. Before the transparent positive is printed down on the tissue, this has had a <u>white-lined</u> screen (because lines must stand up to the top of plate or cylinder) printed down on it, to take the place of the dust grain in photogravure. The tissue is squeegeed down on a copper cylinder (or a copper sheet round a steel cylinder) and etched. Lately attempts have been made to overcome the difficult handling of the tissue by printing directly down on to a cylinder covered with a sensitized layer, but this has obvious difficulties and is still in the experimental stage. The finished cylinder is covered with rectangular cells (if a rectangular screen were employed, but a screen of wavy lines may also be used) of varying depth.

Reproduces. Pictures (photographic or others) and text, but letters are not always sharp because the screen cuts their corners off. The screen does not show up white as in half-tone, but can be discerned.

Points of recognition. A rich, full tone "gravure effect". Screen may be seen. The ink is scraped away from the top of the cylinder by a "doctor blade", and if a grain happens to adhere to this it results in a streak along the page.

Ink. Pigment dissolved in petrol, benzene or xylol, which are all volatile. Dries by evaporation and penetration; the surface hardens almost immediately, though the ink takes some hours to dry thoroughly. The time taken for drying is very important for the quality of the printing. The ink is sometimes sprayed on.

Press. A special rotary press with a "doctor blade" and an ink tank from which the ink is conveyed by various means. Influenced by presses for textile printing.

Paper. Special gravure papers of varying hardness are used, esparto papers are especially good. For high grade work a smooth paper is desirable. Dampened before printing.

Impressions. 75,000–100,000 sheets; rotaries have been capable of 1½ million runs; rotogravure is economic only on long runs. The cylinders are costly and retouching difficult, correction is practically impossible.

Examples.
> BISKEBORN, H: Photogravure machine printing. Pitman 1949. Illustrated London News, Picture Post, Cape Times Supplements; Stage & Cinema (Jhb.)

B.II.3. WOODBURYTYPE.

The principle is the same as for Rotogravure: a recessed surface with depths varying according to the tonal value, but no screen interrupts the recesses, and ink could not be held in them; instead pigmented gelatine was used.

B.III.1. PHOTOLITHOGRAPHY.[1]

Making of plates. Plates of zinc or aluminium are grained and covered with bichromated albumen, or 'Patracoat', and exposed with a photographic negative (line, or half-tone) under arc lamps; inked and the unexposed gelatine washed off. In direct lithography the negative must be reversed by a prism, but if the plate (usually fastened round a cylinder) is printed by the offset method, it will automatically be reversed twice during the process: firstly during photographing, secondly during offset. The offset is made by a rubber-covered cylinder.

Reproduces. Charcoal, crayon, or pastel; line-engravings, etchings, and drypoints, either from photographic negatives of them; or, if the original plates are still extant, from a wet transfer print from them. Out-of-print books, text and illustrations together.

Points of recognition. Greyish tone; no impression mark (squeeze); no ink squash; half-tones go gradually from grey to white.

Ink. Dries by both oxidation and absorption, put on in thin layers, so the colour must be intense, oil-based.

Press. Cylinder, flat-bed, or offset; rollers either rubber, or special vulcanized-oil rollers.

Papers. Offset can take any paper because of the elasticity of the rubber roller; surface must have good ink receptivity.

Impression. 25,000–30,000.

Examples.
>
> HUMPHREYS, H.N: History of the art of printing...100 facsimiles in photolithography. Quaritch 1868.
>
> MONOTYPE Corporation: Twenty-one...[300]
>
> ARDIZZONE, Edw: Lucy Brown and Mr Grimes. Oxford Univ. Pr. 1937.
>
> TANNER, Robin. Tanner, H: Wiltshire village. Collins 1939.

B.III.2. COLLOTYPE.

Making of plates. The sensitized gelatine layer is allowed to dry into wrinkles on the plate in a dark room and is next exposed under the negative, then immersed in cold water

---

1 WOODRUFF: Photo-lithography today. (Brit.Print. 53(375)44–9, 1950)

and covered with glycerine which retains moisture in the unexposed parts of the plate, and which swells. The exposed parts, i.e. the dark parts of the original, remain unaffected and receive the ink when the rollers pass over them. The grain of the gelatine is very fine, but only stands up to a limited number of impressions.

Reproduces. Drypoint, mezzotints, aquatints, oil paintings.
Ink. Two kinds are always used at the same time.
Paper. Usually rag-paper, with matt, or semi-smooth surface.
Impressions. 1,500.
Examples.
> BRITISH MUSEUM: Reproductions from illuminated MSS; 3ed. The Museum 1922–8. 4 Ser.
> ROWLANDSON, Thos: Drawings. Avalon Pr. (1949)

B.III.3. AQUATONE.

A variation of the above, with half-tone dot formation.

B.III.4. DEEP ETCH.

Making of plates. Is actually an intaglio process, but as it is based on the antipathy of grease and water, is placed here. A photographic positive is printed down on sensitized gelatine, the plate is slightly etched and inked before the acid-resisting portions - representing the white in the picture - are removed. The inked, recessed parts of the plate attract ink, while the rest first attracts water, which in its turn repels ink. The life of the plate is quadrupled by this treatment.

B.III.5. PANTONE.

Making of plates. This and the next process have done away with the need for dampening in planographic printing. The Pantone process is based on the antipathy of printing ink and mercury. A copper-plate is chromium-plated all over, sensitized, and printed in the usual way. When the plate is etched the chromium is removed from all the uncovered areas, the acid resist is removed, and the plate placed in an electrolytic bath which deposits silver-mercury amalgam on top of the copper only, i.e. the silver-mercury amalgam repels ink, and does not print, in the parts bared by the etching, which only took place in the unhardened parts of the gelatine, corresponding to the darkened parts of the print with which the plate was exposed.

Paper. Any.

B.III.6. BI- or TRI-METAL LITHO-PLATES.

Making of plate. A steel-cylinder (which may be chromium-plated) with a thin deposit of copper is printed on and etched down to the polished steel (or chromium); copper attracts the ink, the polished steel repels it. Tri-metal on zinc-base, with chromium to retain water, and copper to retain ink.

B.IV.1. XEROGRAPHY.[1,2]

Making of plates. A base plate of electrically conductive material is covered with a photo-conductive insulating material; the coating is sensitized and exposed; where light strikes the plate it becomes conductive and discharges its electrostatic charge into the backing material.

Printing. Powder is dropped over the plate and adheres to the charged parts of the plate (i.e. the parts where the light did not strike the plate, the dark parts of the negative). Paper is then placed over the plate and charged, the powder attracts itself to the paper and is fixed there by heating.

COLOUR PRINTING.

The Chinese artists printed in several colours from the same plate at one impression, by painting the colours in on the plate by hand. This has also been done in Europe in isolated cases, but it has the obvious drawback of being slow and the copies not identical. Stamping-in was the earliest form for duplicating pictures. The early printers of books stamped initials in in a second colour, usually red.

---

1 SCHAFFERT: Xerography & xeroprinting. (Penrose Annu. 44: 96–9, 1950)

2 WINKLER: Xerography & xeroprinting. (Sh.yr Knowl.Rev. 31(2) 15–9, 1949)

A.1. RELIEF.
Wood-blocks were frequently used for adding the colours to impressions in line for the chiaroscuro pictures that were used for book illustration from 1509. The blending of the colours in the spectrum had to be understood before economic, colour-printing could begin. For 40 years from 1704 a 3-colour printing was used. 3-colour printing takes advantage of the fact that all the colours can be produced by mixing (here: overprinting) of the 3 primary colours: Yellow, red, blue. But with no mechanical means of separating the colours, everything depends on the artist'a sense of colour. Colour work with little or no overprinting can be done if the artist transfers the same drawing to each block, and cuts one block for each colour.
> Artists in colour woodcut and wood-engraving: Walter Crane, Randolph Caldecott, Kate Greenaway, Lucien Pissarro, and Robert Gibbings.

A.III.1. COLOUR LITHOGRAPHY.
Examples.
> HUMPHREYS, Henry Noel: Illuminated books of the Middle Ages...examples executed on stone and printed in colours by Owen Jones. Longmans 1849.
> – Penitential Psalms. Day 1850.
> BOYS, Thos Shotter: Picturesque architecture in Paris, etc. 1839.
> WYATT, Sir Matthew Digby: Industrial arts...at the exhibition. Day 1853.

A.III.2. LITHOTINT.
"An intermediate stage between monochrome and colour lithography, developed by Hullmandel. It consists of several neutral tints, scraped down for the white high lights. This technique succeeded chalk and stipple engraving in the reproduction of chalk and wash drawings."[1]
Examples.
> LANE, Richard: Studies...by Gainsborough...in...imitation of the originals Hullmandel 1825.
> ROBERTS, David: The Holy land, etc. Moon 1842.
> SIMPSON, W. Brackenburg, G: Campaign in the Crimea. Colnashi 1856.

---

1   JAMES: English...[328]

B.I. LINE BLOCKS IN COLOUR.[1]

The artist can either submit his design fully made up in several colours, which the printer then separates by means of coloured filters: a blue filter for the yellows, green for red, and red for blue. Or, if the design contains only two colours, the printer can separate the one by means of a filter, and make a plate from the resulting negative, and then draw up the second colour with black on the original and photograph from that. The artist can also provide a key drawing from which several copies are made in black, and the artist then indicates the colours separately, a copy for each. Zincos can be combined with flat colour, Ben Day coloured tints, or with coloured half-tone. During processing the printer must take care to get exact register, and to etch each plate equally long if the inks are going to be of equal strength. When selecting the inks he must keep in mind that the white on the page also affects the visual effect of the picture, and make sure that his inks will print together, i.e. that the ink first printed will "take" the next. If the area is being reduced then colours should be reduced correspondingly.

B.I.2. THREE-COLOUR PROCESS.

The 3-colour process is a half-tone process. But one can also print half-tones in two colours. For the 3-colour process the original is photographed through filters as above, and each of the 3 plates etched in the usual way. Some retouching is done afterwards. In theory these 3 colours should be able to produce all the colours of the spectrum, but in actual fact one usually prints a fourth plate in black. In order to avoid a _moiré_ effect the original is tilted about 30° between each exposure. For the 3-colour process a fine screen is used for forming the dots and, therefore, art paper is used.

Examples.

MEMPES, M. _and_ D: War impressions. Black 1900.

    The first book to be illustrated throughout by this process.

RACKHAM, Arthur. Barrie, J.M: Peter Pan. Hodder 1906.

---

1   JARROLD; Reproduction. (_Int.Print._ 2:19–24,1950)

B.II. COLOUR GRAVURE.[1]

As the colours in this process extend over the whole area with no whites between dots to impair its brilliancy, 2-colour photogravure gives nearly as good an effect as 3- or 4-colour in any other process. The colour separation takes place in the same way as above. A brown key plate is usually printed with the others, and gives the special gravure effect. Great care must be taken not to stretch the tissues on transfer to the cylinder, or the register will be spoiled. The Holbein multi-colour-machine takes 3,000 sheets per hour.

Examples.
    HODGKIN, J.E: Rariora. Sampson Low 1902. 3v.
    FISHER, J: Bird recognition. Penguin 1947–5? 4v.
    HOGBEN, Lancelot: From cave painting to comic strip. Chanticleer Pr. 1946.

B.III. CHROMO-LITHOGRAPHY.

Usually at least 6 plates are used. The offset roller gives a blurred effect to the finished print.

Examples.
    SALA, Geo. A: Paris herself again. Golden Galley Pr. (1948)
    GROSS, Anthony. Galsworthy, J: Forsyte saga. Heinemann 1949.
    Insel–Bücherei, Leipzig, combined hand- and photo-lithographed plates with diamond engraved stone plates as key plates for some of their Insel-books such as No.255: Goldfischteich; 351: Tropenwunder.

B.III.2. COLOUR COLLOTYPE.

Examples.
    BURCHELL, Wm J: South African drawings. Johannesburg: Witwatersrand Univ.Pr. 1938–52. 2v.
    NEW Statesman and Nation, with Lund, Humphries, produce the 'Ganymed' reproductions and 'Turnstile' prints.

---

1 CONRAD: Sheet colour photogravure in Europe today. (Int. Bull. Print.all.Tr. (56)18–20,1951)

SPECIAL. 1. BAXTER COLOUR-PROCESS.
Many wood-blocks printed in oil colours.
Examples.
BAXTER, Geo: The parlour table-book. Woodward 1835.
DICKES, W. Gosse, P.H: History of the British sea-anemones, Van Voorst 1860.

SPECIAL. 2. LUMIPRINTING.
Tool. Glass.
Artist. Di Gemma.

SPECIAL. 3. SILK SCREEN, or SERIGRAPHY.[1,2,3]
Stencils have been used for textile printing since time immemorial, and in Japan up to our times. The difficulty has bees the stencils' fragility, and the difficulty of connecting the various parts of the pattern. The silk screen does away with the necessity for connexion and the mesh does not show in the actual print. The design can be hand-cut and pasted on, or painted on, or photographed on to the mesh. Oil colours are pressed through the mesh. It can print on practically every kind of material.
Artists: P. Nash, Barnett Freedman.

SPECIAL. 4. STENCIL, or POCHOIR.[4]
A key plate is prepared by collotype, and the colours applied to this plate through stencils with special brushes and water-colours printed on china paper.
Examples.
KAUFFER, E. McKnight. Bennett, A: Elsie and the child. Cassell 1929.

---

1   KYLE: Silk screen process. (Paper & Print. 21(2)150–2,1948) also in S.Afr.Annu.advertising art 1949.
2   MACKENZIE: Screen process printing. (Penrose Annu. 43:138, 1949)
3   ZIGROSSER: Ten years of serigraphy. (New Colophon. 1(1)58-66,1948)
4   MACKENZIE: The stencil. (Penrose Annu. 44:67–70,1950)

SPECIAL. 5. ELECTRONIC COLOUR-PRINTING.
Electronically controlled jets spray colouring matter on to sheets of ordinary paper. Not commercialized yet, but should eventually make colour reproduction much cheaper.

The classification of illustration processes is according to the method and not according to the material used. Lithographic stone can be exchanged for zinc or aluminium; copper for zinc, etc. Magnesium may one day completely replace both copper and zinc.

> "I opened before her Vecellio's Collection of costumes; not, if you please, the banal reproduction so meagrely executed by modern artists, but in truth a magnificent and valuable copy of the editio princeps".
> Anatole France: Sylvestre Bonnard

X

FACSIMILES AND NEAR-PRINT

A facsimile has been defined as "a reproduction which copies the original...as accurately as is possible within the limits of the reproductive process employed".[1] The expression can of course be applied to illustrations as well, but this aspect has already been treated in the previous chapter. We are here concerned only with reproductions of books as a whole, text-matter or MS. Weitenkampf says that "every facsimile is a copy, but not every copy is a facsimile", and further that "before 1870, the use of the word had no justification whatever".[2] Contrast a saying by another prominent bibliographer, that "photographic reproductions [are] reliable but illegible, reprints are legible but unreliable".[3]

---

1 DULKA: Facsimile reproduction of books. Unpublished, M.Sci. thesis. N.Y: Columbia Univ. 1947.
2 WEITENKAMPF: What is a facsimile? (Pap.bibliogr.Soc.Amer. 37(2)114–30,1943)
3 "Facsimile" reprints of old books. (Libr. s4,6(4)305–28, 1926) p.322.

The user of facsimiles must make his choice according to his requirements. The word "facsimile" was known and used long before 1870; apart from the reproduction of pictures they were used as precepts when the interest in handwriting awakened. Today they are used widely by scholars for critical editions, where every existing copy of an early, rare book should be examined; for research purposes when inaccessible materials are wanted; for literary students who may be satisfied with a reprint in one form or another; by scientists for articles in periodicals; by the general public for whom early editions have an aesthetic appeal; and lastly, by those individuals who fabricate old and rare editions, of whom more later.

The categories fall into the three well-known groups: relief, intaglio, and planographic, each again within the two groups: non-photographic, and photographic.

A. NON-PHOTOGRAPHIC.

I. Relief.
   1. Type-Facsimiles. Type-facsimiles strive to imitate one specific edition of a certain work, not one specific copy. Type-facsimiles are usually made after comparison of several original copies, usually set following the original, letter by letter, line by line, page by page, with the same impositions and, sometimes, the same margins, also misprints and readings, setting and spacing, spellings, etc., and of course in a type-face resembling the original as closely as possible. It is a bone of contention between editors of this type of work whether the fac-simile should also introduce a letter in another

type-face when it is evident that the printer of the original only did so for want of enough sorts in the main type-face. The danger here is that new errors are apt to creep in, despite careful proof-reading; but for students of literature good type-facsimiles are adequate. For scholarly work the ideal would be a book where a photographic reproduction faced a transcription in type recording other variants in other copies.[1] Type-facsimiles lend themselves very easily to deception, as Mr Chapman pointed out in his letter to the T.L.S., cited on p.224. He also mentioned two safeguards: to print "Facsimile" with date, etc. on the verso of the title-page, or/and to print on a paper with a modern, and preferably dated watermark.

It is always important to reproduce a relief process with another relief process; intaglio with intaglio, etc. And as the photographic relief processes: line-blocks and half-tone, are etched and, therefore, blurred in their outlines, type-facsimiles will always have an added aesthetic appeal.

Examples.

1710? PRIMER... Grafton 1546.
Found by Pollard and regarded as the earliest known type-facsimile. The date is approximate and the printer is unknown. The type used is a poor, 17th century fount.

1778 George Steevens' reprints of 18 Shakespeare Quartos. Was this a rev.ed. of 20v. in 10, issued 1773?

1807 SHAKESPEARE, Wm: ...Comedies, etc.
From the 1623 edition; repr. by Wright.

1810–20 J. Sturt publishes reprints of 17 tracts originally printed 1628–87; repr. by Jas Barker.[2,3]

1855 GAME of the Chesse. Repr. by V. Figgins from Caxton's 2ed. 1474. Done with newly cut type, engravings on wood from tracings of the cuts, by Mary Byfield.

---

1   Gaselee in a discussion following the papers called "Fac-simile reprints of old books" quoted in Libr. s4,6(4)327, 1926.
2   HAZEN: J.Sturt, facsimilist. (Libr. s4,25(1/2)72–9,1944)
3   MACDONALD: J.Sturt, facsimilist. (ib. s4,26(4)307–8,1946)

1861   SPECULUM Humanae Salvationis; ed. by J. Ph. Berjeau and published by Stewart, from tracings engraved on wood(?)
1864   SHAKESPEARE: A Repr. of his collected works as put forth in 1623.
This repr. by Lionel Booth is perhaps still unsur-passed for exactness.[1]
1886–92 SHELLEY Society: Publications. 2nd ser. Begun with the repr. of the 1ed. of 'Adonais'. Published under the supervision of Thos Wise. Wise & H.B. Forman had each privately issued facsimile reprints before the inauguration of the Shelley Society[(1)] without what are now regarded as the necessary safeguards, i.e. dated paper, prominent imprint.
1907–38 MALONE Society: Reprints. 77v.
Edited by W.W. Greg. Publication resumed.[2]
1906–14? TUDOR and Stuart Library. Oxford: Clarendon Pr. This series started as "period printing". With Religio Medici published 1909, under the supervision of R.W. Chapman, the series was transformed into a series of type-facsimiles following the lines and pages of the original, including wrong pagination, but not purely typographical errors such as turning of right sorts, etc. Others were Shakespeare's "Sonnets" 1907; his "Merry Wives" 1910, which followed the Malone and Capell copies; the 1786 Burns, 1768 Gray, 1820 Keats, 1842 Tennyson, etc. Set up from originals or rotographs of them.
1914+   Reprints of first editions of 18th century poetry in Fell and Caslon types under the editorship of R.W. Chapman.
1926?+ Haslewood Books. Shakespeare Head Pr: Etchells and MacDonald. In "The Phoenix nest" 1926, short "s" has been substituted for the long "s". Other Hasle-wood books are "Hero and Leander"; repr. from the 1598 ed., and "England's Helicon", 1600.

---

1 MCKERROW: Introduction...[36] p.232n.
2 (Libr. s5, 7(1)68–70 Mar.1952)

1927	KEATS: Endymion; ed. H.C. Notcutt. Oxford Univ.Pr.
1935	BROWN, C.B: Alcuin. New Haven: Rollins. Set in the same fount as used for the original (1798) ed.
1940	POE, E.A: Tamerlane. Baltimore: Wirth Bros.

A.1.2. PERIOD PRINTING.

"The production or reproduction of books, not on the model of any particular edition, but in the style of the period when the book was first published, or with which... it is concerned."[1]

Strictly speaking all incunabula reproduce period printing, because they were imitating contemporary manuscripts, and only slowly evolved into a form determined by the medium. The supposed first English piece of period printing is

[1690]	"The ORDER of the Hospitals of King Henry VIII..." dated 1557, but printed from a MS.
1844	LADY Willoughby's "Diary". Printed by the Chiswick Pr. and famous also for being the first (?) volume in which the revived old-face type was used.
1906–9	The first part of the Tudor and Stuart library. See above.
1926	MALTHUS, T.R: First essay on population. Macmillan for R.Economic society.
1932	EVELYN, J: Directions for the gardener at Says-Court... Nonesuch Pr. Designed by Francis Meynell and printed with Janson types at the Fanfare Press.
1942	"BOKE for a Jvstyce of Peace, etc." Four Oaks, War-wickshire; Bracebridge Pr. Original printed by Thos Berthel(et)

A.I.3. STEREOS.[2]

Replicas of standing type or of half-tones, for which a coarse screen (up to 85 lines to an inch) has been used, can be

---

1 POLLARD: "Facsimile" reprints of old books. I. (<u>Libr</u>. s4,6: 305–13,1926) p.305.

2 PLATE duplicating. (<u>Paper & Print</u>. 21(3–4)p.193–8,309–12; 22(1–3) p.40–4,156–60,256–60,1948–9)

made by pressing papier mâché hard down on the original (it may be either wet flong prepared in the printing office, or dry flong from a paper mill). When the paper dries it retains a sharp image of the original, from which up to 6 replicas can be made by pouring molten metal into them. If nickel-faced, stereos will give up to 100,000 satisfactory impressions. Stereos are much used for newspapers, where the type is set once, and stereos taken, from which several printing machines can simultaneously produce copies of an identical edition. Also used for reprints of books, when the stereos can be stored for future use and the type metal melted down. Plaster of Paris or Plastics can also be used.

A.I.4. ELECTROTYPES.

Electrotypes, which are extensively used for those illustrations for which a screen of up to 150 lines per inch has been used (finer than that, another original etched block should rather be made from the original) are made by taking a wax mould of the type or plate to be facsimilied; this mould placed in an electric bath and copper deposited on it in a thin shell, which later is reinforced by being filled with molten metal. It can be further strengthened by being nickel-faced, in which case one can take up to half a million satisfactory impressions from it.

A.II. INTAGLIO.

This method was never widely used for facsimiles, but was found useful for some kinds of work, until the invention of lithography superseded it.

1626–33 Between these years an attempt was made in Antwerp to reproduce a MS Martyriology of St Jerome. The book was not finished and the fragment was first published in 1660.
17th–18th century used for plates reproducing ancient handwriting or incunables.

A.III. AUTO-LITHOGRAPHY.

This, as well as A.II. and some wood-engraving reproductions of illustrations, were all done from tracings which were then transferred and finished in the medium chosen. All depended on the capability and exactness of the scribe. Some critics are inclined to deprive these methods of all merit.

1808   Gutenberg's Turkenkalender (1455) as a Suppl. to a book by Arctin.

1860   CANTICUM Canticorum.
       One of Berjeau's facsimiles of block-books. This one dated from 1465.
1862–71 Facsimiles of rare 16–17th century pamphlets in quarto, done by E.W. Ashbee for Halliwell-Philipps.

About 1880 photographic reproduction technics took over from all the above methods, but colour photography was not sufficiently developed yet, so chromolithography facsimiles were still produced for a number of years.

1856–97 ARUNDEL Society: Works of ancient masters.

B. PHOTOGRAPHIC PROCESSES.

From the very beginning it was realized that photography would be important for the reproduction of printed pages or MSS. Fox Talbot in 1840 photographed some MS. pages, and "The pencil of nature" included a photograph of a printed page.

Photography will reproduce faithfully, but that means that the background, greyish, often dirty, foxed paper, and all will photograph, and the photographer likes the pages to be flat - nearly impossible in a folded sheet, bound into a book.

B.I. RELIEF. 1. LINE-BLOCKS, OR ZINCOS, OR PHOTO-ZINCOGRAPHY.

Zincography, being an etched process, will by necessity give a blurred impression, which is fatal if the original is already blurred. But it is often combined with type-facsimiles and "period printing" for reproducing title-pages, large initials, fleurons, etc.

1909   RUSSELL, J: Propositio Johannis Russel. (John Rylands Facs. 1)
       First printed by Caxton in Brughes 1476(?)
1904–10 SHAKESPEARE: ...Comedies, etc. Methuen. 4v.
       Reproductions of the editions of 1623, 1632, 1664, 1685, i.e. the First to Fourth Folios.

1936 MONTESINO, A: Coplas sobre diversas devociones...British Museum.
Printed by Emery Walker, ltd. without the photographs or the plates being retouched.

B.I.2. HALF-TONE.

Very seldom used.

1929 BRUSSELS. Bibliothèque roy. de Belgique: Le bréviaire de Philippe le bon... Ch.Weckesser 1929.[1]

B.II. INTAGLIO. 1. PHOTOGRAVURE.

Type, when reproduced by photogravure is apt to look blurred because the screen cuts off corners. Long runs required to make it an economic proposition.

1904 BLAKE: Illustrations of the Book of Job; new ed. Methuen. (Illus. Pocket Libr. of plain & col. Bks)

B.III. PLANOGRAPHIC. 1. PHOTO-LITHO.

Great care must be exercised when reading about early reproduction techniques to distinguish between Line-blocks, also styled Zincography, and Photo-zincography, which was the name used in the early days of Photo-lithography when the plate employed was of zinc, as opposed to the lithographic stone proper.

Photo-lithography[2] was first used for the reproduction of books in

1855 when the University of Moscow published a book on classical calligraphy, illustrated with reproductions.

The process was further developed and zinc plates used in the Ordnance Survey Office in Southampton for the production of maps.

---

1 DULKA: Facsimile reproduction of books... Unpublished M.Sci. Thesis. N.Y: Columbia Univ. 1947. p.41.
2 REDGRAVE: Photographic facsimiles. (Libr. s4,6(4)305–28, 1926) p.313–7.

1861–2 DOMESDAY Book. Reproduced by the Ordnance Survey Office.
1866 SHAKESPEARE: First Folio[1] Day & Son.
For this ed. plates made 1861 by the Ordnance Survey, covering a large part of the Folio, & plates made by Preston for the parts not reproduced by the Ordnance Survey Office, were used. The edition was supervised by Henry Staunton, who in 1864 had issued a facsimile of the quarto of "Much Ado About Nothing".
1869–92 HOLBEIN Society: Fac-simile reprints. 18v.
1880–9 SHAKESPEARE-Quarto Facsimiles, 43v.
Executed partly by Wm Griggs (in photo-lithography) & partly by Chas Praetorius (in photo-zincography); superintended by Dr F.J. Furnivall, who wrote that "Mr Griggs guarantees the substantial accuracy of his work, and my testing confirms it" ("Hamlet", 1603, xii), but soon found reason to complain and, by 1886 was calling for "subscribers willing to undertake the hanging or burning of a photolithographer or two, - to encourage the others!" ("Corrections" at end of "Henry V", 1600). W. Aldis Wright (Cambridge Shakespeare in Preface to 2ed., vol.9, p.xxxvi–vii) concludes: "all confidence in the facsimiles as trustworthy authorities disappears". Professor Hemingway recently continued: "The so-called facsimile of Q 1, published by Griggs in 1881...is full of inaccuracies". ("I Henry IV"; variorum ed.)
1893 COLONNA, F: Dream of Poliphilus; facsimiles of 168 woodcuts... Dept of Science and Art.
Made by W. Griggs.

B.III.2. COLLOTYPE.

The most faithful and accurate process; also called Albert-type, Autotype, <u>Licht-druck</u>. In good collotype reproduction what is in the original is reproduced with the greatest exactitude. Now nearly always used when good work is wanted for the reproduction of MSS and illustrations.

---

[1] Shakespeare's works were issued in the following manner: The plays singly from 1594 to 1622; the first collected edition called...Comedies... was issued 1623, and is called the First Folio; the reprints of this (with some additions) appeared 1632 (2nd Folio), 1664 3rd Folio) and 1685 (4th Folio)

1873–83 PALAEOGRAPHICAL Society: Facsimiles of MSS and inscriptions.
Collotype plates from original negatives prepared by Chas Praetorius.

1900–9 TYPE-Facsimile Society: (Limited to 50 members) Portfolios; ed. by Robert Proctor and Geo. Dunn. O.U.P. 5v. 242 plates of reproductions of early printing.

1902 SHAKESPEARE: First Folio in facsimile edition, Sir Sydney Lee. Oxford.

1905 – Pericles, 1809. Sir S. Lee, ib.

1907–14? TUDOR Facsimile Texts.

1913–4 Gutenberg's 42–line Bible. Leipzig: Insel-Verlag. In colour.

1916 SHAKESPEARE: Richard II, 1598. A.W. Pollard. Quaritch.

1922 CANTICUM Canticorum. Berlin: Marées-Ges; Ganymedes. "Collotype used to reproduce also the adventitious effects, such as spots, discolorations, tears". Compare with the autolithographed copy, p.215. In colour.

1924 MORISON, Stanley: Four centuries of fine printing. Benn.
Not to be confused with the 1949, 2nd rev. demy 8° ed., with plates in half-tone.

1927 SYMBOLUM Apostolicum. Paris: Pegasus Pr.

1931 SHAKESPEARE: Hamlet, 1603. Cambridge, Mass: Harvard Univ.Pr. (Huntington Libr.Publ.)

1936 – Titus Andronicus, 1594. (Folger Libr.Facs.)

1938 – Hamlet, 1605 (the Second Quarto). Cambridge, Mass: Harvard Univ.Pr. (Huntington Libr.Publ.)

1939–51 - Shakespeare Quarto Facsimiles. Shakespeare Ass. and Sidgwick & Jackson. 7v.

1940 TICKHILL Psalter. N.Y: Publ.Libr. & Princeton Univ. Front. in colour.

B.III.3. PHOTO-LITHO-OFFSET.

This process is most often used for new editions of books, either by the same publisher and in the same format as the first edition, or as a cheaper reprint in some of the reprint series, in which case they may be reduced in paper size and some of the plates of the original may be lacking. Although the same process is used, with slight modifications, by most of the following printers or publishers, they all use trade names to distinguish their products.

ADPRINT. Turner, W.J., ed: Impressions of English literature. Collins 1945. (Britain in pictures)
BALDING & MANSELL. Tunnicliffe, C.F: My country book. Studio 1942.
BRADFORD & DICKENS. Conrad companion. Dent 1947.
FACSIMILE FIRSTS. [1947?] Philadelphia: Edw. Stern & Co.
HELIOPLANDRUCK. Graesse: Trésor...[686] repr.1922; Hain: Repertorium...[787] repr.1925.
HENDERSON & SPALDING. Straus, R: Portrait of Dickens. Dent 1938. (Aldine Libr.). (No Illus; cf. with 1928 ed.)
KIMBLE & BRADFORD. McCurdy, E: Mind of Leonardo da Vinci. Cape 1932. (Life & Lett.)
LITHOPRINTING. (Edwards Bros., Ann Arbor) Augustan Repr.Soc: Publ. 1946+; British Museum Cat...[688]; Library of Congress Cat...[693] (for this Catalog a special technique was employed; it was photographed from cards, which were then reshuffled, cumulated, or arranged for the Subject Catalog[1]; Music reprints, e.g. Bach, Beethoven.
NOVOGRAPHIC (Lowe & Bryden). Timlin, W: South Africa. Black 1927; Trevelyan, G.M: English social history. Longmans 1944.
OBRALDRUCK (Oscar Brandstetter, Leipzig) Hetherington, H.J.S., and Muirhead, J.H: Social purpose. Allen & Unwin 1922.
PHOTO-LITHOPRINT. See Lithoprinting.
PHOTOLITHOTYPIC Reprints. Davenport, C: The book. N.Y: Peter Smith 1930.
PHOTOTYPE. Rolland, R: Mahatma Gandhi... Allen & Unwin 1942.
PLANOGRAPHING. See Lithoprinting.
REPLIKA (Lund, Humphries & Co.) Hubbard, E.H: On making... etchings. Print Soc. and Batsford 1923; 'Joint Code' 1935; 'Cutter' 1935; Shakespeare Ass: Facs 1931–8 in 15v; Jeanneret-Gris, C.E. (pseud. of "Le Corbusier"): City of tomorrow. Archit. Pr. 1947; Catalogue of Un.Period.[805]
RODAR Prozess. (C.G. Röder, Leipzig). Bonar, J: Malthus. Allen 1924; Gaster, M: Studies and texts in folklore. Maggs 1925–8. 3v.
ROTAPRINT. (Kaye's R. Agency, ltd) Map showing spread of printing in S.Afr. (S.Afr.Libr. 6(2)Oct.1938); S.Afr.Libr.Ass. Repr. 1–2. (Suitable for single sheets only; can do half-tones)

---

1 See foot-note p.81.

SCHOLARS Facsimiles and Reprints. N.Y. 1938+

The complete negative for photo-litho-offset printing includes one whole side of a sheet, but in order to avoid distortion only one or two pages are photographed at a time.

All the above-mentioned examples have had one thing in common: that there has been a big enough demand to print, or reprint an ordinary edition. But quite a lot of scholarly books are so much in demand that microfilms (about which later) are insufficient, but on the other hand so special in their subject that an ordinary commercial edition will not pay. Here Near- print serves.[1,2]

In near-print the book is not set in type-metal, but the copy is either (a) typed and then photographed; or (b) typed directly on to thin, aluminium-paper sheets for direct offset.

In order not to look too amateurish the typing must be very well done, preferably on one of the typewriters specially constructed for this type of work, e.g. with half-spacing; one-time paper ribbon; electric working of the keys (for even pressure); automatic justifying, etc., and fitted with a book-face (Vari-typer, Justowriter, etc.). Or photographic type composition can be employed. Copy is often reduced 5 diameters.

(a) CIBELLA, Ross C: Directory of microfilm sources, etc. N.Y: Special Libr.Ass. (1941)

(b) UNION of South Africa. Dep. of Native Affairs. Copper miners of Musina...Zoutpansberg...ed...by N.J. van Warmelo. Pretoria: Govt Print. (Ethnological Publ.8)

C. DOCUMENTARY REPRODUCTION. I. DIRECT PHOTOGRAPHY. 1. PHOTOSTAT OR ROTOGRAPHS[3]

The original is copied directly down on to the sensitized paper, the original can be enlarged or reduced. Used for

---

1 SILVER: "Near-print" draws nearer. (J.Docum. 5(2)55–68, 1949)

2 – New methods of printing & reproducing scholarly materials. (Amer. Docum. 2(1)54–8,1951)

3 BENDIKSON: Photostat reproductions of valuable source material. (J.docum.Repr. 3(4)227–8,1940)

editions of less than a dozen. White on black is adequate and cheaper for articles from periodicals. Rotographs are used for preparation of type-facsimiles (see 1914 and 1926 thereunder) used in the collections of the Modern Language Association of America until they began using microfilms; by the Massachusetts Historical Society and the Huntington Library.

C.I.2. MICROPHOTOGRAPHY.[1,2,3,4,5,6,7,8,9]

John Benjamin Dancer made the first microphotographs in May 1853, but it is only in this century that greater use has been made of them. By microphotography the copy is usually reduced to such a degree that the result cannot be read with the naked eye, so that an enlarger must be used. Unless the institution in which the user of the microphotograph works is the owner of several viewers and allows the reader the use of more than one, he is prevented from referring to several texts at the same time if these are available only in microphotographic form. Another disadvantage is that the human eye gets tired of reading the viewers. Against this we can set the many advantages: reduction of bulk, resulting in less postage and quicker transport by air and, if many are used, as envisaged by Fremont Rider, the smaller buildings. The scholar can get access to copies of rare books seldom lent out. (That is if he is interested in the subject matter only; for textual criticism he will have to use collotype, or another reproduction in the same size as the original). Microphotography is really the tool of the scientist as opposed to the humanist.

---

1 COBLANS: Some notes on American practice in documentation. (J.Docum. 6(4)206–12,1950)
2 – Some recent developments in microcopy. (S.Afr.Libr. 19(3) p.77–81,1952)
3 ERICKSON: Microprint. (J.Docum. 7(3)184–7,1951)
4 LUTHER: The earliest experiments in microphotography. (Isis 41:277–81,1950)
5 TATE: Appraisal of microfilm. (Amer.Docum. 1(2)p.91–9,1950)
6 UNESCO survey of microfilm use. (UNESCO Bull. 5(5)161–7, 1951)
7 VAN DER WOLK, & Tonnon: Microcopy on flat film as an aid in documentation. (Rev.Docum. 17(5)131–41,1950; 18(8)216–38, 1950)
8 WILSON: MSS in microfilm. (Libr.Quart. 13(3)212–26,1943)
9 – A plan for a comprehensive medico-historical library. (ib. 21(4)248–66,1951)

Microfilms are either made of articles in periodicals at the special request of an individual scholar, or used for publishing theses, etc. When not in use the films are kept in special containers and, because of their form, are stored apart from the books. For this reason, the flat form (micro-fiche) is more used in Europe, especially France, than the roll form. During the war about 10,000 films of research material in Britain were made for the use of scholars in the U.S.A. Unlimited numbers of positives may be taken from the negative microfilm, and most libraries in possession of a long run prefer to give a positive instead of running the risk of having their negative damaged during inter-library-loans. <u>The Times</u> is available on 35mm. microfilm from its very beginning up to one year in arrear of the current issue. The reduction is 10–35 diameters.

<u>Dissertation Abstracts</u> [830] lists microfilms.

Microcards, positives printed on opaque paper with 100 pages to one page of microcard, are not made to order - that would be too expensive - but are made as an edition of certaintypes of material, e.g. out-of-print periodicals; Early English Text Society's Publications; Rolls Series; Hakluyt Society Publications, etc. Easy to read. Titles available are listed in <u>Microcard Bull.</u> [798] The title may be printed in ordinary size letters, on the first page of the card.

Microprint is really a printing process, where the text is printed with ink on paper, only the reduction makes it differ from ordinary photo-litho; with a reduction of 3.2-6 diameters they are called miniature facsimiles. They can be read without the aid of a viewer. The larger sizes may also be produced by letterpress.

C.II. PHOTOGRAPHY BY REFLEX.[1] 1. CONTOURA.

It photographs by reflected light from bulbs in the machine (first passing through the sensitized material and then reflected back from the object); the light from these bulbs is equalized. It is possible to photograph pages in a bound volume in ordinary light. The copy can be read by means of a mirror (it is reversed) or another unreversed copy can be made by repeating the process.

C.II.2. GESTEPRINT.

A combination of reflex copying and duplicating techniques.

---

1 JONES, Graham: Progress in reflex copying: Diazo & after. (<u>Libr.Ass. Rec.</u> 55(1)10–13 Jan.1953)

C.III. PHOTOGRAPHY BY CONTACT. 1. BLUE-PRINT.

The original, drawn on transparent paper is used as a negative. The dark lines in the original show up as white after exposure.

C.III.2. DIAZO-COPYING.[1]

The sensitizer consists of two components that unite and form a dye when exposed to ultra-violet light and dampness. Can also be used as a reflex copying method.

C.IV. OTHER. 1. ANASTATIC PRINTING.

The original, which preferably should be recent, is immersed in chemicals which either make the ink already on the paper transferable, or receptive to lithographic ink; the image is transferred on to a lithographic plate which is then etched in the usual way.
DU CANGE, Chas du Fresne: Glossarium mediae et infimae latinitatis; ed. L. Favre. Breslau: Koebner. 1890–1. 10 fasc.

C.IV.2. TELETYPE.

An electric typewriter or a special Linotype keyboard attachment is operated by impulses sent over a wire; much used by small newspapers in America.

C.IV.3. "FACSIMILE" or ULTRAFAX.

The word used for the product of radio impulses sent from a scanner; the product is on paper.

C.IV.4. DUPLICATORS.[2]

These processes are many and varied, usually either onset or offset, and with capacities varying between 150-5,000 good impressions.

---

1 GORTER: Principles & possibilities of diazo-copying processes. (J.Docum. 5(1)1–11,1949)
2 NEWBURY: The duplicator in the library. (Libr.Assistant. 43(2)19-24,1950)

"Are not the publishers [of a new facsimile reprint of Poe's "Tamerlane"] courting unnecessary risks? If they are successful in 'completely reproducing all details', how is a (suitably soiled and frayed) copy to be distinguished from the authentic piece?"[1]

FAKES.[2]

It is often difficult to draw the line between type-facsimile and fake; the criterion must be the intention of the printer or publisher and, of course, of the person who later will erase or cut out the imprint of the reprint in order to sell it as an original.

We have already mentioned that the early printers undoubtedly tried to make their books look as much like MSS as possible. There was no respect for the copyright of the printer until recent times, and printers would cheerfully copy pictures from other books, however badly they might suit the subject of the new title; or reprint a best seller, title-page, imprint, and all. Two famous examples of this are Virgilii Opera, printed by the Elzeviers in 1676, and reprinted with the same title-page in 1724; the reprint is distinguished from the original by 11 printer's mistakes, one of which is the page number 32 instead of 24, and the other is Boccaccio's Decamerone printed in Florence by Giunta in 1527, famous for its beauty and reprinted on

---

1   CHAPMAN in T.L.S. 14/3/31, p.390.
2   HOLSTEIN: A five-foot shelf of literary forgeries. (Colophon. ns 2(4)550–67,1937)

numerous occasions; in 1729 by Pisanello, with the same date as the original. The easiest way to distinguish between them is by the wedge-shaped lower-case "a" in the original where the reprint has an ordinary "a".[1]

With the increase in prices of rare books came the temptation to insert facsimiles of missing leaves, or to combine two incomplete copies in order to make one complete, both proper practices as long as the buyer is made aware that it has been done, and exactly what has been done. Modern reproduction techniques give the prospective faker a wide choice, but booksellers and bibliographers are also more wary. The last 30 years have seen some astonishing detection of forgeries, some of which dated at least 300 years back.[2]

Quite apart from any technical tests, internal evidence will often damn a forgery right away, as was the case of the forgery of the quarto Spanish Columbus letter printed in 1497. The forgery repeated some mistakes which had crept into a facsimile in 1866 (made by pen and transferred to a lithographic stone) and could, therefore, not be prior to the date of a facsimile, that is commonly believed to have been executed about 1882.[3] One

---

1 NODIER: Den boggale...forsynet med noter...af Ejnar Munks-gaard. Khb: Carit Andersen 1946. Notes 48 & 67.
2 WEITENKAMPF: St Christopher in a comedy of errors. (Bull. N.Y.publ.Libr. 47(6)390–4,1943)
3 THACHER: A bl romance. (Bibliographer 1:269–84,1902)

of the copies was sold for £4,000. External evidence of the faking was provided by the fact that descenders dropped farther than ascenders went up.

Paper comes second in value for evidence of forgery. If only a single leaf has been forged, the forger usually will use either old paper, in which case chainlines and watermarks must be examined to see whether the particular leaf fits into the sheet of which it is supposed to form part; or, he will try to give it the same colour as the rest of the book. This is a dangerous practice as the faked leaf after some years will probably fade differently from its "conjugate" one. Another method for establishing the verity of whole books is somewhat similar to "the natural history method" used by Proctor for dating incunabula. When Mr Hazen was writing the bibliography of the Strawberry Hill Press he examined the paper on which each copy had been printed and thus established what batches of paper had been available at certain times. This was a great help in weeding out doubtful copies. The Strawberry Hill forgeries are numerous, and some done by Kirgate were actually reprints made at the press itself![1]

If the watermark is dated, or if it is known that a special kind of paper was not manufactured before a certain date, the book printed on it can only have been printed after that date, printed date on title-page notwithstanding. In the most famous

---

1   HAZEN: Watermarks & forgeries. (Print. 2(2)21–31,1941)

of all bibliographical forgeries (to be distinguished from literary forgeries, as bibliographical forgeries are usually genuine pieces of literature, ante-dated) the case of the faked 19th century pamphlets[1] the investigators were greatly assisted by the fact that certain of the pamphlets, dated before 1860, were printed on paper containing esparto (commercially available only after 1861) and chemical wood (first manufactured to any extent 1874+). The last piece of evidence in these Thomas Wise forgeries was supplied by the kernless fount used, which had only been available since 1880; also the fact that the type used was in fact mixed, which in the end took Messrs Carter and Pollard to the firm which had printed the pamphlets.

In the case of the Shakespeare Quartos, the evidence of the faked dates was derived from a combined study of watermarks and typesetting. The study of watermarks showed that the same lot of paper had been used for some books whose dates vary over some 20 years. Common sense suggested that the printer would certainly not antedate his products, so the last date could be taken as the date for the lot. Examination of the title-pages showed that the printer had used exactly the same set-up for all the title-pages, only altering the titles themselves, and the dates, though even they had been forgotten in some cases.

---

1   SYMONS: Detection of a bl forgery. (Penrose Annu. 40:33–7, 1938)

"There Caxton slept,
With Wynkyn at his side,
One clasp'd in wood,
And one in strong cow-hide"[1]

XI

BOOKBINDING

Even the oldest "books" of baked clay were enclosed in shells of similar material. The papyrus, or parchment rolls of classical antiquity were kept in vases, with a title slip attached to the "umbulicus" round which they were wound; in larger libraries they would be lying on shelves along the walls.

Binding as we know it to-day is supposed to have evolved from the diptycha which had reached perfection about the time when the roll was superseded by the codex of folded vellum leaves. It was natural to put these valuable ivory plates to some use in the churches as protection for the sacred books. The bindings there throughout the Middle Ages resembled jewellery rather than binding in the sense we use that word now; made with enamel and precious stones. The shape of the top and bottom covers differed because the latter had to be flat. But at the same time the binding of to-day was evolving. The sheets of vellum were folded once and put one inside the other, four together forming a quire, sewn on strips of leather, and encased

---

1 POPE: <u>Dunciad</u>. I, 149–50.

in wooden boards, which were covered with skins of deer, first as a half-binding, later all over. The decoration of these first bindings in leather was probably (a few are still extant) done by the cuir-cisélé method. The skin was dampened, cut lightly, and shaped with tools into various patterns. This form of decoration went out of fashion but returned and reached perfection, especially in Germany, between 1350 and 1500. Books were expensive things and, for safety, were chained to desks or shelves. The titles were written on the fore-edges, so as to show when the books were lying down. Books were still very large.

12th century.	Stamping of books began. Figured metal stamps were impressed in "repeat pattern" on the binding. Top and bottom halves of the books were in different patterns. Calf, ox, and deer-skins, cured in the monasteries, were used for these blind-stamped bindings.
Invention of printing.	From the East came the art of gold-tooling with small hot irons through gold plate. Bindings had had gold decoration before but then it was painted on. This new technique was called à petits fers, and became common from about 1550.
16th century.	Books were no longer so expensive and the decoration on them no longer worth so much trouble. Rolls for decoration came into use, common from about 1600. Books were smaller now and had paste board covers instead of the wooden ones. Cold tooling was done with large stamps which might cover a whole side. These stamps were in intaglio and the decoration stood out in relief. Rounding and backing after sewing was necessary with the paste board covers. Lettering done on spine instead of on fore-edge or side, because books were smaller and more numerous, and now stood up on shelves. They had to be top-gilt to prevent dust from settling on top.

± 1550

Italy led in book-binding from about 1450 to the middle of the 16th century. The one isolated instance to challenge this was the library of the Hungarian king, Corvinus, and even he got his binders from Italy. Outstanding are the so-called "Cameo bindings" made for the Duke of Farnese. From Italy the initiative passed to France which kept its position until the advent of the machine-age just after the French Revolution. The names of individual binders are rarely known and the bindings from this period are mostly named after the collectors for whom they were made. The general trend in the first half of the 16th century was towards fine gold-tooling in simple, geometric patterns. Thomas Mahieu, secretary to Catherine de Medici, had his bindings made with flat backs, and sewn on flat strips of parchment or leather. Another great collector was Jean Grolier who collected a library of about 3,000 books. His earliest treasures were bound in Italy, but he lived long enough to be able to employ good French craftsmen. On all those books thus bound for him appears his 'liberal and well-known inscription': Io Grolierii et Amicorum. Wonderful work was also done for François I; a few are known which were bound for Geoffrey Tory, but the most famous from that period are those made for Henri II, his queen Catherine de Medici, and his mistress, Diane de Poitiers.

± 1575–1600

The style then reigning: à la fanfare, is ascribed to Nicolas Eve; it consists of a geometric pattern of curved lines covering the whole of the side.

17th century.

"Le Gascon", of whom hardly anything is known, is said to have started the pointille style, for which numerous very small, dotted tools were used. This was a lengthy business and, therefore, very expensive, so for ordinary bindings it was soon superseded by a pattern of a few straight lines, skilfully combined with a little pointille tooling.

18th century.

Mill board, covered with calf, replaced vellum about the middle of the century. Doublures came into use. "Sawing-in" began, and the calf bindings were stained by acids into a conventional pattern: "Tree calf"; both methods did much towards ruining the craft. The reigning style was called dentelle, imparting a lace-like effect along the edges of the binding, pointing towards the middle. It is said to have been invented by A.M. Padeloup, who is also known for his mosaic bindings, inlaid with coloured leather. Another famous binder was N.D. Derome. The Revolution marked the end of the French era in bookbinding. The lead was now taken by England, which had shown originality only once before, with her blind-tooled, Romanesque bindings. This style prevailed till about 1540; then influenced from France, except for the embroidered bookbindings for Prayer Books which, however, were not the work of book-binders, but of noble ladies.

16th century.	Thomas Wotton ordered many fine bindings in the style of Grolier. He used brown leather and black decoration.
± 1650	The Mearne bindings, which may not all have been executed by Mearne himself, were in the manner of Le Gascon, but the arrangement was "rectangular", "cottage", and "all over". These bindings also contained the first hidden, fore-edge paintings.
Last half of 18th century.	Roger Payne made his decorations in the <u>pointillé</u> style, but the colour and the grain of the leather formed an integral part of the design.
± 1780	Labels for the backs came into use.
	The beginning of the 19th century was a turbulent time and no definite style was formed. The increased demand for books at small prices made the publishers look for binding cheaper in both labour costs and in materials. Books were still sold in sheets to booksellers, and people often bought them like that and had them bound in their favourite material. In the 1820's silk was used.
1821	Pickering had the 'Diamond Classics' and others bound in full cloth.
1834–43	Half-cloth.
1830±	Grained cloth, and "Morocco cloth" came into use, as well as paper-labels.
1832	Gold blocking on cloth became possible, and publisher's casing was introduced.

1860	Buckram made; first in common use 1880.

Cloth bindings were made in the worst possible taste (paper boards, so-called 'yellow-backs', existed alongside from 1855–65; their picture-covers developed into present-day dust-wrappers); William Morris's influence made itself felt here as in other branches of book-production, but it was Cobden-Sanderson who, using original flower motifs, first had any practical influence on leather bookbinding. Other influential binders from this period are, or were : Bedford, Sarah Prideaux, Revière, Sangorski, and Zaehnsdorf. Douglas Cockerell, a pupil of Cobden-Sanderson, has also influenced the binding of books considerably; the firm is carried on by Sydney Cockerell, his son.

It is well to remember what Diehl says: that a book is bound only when the cover-boards are laced on to the back of the book with the ends of the cords, over which the sections are sewn together.[1,2,3,4,5]

Binding of a new book by hand begins with the folding of the sheets and the subsequent gathering into the right sequence by following the line of "steps" on the backs of sections; or

---

1 DIEHL: Kinds of binding. (Dolphin. 2:131–43,1935)
2 HARRISON: What to look for in a modern binding. (Book-Coll. Quart. ((13)31–41,1934)
3 MASON: Bookbinding to-day. (Brit.Print. Jan./Feb.1947–Sep./Oct.1948)
4 WALL (of Cedric Chivers): Modern binding for modern books. (Paper & Print. 10(39)264–7, 1937)
5 ZAEHNSDORF: Book-binding. (Station.Co.Craft Lect. 1923:48–61)

by signature checking. Good binding depends to a large extent on the paper the sheets are printed upon. The direction of the fibres should run parallel to the spine of the book, otherwise the paper will cockle if exposed to dampness; the correct direction of the fibres gives greater flexibility. If plates on coated paper are included, however, they should have the fibres running across the page.[1] After folding, the plates are placed in their proper position for sewing. They should be sewn with the rest of the book, not just tipped, or pasted in; and cancels substituted for cancelled pages, if any.

The endpapers, which protect the first and last pages of the book, are made next. They too should, of course, be sewn with the rest of the sections and, in order to make them strong enough to resist the pull of the sewing thread, at least two sheets should be folded to form the section at each end.[2] Douglas Cockerell is the inventor of the so-called zig-zag endpapers, where pleating takes some of the strain on the joint. Part of this section is later to be lined down on the board; the rest constitutes the fly-leaves. Endpapers may be marbled, or coloured; of silk or other fabric.

---

1 CHIVERS: Bookbinding. (J.roy.Soc.Arts. 73(3807)1077–96,1925)
2 MIDDLETON: Book end-papers and their attachment. (Paper & Print. 23(4)431–6,1950)

The book is next pressed, or rolled through a press between metal sheets; in olden days the sheets were beaten with a hammer.

The next step is not compulsory, but depends on how the customer wants his edges. Some collectors prefer their books untrimmed, i.e. uncut (not to be confused with unopened). But the head of the book will then collect dust which, in the long run, will ruin the book. At least the top edge should be cut, but no more than is necessary. A cropped book is unsightly and, even if a binding theoretically, and ideally should last for eternity, the book may have to be rebound and recut later. If the book is to be "gilt-in-the-rough" it is first "sanded" lightly, and the gold laid on after glaire (a mixture of egg-white and water, or vinegar). If a more solid edge with marbling or gold is wanted, and perhaps a fore-edge painting[1,2] the gilding will have to be done after sewing and lacing-in.

The book is now ready for sewing. There are numerous ways of doing this, and even apart from the fact that some are much stronger than others, the binder must take the nature of the paper into consideration. Thick, fluffy papers demand a thick thread that does not cut easily through the paper. Thin and M/G papers, on the other hand, should be sewn with a thin thread,

---

1 HANSON: Edwards of Halifax. (Book Handb. (6)329–38,1948) p.330-2.
2 HOBSON: On fore-edge painting of books. (Folio Sep./Oct. p.8–11,1949)

because the back will be too bulky if a thick one is used.[1,2,3] The best method for good paper is still the one used for "extra" binding ever since the Middle Ages, called "flexible", where the sections are sewn round cords that are later laced into the boards. For large books "double flexible" sewing round two cords, at a time should be employed (again only if the paper is good). The purpose of sewing is to keep the leaves within the signature, as well as the sections together. Each single sheet is sewn, the thread running inside, slipping out at intervals, going round the one or two cords, to appear again inside, to the next cord, and so on. At the ends, the sections are kept together by the so-called "kettle" stitch. When the book is later covered with leather these cords show up on the back. This is sometimes regarded as ugly and the cords are recessed into a small groove sawn into the backs of the sheets. This weakens the binding, and "extra" (fine) binders regard it with mistrust; on the other hand many library binders employ it with moderation. There is always the danger of glue seeping through into the book proper. When the cords are sawn-in the thread goes across, not round the cords. This form of binding is often used with a hollow back, and for cheaper books. Instead of sewing on cords, tapes can be used,

---

1 MIDDLETON: Scale in book-binding. (Paper & Print. 23(2) 202–6, 1950)
2 – Notes on the hand-sewing of books. (ib. 24(1)45–8,24(2) 161–4,1951)
3 – Notes on the art of covering with leather. (ib. 25(3–4) 316–21,430–5,1952)

to give a flatter back. Here again the thread goes across the tapes instead of round them. If the paper is very thin and the binder realizes that the back of the book will swell unduly, he may saw "two sheets on", that is, he sews between one cord or tape and the next in one sheet, but for the next section in the next sheet, he changes back to the first for the third section, and so on; but end-sections should always be sewn "all along". If the grain of the paper runs the wrong way, or if the paper is very bad, the binder may decide to oversew the book, i.e. over-cast the sheets all along; this gives little flexibility, but is often used for rebinding of library fiction, because of its solidity. The ends of the cords, frayed out, are called "slips". The book is then glued along the back. Binders' glue is mostly made from animal glue, from skins and hides, with an admixture of glycerine; in recent years, however, synthetic glues[1] have come into use. They have the advantage that the many parasites on books, which mainly thrive on glue and size, do not eat these.

The book is now rounded. The early books were not rounded, but the binders soon realized that that meant a concave back in the book's later life. The degree of rounding is a matter of taste, the most usual being not more than one third of the full circle. Both the rounding and the backing following this, are

---

1 LAWRIE: Synthetic resin (Polythene) instead of glue & paste. (<u>Libr. Ass.Rec</u>. 46:114–7,1944)

done by means of a hammer; the backing is done in order to provide the necessary grooves, or shoulders to receive the boards.

The book is now ready to receive the boards. They may be either mill-boards, made from old rope, or split boards, which actually are two boards glued together. The "splits" are laced through grooves in the boards and securely fastened together by means of paste. The last leaf of the endpapers is pasted on to the boards, and prevents them from warping. If the book was not 'gilded-in-the-rough' it must now be trimmed and this is best done with an instrument called a "plough". Decorative headbands are next sewn on (they may also be pasted on, but not in good binding). Old headbands were sewn at the same time as the book. Headbands serve to even the discrepancy between the height of the board & the back; to add strength to the binding as a finish; & to take the strain when removing a book from the shelf. If the book is to have a "hollow back" the back of the sections is lined-up with a backing cloth or paper, and a tube of paper pasted on to the lining and the leather covering, in its turn, pasted on to the tube. "Hollow back" makes the book easier to open, but it is anathema with many English-speaking librarians. The alternative, a "tight, or fast back", is glued direct on to it.

The covering material is now cut to the desired size and pared, i.e. thinned, where it passes over the joints; this must be done with care, because excessive paring shortens the life of the binding. The cover is now pasted on to the book. It may cover it completely and is then termed full leather; or extend well on to the front and back boards, plus the corners, this is half-binding'. Covering still more of the boards and corners is called '3/4-binding". Quarter binding has no corners, and very little leather beyond the joints. This completes that part of the process called "forwarding".

Then follows the "finishing", i.e. the decoration of the "forwarding" structure. First the leather covering is polished, and some binders crush, i.e. dampen, and press heavy-grained leather. The tooling is either "in blind"; or in gold, when it is first done "in blind" and then repeated through gold leaf, a very exacting process. The tools are made of metal and in various patterns: dots, straight lines ("fillet") curved lines (gouges), etc; then washing and, finally, more polishing.

The above describes what is now called "extra" binding, but which was formerly the common fashion; to-day it is accorded only to 'well-dressed literature'. The demand for cheaper books and larger editions at the beginning of last century was the back-ground for the "casing" of books in publishers' cloth, or for 'edition binding'.[1]

---

1 GOULD: Mechanization of bookbinding. (Station.Co.Craft Lect. 16:61–83,1937)

The books arrive from the publisher in sheets and are folded on machines at the rate of 100's per hour. If the sheets were printed in perfect "register" they will be folded in correct register by the folding machine. Next the sheets are gathered in correct sequence, also by machine, or by girls seated around a revolving table, or staircase-wise along an escalator. The sheets are then fed, one book at a time, into an iron, power-driven smasher, that reduces them in thickness and makes them solid (also called "knocking-down").

The sewing is also done by machine. It may be done over linen tapes, but usually the sections are just jog-stitched together, the sewing running horizontally through the back of the book, contrary to hand-sewing, where it runs the length of each section. The endpapers are not sewn on but merely tipped, or pasted on to the first and last sections of the book. The edges are cut in a machine called a guillotine, and may be top edge gilt (t.e.g.), but more often spray-tinted. The book is then glued, rounded and backed, and "lined-up" with a strip of coarse muslin called mull in U.K., scrim in South Africa, and super in U.S.A. This is cut wide enough to extend 3/4" over each side, to serve later as a reinforcement to the endpapers. Machine-made headbands, if specified, are now glued on at head (and tail). In better class work the back has a strip of paper glued over the mull and the headbands. The machine known as "Flexiback" glues and backs the book with a linen strip, in one operation. The cover of the book, including boards and linen, is made separately. The full cloth casings are made on machine, while cloth backs with paper sides (as for <u>Libr.</u> [79]) are usually made by hand. The casings go next to the blocking, or stamping press, where they are sized and laid with gold leaf, metal (copper) foil, etc., and then placed in the machine to have their titles and decoration stamped on. Without any intervening media this operation is called "blind blocking". Following this the casing-in machine pastes the lined-up books into their cases, so that the books and their covers are held together solely by the endpapers; or, at best reinforced by a strip of mull. Finally the books are put in a standing press and kept under pressure there until dry.

The <u>re-binding</u> of old books follows the procedure outlined under "extra" binding, except for the initial stages, which consist in 'pulling', i.e. separating one section from another by removing the glue, and cutting the sewing threads. The pages may be damaged or may already be cut through by the threads and have to be mended; the folds are 'reinforced' by interlocking, serrated bank-paper, or linen. Too many guarded sections produce a swelling at the back and sometimes the binder may have to paste each leaf or section on to a guard which then is sewn in the ordinary manner, instead of the sections themselves. The pages may be dirty and foxed. Foxing is said to be caused either by colloids, minute particles of metal from the types, or, by moulding of the size in the paper. There are several methods of eradicating these brown spots, the most drastic of which is by dipping in chloride of lime; another is resizing, and yet another: interleaving the book with paper impregnated with "santobrite". Before resewing, the book should be checked by signatures, and an old book should be carefully collated.

New sheets of books with small back margins, or on very thick paper, can be mounted on guards as described above and then sewn through the guards. Pamphlets, or books of single, roneod leaves can be stapled, stabbed, or tape-slotted.

The newest development for the assembling of leaves into books in covers is the "unsewn" method which, for many years, has been employed for telephone directories.[1,2,3,4,5] It is only lately, however, that it has been used largely for novels and other cheap editions. No sewing at all is done. The back edges of the sheets are cut, or sanded off, and the edges bound

---

1   BINDING with electronics. (Bookb. BkProd. Jul:44-6,1948)
2   NEW York public library; plastic jackets safeguard library bindings. (ib. 51(1) -.45-6, 1950)
3   CARSON, & WEBER: Performance of the "perfect" book binding. (Libr.J. 73(12)918-23,1948)
4   CLOUGH: Perfect binding. (Libr.Ass.Rec. 51(10)310-2,1949)
5   FRENCH: Plastics for printing. (Bookb. BkProd. Mar:41-3, 1948)

together by means of a plastic covering. The strength depends partly on the plastic employed and partly on the paper. A heated controversy has been going on: one librarian contends that "the perfect binding" is at present suitable for about 80 per cent. of papers, and in a few years, maybe for 90 per cent. Binders, on the other hand, say that it should only be employed for books which it is not intended to re-bind. Re-binding, if at all, will have to be done by the same method. Plastic as a covering was employed, e.g. for J. Summerson's Heavenly mansions.[1]

Spiral binding is used in a few cases for books consisting of single leaves. It has not got much to recommend it for a book that is meant to stand on a shelf, and the spiral has the added disadvantage of being wider than the body of the book.

Materials.[2,3]

> "Punch" defines 3 grades of modern bindings; "Leather", "Something like leather", "Nothing like leather".
>
> Vellum (calf) and Parchment (sheep or goat) were the first materials used for bindings. Modern parchment is usually split, the upper, hair, or grain side becomes 'skiver', and only the flesh, or underside is made into parchment. Both are very strong, but mice like them, and they stretch when damp. They are easy to clean, but become brittle under much light. Vellum is used for large volumes, parchment for small.

---

1 Cresset Pr. 1949. (cf. P.317 here)
2 JACOBSON: Leather for bookbinding. (Bookb. BkProd. Apr: 47; May: 41–2,1950)
3 WARNER: Modern bookbinding leathers. (Libr.Ass.Rec. ns 7: 153–64,1929)

Vellum and parchment are not tanned and, therefore, are not regarded as true leathers. The word parchment derives from Pergamum, city in Asia Minor; vellum from <u>vitulus</u>, a calf.

Sheep. The old sheepskin bindings from the 17th and 18th centuries are astonishingly good, but to-day's sheep-skins are poor. The skin is thick and split into 'skiver', and 'flesh'. It takes very well the grain of other skins fraudulently impressed on it, but is weakened even more by this. Roan, tanned in sumach, imitates ungrained Morocco; Basil (<u>basane</u>)

Calf. The grain resembles Morocco but it is a weak skin, and most suitable for pressed bindings. Tree-calf is stained by acid. Old tree-calf has had the "tree" fall out(!) Russia leathers from 1869+ rot away. Divinity Calf; Law Calf.

Morocco (goatskin). Best from skins of well-fed goats from warm climates where their energy does not go into making hairs. Levant Morocco, from a now extinct goat, is the best of them all (L.M. is often crushed, which does not improve it); Nigerian leathers are tanned by the natives; Cape goat not quite so good as the above. Others are "Oasis Morocco", and Persian Morocco (the goat is said to be miserably fed, with dire results to its hide). Goat hides have a lovely grain and are the best for gold tooling.

Pig. A very strong skin if it is left in its natural, white state. For binding of large volumes.

Seal. Dear, but durable. Greasy; must be handled often.

Bookcloths. Buckram (English) Linen; American Cotton, e.g. Holliston, Winterbottom's imperial Morocco cloths, thick and coarse, for large and heavy books. When cut care should be taken to let the grain run along the spine of the book, books bound in cloth or buckram must necessarily have 'hollow backs', owing to the stiff nature of the materials; Canvas; Durabline: Chivers' waterproof cloth with a watered-silk pattern; Keratol, a washable cloth, useful for juvenile books.

Leatherlen. A latex, impregnated material of cellulose fibre combined with approximately 40–50 per cent. shredded leather.

Other substitutes. Leatherette: paper or cloth having a surface in imitation of leather; Pegamoid; Pluviusin; Rexine, etc. Plastic coverings are washable, the design on the paper under the covering can be in any form and colour desired. The covering with a transparent plastic is called lamination. A similar effect was earlier obtained by means of transparent vellum.

Various odd, association bindings have also appeared, e.g. Shakespeare's Works bound in oak from the church in which he was baptized, and Hitler's <u>Mein Kampf</u> bound in skunk skin.[1]

Nylon thread is coming more and more into use; it is cheap and has no joins, but it can suddenly spring back when it is cut.

The care of the finished binding depends on a knowledge of the various factors in its decay[2,3,4,5,6]. Research dates back to the beginning of this century when binders and collectors began to worry about the decay of leathers. The Committee of the Royal Society of Arts found that the leathers tanned by manufacturers in England were inferior to those tanned by the natives of Nigeria, and that it was the sulphuric acid in the dyes

---

1 THOMPSON: Bibliopegia fantastica. (<u>Bull.N.Y.publ.Libr.</u> 51(2) 71-90,1947)

2 HARRISON: Care of books. (<u>Book-Coll.Quart.</u> 3:1-14,1931)

3 INNES: Bookbinding leathers & their deterioration. (<u>Station.Co.Craft Lect.</u> 10:73-91,1932)

4 – Causes & prevention of decay in leather. (<u>Libr.Ass.Rec.</u> s4,1:393-9,1934). Also in <u>Leather world</u> Sep.1934.

5 – Preservation of bookbinding leathers. (ib. 52(12)458-61,1950)

6 MIDDLETON: Deterioration of bookbinding leather. (<u>Paper & Print.</u> 23(3)326-30,1950)

employed that caused the decay. This finding was revised by a committee of the British Leather Manufacturers' Research Association and PATRA (PIRA then) because it had been found that leathers treated in the way recommended by the Royal Society of Arts' Committee still decayed, and tests showed that these skins now contained sulphuric acid. It has since been found that certain salts, "non-tans", that neutralized the acids, were being washed out by the manufacturers, and that the bindings, therefore, became infected by sulphuric acids in the atmosphere, especially from gas fires, which should never be tolerated in libraries. Skins should be treated with 7 per cent, solution of potassium lactate. Skins so treated are stamped "Guaranteed to resist the P.I.R.A. test". During tanning, only agents of the pyrogallol class should be used, as opposed to the catechol class, to which belongs the birch bark, commonly used for tanning Russia leather (which had decayed badly). Alum and chrome tans are said to be safe.

Other causes already mentioned are excessive paring of the skins, and the making of 'tree-calf' by means of acid (copperas) staining.

Ammonia from tobacco-fumes is also dangerous in a library.

Various dressings (British Museum, U.S. Bureau of Standards) are on the market and should be employed at regular intervals, but one must realize that these will not stop chemical action in the leather, but they can close up the pores of the skin and prevent atmospheric fumes from getting in. They also feed the necessary fats to the skin. For the same reason it is recommended that leather bindings be handled often, though warm hands secrete salts which, in turn, are harmful.

Books left untouched on tightly packed shelves are in danger of being attacked by mildew[1]: minute colonies living on the starch and other organic materials in the book. It can be counteracted by using synthetic adhesives instead of glue, and starchless cloth. This holds good also for all the other parasites of books, such as silverfish, etc.[2] Of course books should never be tightly packed, though all bound books should have some support, and with fresh air circulating around them. Ideally, books should be kept in air-tight, air-conditioned dark rooms with a temperature of 65°–75°F., and a humidity of 50 per cent. This may be obtainable in a library; a book-lover could certainly not do it; but a deep bookcase, with locked doors, and a saucer of water in the room, will help.

Re-binding takes a great deal of a library's budget, and the librarian will have to determine each case on its merits.[3,4] The

---

1 ARMITAGE: Cause of mildew on books and methods of prevention. (PATRA Bull. (8)1949)
2 EVANS: Life & death of a bookworm. (PATRA J. 12(4)14–6,1949)
3 DAVIS (of Riley): Bookbinding and the school librarian. (Sch.Libr. 4:240–5,1949)
4 HOWARTH: In search of a popular binding. (Libr. & Bk World. 41(2)21–3,1952)

quality of the paper sets the standard for the binding. Consider the ratio of coat of binding (up by 110 per cent. since 1939) to the circulation, and the use and value of the book. Replacement may offer an alternative. Bind too soon rather than too late, and use leather on those books that are to receive hard usage. "Pegamoid" which South African fishmoths and cockroaches do not eat, should be preferred to cloth, which they do like. When books are sent to the binder, a full list, giving style, material, colour, lettering (including class numbers) should follow, or accompany them. Periodicals should be complete, including title-page and index, rubbings of previous volumes, to ensure binding "to pattern". Decide whether the advertisements should be bound separately at the end of the volume, or not be included at all. If a new binder is employed state in the specification how the books should be bound, e.g. on cords, or tapes; plates to be guarded; if oversewing wanted, etc. etc.

Bookjackets[1] which first appeared on Heath's Keepsake for 1833, but first became common at the beginning of this century, are often a sore point with the binder. Very exquisite jackets which the owner wants to preserve can be bound with the endpapers (often done for Scandinavian library books). They may be superseded by a suitable design on the boards, covered with a layer of transparent plastic.

---

1   ROSNER: The British book-jacket. (Brit. Book News. (119) 445–50, 1950)

> "It should be a point of honour not to inflict upon printer and publisher the burden of irritating afterthoughts and infirm vacillations."[1]

XII

PRACTICAL AUTHORSHIP

Author and Printer Publishing and Bookselling
- Copyright Book-Collecting

> "...Let us emphasize again the simple fact that if you wish your work to be printed properly you should make your copy read just as it is to be printed... proofs are not submitted to an author in order that he may rewrite his work in proof."[2]

AUTHOR AND PRINTER.

The student should have realized by now that most books consist of: I - Text, and II - Illustrations, and that the Text is often divided into (a) Preliminaries ('Prelims', or Front matter); (b) Main Text, or Body; and (c) End matter. The detailed enumeration appeared in Chapter V. Simon [173] is a safe guide on such matters as format, type, and design. (See Chapters VII–IX and XI for Paper, Printing, Illustration, and Binding).

---

1 CHAPMAN in Collins: Authors'...[462] p.xv.
2 BENBOW: Manuscript...[465] p.18–9, 51.

In the preparation of manuscript (MS.) or typescript (TS.) for publication there are three main stages: From the author's MS. to the typist's finger tips; From the TS. to the printer, including his proofs; The final production, including Distribution: Publishing, Bookselling, and Copyright.

Although the student may have decided to use 3" x 5" cards for his bibliographic entries, he will wisely use divisions of post 4to sheets (10" x 8") for his notes. An experienced writer would probably scribble straight on to half-sheets (5" x 8") but the student should begin on slips (2½" x 8"). Both sizes can later be arranged, re-arranged, and be easily rewritten, before their final pasting down for the typist.

"Is it unreasonable", asks Sir Stanley Unwin[1] "...to suggest that they [typists] should have a 'Rule of the House' as a book printer does, and thus preserve some measure of uniformity in such matters as the spelling of proper names and the use of capital letters; that they should know that single underlining indicates italics, double underlining 'small caps', and treble underlining 'large capitals'; that they should single space and indent quoted matter...?"

The MS. should be type-written, double-spaced. It should be typed on one side only and on sheets of uniform size, preferably quarto. Avoid stiff or tissue paper, or any kind with a glazed or slippery surface. A margin of about one inch

---

1   Truth...[498] p.112.

should be left on all four aides. With a maximum length of line up to six inches, and an equal number of lines typed to each full page, "casting-off" and estimating cost will be facilitated. Sheets 8" x 10" provide for such a type area. They should be kept flat, be numbered consecutively throughout in the top right-hand corners, and fastened securely together at the top left-hand corners, section by section, or chapter by chapter, in batches not usually exceeding about 24 sheets each. Begin a new chapter or other large division on a new page. New paragraphs should be indented three, preferably four, or even five spaces. Provide half- and title-pages, and on the protecting end-sheets, front and back, put your name and address before dispatching the completed TS. to the publisher.

<u>Consistency</u>. Careful and consistent preparation throughout should be the aim of all concerned in book production, particularly regarding the following points: Abbreviations and Contractions; Brackets; Capitalization; Figures and Numerals; Footnotes and Bibliographical References; Headings; Hyphens; Punctuation; Quotations and Extracts; Spelling and Word Division. Many of these points are classed as <u>style</u> by the printer; they are equally the concern of author, editor, and typist.

<u>Abbreviations</u> should normally be followed by a full stop, otherwise point, or period. Use the full stop sparingly. It is unnecessary following a true <u>Contraction</u>, i.e. one containing

the last letter of the abbreviated word, e.g: Capn, Dr, Messrs, Mme, Mr, Revd, St (Saint or Street). Abbreviations, particularly of the titles of periodicals, are to be encouraged but only in accordance with one system: The World List [804] as used in the C.U.P. [807] Abbreviations should not be used in the text.

Be sure to use Brackets in pairs: called 'curves', parentheses, or round brackets: (), and the square ones: [] to enclose interpolated matter, not occurring in the original matter.

Capitalization.
"...it is barbarous to use small initials in German nouns, contrary to the usage of that language."[1]

When the name of a periodical is cited do not capitalize the word the which precedes it, even if it is part of the name, except: The Times, of London.

Figures v. Numbers. Use figures to express a specific number, as: The Library had (exactly) 225,000 volumes; but: Its estimated capacity is one million (a round number). Dates. Figures should be used in referring to the year and, of several possible forms, prefer 6 February 1952, with no punctuation, i.e. "Begin at day, ascend to month, ascend to year."[2] In

---

1 VAN HOESEN: Bibliography...[38] p.29.
2 HART: Rules...[472] p.82.

numbers from 21 to 99 use hyphens to separate tens from units, as: fifty-two.

Footnotes should be typed, preferably between horizontal lines, and directly below the line of text in which the reference occurs; or, they may be typed at the foot of each folio, not more than one per page if indicated by an asterisk; or, alternatively, on separate sheets for each chapter. The superior figure or asterisk in the text is printed outside and after all punctuation marks.

The methods of bibliographical reference approved by the British Standards Institution (B.S.1629:1950)[112] are acceptable to librarians, but not those in B.S.1219:1945 [469].

Their position may be:

1. In the text itself, with the author's name, and page number, plus the year of publication if necessary, all within parentheses, as used in the S.Afr.J.Sci.[1] where all the references so cited in the text are then grouped alphabetically by authors at the end of the paper.
2. At the foot of the page, a common practice if references are few, as in Part 2 of these Notes.
3. At the end of the chapter, as in Esdaile.[2]
4. In a special chapter, as in these Notes, for references to books.
5. At the end of the book, as in Van Hoesen.[3]

---

1 SOUTH African Association for the Advancement of Science: Information for authors. (S.Afr.J.Sci. 47(10)iii–iv May 1951).
2 ESDAILE: Student's...[34].
3 VAN HOESEN: Bibliography...[38]

Their form:

(a) For a Book, it is only necessary to modify ordinary library cataloguing practice.
(b) For a Periodical. The titles of periodicals should be enclosed within parentheses; be underlined singly for italics;[1] and be set down in the abbreviated form appearing in the World List,[2] or in the C.U.P.[3]

The recommended order of the items is: Series, Volume, Number (or Part)*, inclusive Pagination, Day*, Month*, and Year, as: (Ann. Mag.nat.Hist. s5,1:491–9,1952)[4,5,6]

Inclusive Pagination. One cannot think that Drs Billings, Cushing, Osler, or Fulton would have endorsed to-day's annoying practice, or malpractice, prevalent mainly among "Medicals", of citing the commencing page only. The omission leads to errors and delays, especially when photographic copies of articles are required from afar.

Ensure that all Headings and sub-headings are consistently used, i.e. typed in a uniform style. Omit the full point after

---

* if known, or considered necessary.
1   WILSON, firm: Style...[477]
2   WORLD List...[804]
3   C.U.P...[807]
4   HIGGINS: B...[116] p.15–33.
5   SHORES: Basic...[108] p.237–45.
6   WORDS...[478] P.33–5.

a centred heading, i.e. a <u>displayed</u> line: it throws it out of balance and says nothing, e.g.

The Hyphen-Hazard

not

The Hyphen-Hazard.

Instruct the typist not to divide any words but to begin a new line whenever there is not room enough left in a line for the whole word. Alternative methods are (a) to draw an arrow pointing to the hyphen and say: "Keep hyphen"; or, "No hyphen"; or (b) - and better - in the case of a word to be hyphenated, to type <u>two</u> hyphens: one at the end of the line and another at the beginning of the next, as: to-day; to-morrow; out-of-date; up--to-date; but none for layout (one word) or for out of print (three words).

Punctuation.
"...the best bibliographical usage includes the library devices of three dots to indicate omission, square brackets for insertions, the semi-colon separating main title from explanatory title, the colon between independent titles as set forth on the title--page..."[1]

The <u>dash</u> - in the form :- is superfluous and should be avoided.[2] In our book-lists we have used the <u>colon</u> to separate the author from title, following on the same line; and to separate place of publication and publisher, e.g. Edinb: Grant;

---

1 VAN HOESEN: Bibliography...[38] p.29.
2 But cf. VAN HOESEN p.29, & 425 no.1.

N.Y: H.W. Wilson, rather than N.Y., H.W. Wilson.

Double <u>quotation marks</u> are preferable to single ones. Use single marks for a quotation within a quotation. <u>Extracts</u> should have single-spacing, or appear with indentions at <u>both</u> sides of the page. Those to be set in two sizes less than the text type need not be enclosed between quotation marks, but their source should be made clear in the context, or by reference.

Avoid the use of varying forms of <u>Spelling and Word Division</u>, as: year-book (hyphen), yearbook (one word) and year book[1] (two words); the last form is best. Endeavour to be both correct and consistent in the spelling of your 'Authorities', but copy, punctuate, and quote your sources <u>exactly</u>. Pay particular attention to the uniform use of -ise and -ize.[2,3]

<u>Types</u>. The use of <u>italics</u> should be confined to foreign words and phrases, to titles of books cited <u>in the text</u>, and to give emphasis, e.g. in sub-headings; they should always be used for the titles of newspapers and periodicals, and often are for poetry.

The processes available for reproduction of <u>Illustrations,</u> maps, diagrams, etc. are so varied that the student should

---

1   In law, always Year Book.
2   HART: Rules...[472] p.12–4.
3   COLLINS: Authors'...[462] p.193–4.

re-read Chapter IX, and an author should consult his publisher or printer. Line (Black and White) Drawings should be drawn on Strathmore pro-ply, plate-finish, Bristol board, or equivalent, in undiluted, black, waterproof drawing ink, e.g. Higgins, and be made about twice the size intended for the finished reproduction. Keep separate from the text all those illustrations requiring the making of blocks, e.g. line-blocks, wood-engravings, or half-tones. They must be numbered consecutively according to the order in which they are to be used. In the text itself clearly mark where each illustration is to appear. They should bear on the back the author's name. Their captions, legends, or under-lines can well be typed on a sheet (or sheets) and a number can be given to each corresponding to the number given to each original. With unmounted photographs it is very important to remember that any writing should be done lightly with a very soft pencil. Any indentation, however slight, will be likely to show as a blemish in the reproduction. Glossy black prints are better than 'art' photographs on rough or mat papers.

From the Typescript to the Printer.
Unwin[1] lists eleven "Points raised by the printer".

---

1   UNWIN: Truth...[498] p.39.

Co-operation between author and typist could obviate most of them, though publishers will still follow a certain, prescribed "House Style" unless instructed to the contrary.

"When type face; type size, and margins have been chosen provisionally, a <u>cast-off</u> can be made of the TS., which will be shown to make a book of x pages."[1]

Cast-off is very simply done in a rough and ready sort of way by counting the number of words on a few typical pages and multiplying their average by the total number of pages in the TS. But a printer will count the TS. word by word, or character by character, adding at the foot of each page the exact number of words, or characters occurring on each page; allow for blank spaces at the beginning and end of chapters; for half-and sectional title-pages; single-spaced material; footnotes; tables; exotic words; etc, etc. <u>Spacing</u> cannot be so finely differentiated on a typewriter as it can be by hand- or machine composition: whether tight or loose; and between letters, words, sentences, and paragraphs.

A <u>Specification</u> forms part of a contract. Only a complete tabulation of the processes described in these chapters would cover all the variable factors that should be submitted, in fairness, to printers tendering for an identical work.

---

1   SIMON: Introduction...[173] p.23.

PRACTICAL AUTHORSHIP: SPECIFICATION

Here we can only summarize the essentials:

Publisher (if not given in the letterhead) ...
Printer.   Name:
           Address:

Author:
Title:
Price:
Copy: MS., TS., or Letterpress.

Approximate number of words. Language.

Edition to consist of ... copies.
Number of Pages (approx...)
Paper Stock: Make, Weight.
Printing Process.
    Setting: Hand, or Machine; Type Face. Point Size; Format[1]; Margins; Leading.
    Style: Spacing. Headings: Size, Position, etc.
    Illustrations: Number. Kind: Line, Half-tones, Inks, Coloured, etc.
Proofs. Corrections.
Binding: Material. Style. Sewing. Trimming. Lettering.
Dummy: Specimen pages (Samples of Paper, Type, Casing, etc.)
Delivery Date. Mailing. Standing Type.

---

1   format (-ah) shape & size of book, as: crown 8vo (7½" x 5") post 4to (10" x 8"). "All departures from standard sizes...involve the special making of the paper..." (Unwin: Truth...[498] p.114)

Type Differentiation.

Quotations or Extracts in a book are often set in type a size smaller than the main text, or with different "leading" or indention, when they must begin a new line, for the smaller type is seldom part of a line of the larger text-type. Footnotes are still contained within the type area, and set in a size two points smaller than the text size; likewise the index, and the captions to illustrations, and each caption should bear a number for ready reference when the illustrations are of a documentary nature.

Preface and Introduction. It is often expedient to introduce some moderate typographical difference between introductory pages and the text. This can be most happily achieved by setting these pages in type a size smaller than that used for the text; likewise the Appendix, Author's Notes, Glossary, and Bibliography.

Half- and sectional title-pages, a glossary, a vocabulary, or an index should...begin on a recto.[1]

Proof Correction Marks will be found in B.S.1219:1945 [467]; Collins[2]; Hart[3], and elsewhere. All corrections are to be

---

1 SIMON: Introduction...[173] p.80–7.
2 COLLINS: Authors'...[462] p.313.
3 HART: Rules...[472] p.128–9.

made in ink, and attention called to them in the margin - the left one for errors occurring left of an imaginary centre line of the galley proof, or page, and right for the others. All punctuation marks, as full stops, etc. are to be encircled. Do not be disturbed either by a "slug" turned upside down, and which prints in the page proof like a black smudge; or, by a "turned letter", showing as two black marks. The first is a "make-line" indication, and the second to show that no type of the right letter is available at the moment.

The most frequently occurring of printer's errors ("literals") is the use of the small figure 1 instead of the lower-case letter i. Note, however, that in some type faces, e.g. Bembo, Garamond, and Scotch Roman, the lower-case (l.c.) letter i, following the letter f, is not dotted: in Rembo this is a distinctive feature; in Garamond and Scotch Roman, because it is ligatured.

The page proof follows the galley proof. Read through and check all galley corrections and the page sequence; see that all pages are of the correct length; and ensure the correct placing of running headlines. The verso pages usually carry the title of the book, and the recto the chapter, but chapter heading as verso and topical heading as recto is preferable, though frequently more expensive to arrange. If the job has been lino-set, carefully check the whole line which will necessarily have been recast in making even one correction in it.

Particularly watch for the transposition of lines, and continuity from page to page, and for indistinct lines of type. See that ends of lines are not damaged, or out of alinement; that footnotes correspond with their markings in the text; that there are no drop-outs; or wrong fount (w.f.) types remaining, and no broken letters; that the illustrations, figures, tables, etc. are in their correct positions; and remember that the pages are now filled in on the lists of contents and illustrations. Already the student has no doubt discovered for himself that proof-reading should be rationed in the interests both of his eyes and of accuracy.

It is only at the page proof stage that the Index can be compiled, and the late Canon Gould said[1] "An index should be imposed by law upon the author of any factual work of over 50 pages." Model indexes occur in the Cook and Wedderburn Ruskin; in the 3v. edition of Morley's Life of Gladstone, and elsewhere.

Is the Index to be short, medium, or full? Its purpose is to facilitate reference, therefore, put yourself in the user's place. To avoid disappointment it will have to assume analytical scope so, in addition to 'main' entries, the added, secondary ones must also include: Catchwords (First words, Important, Informative, or Keywords); Form entries; Names (Corporate, as Societies; Individual, as Authors, Editors, Illustrators,

---

1   GOULD: Author...[480] p.23.

Translators; and Place-names); Series; Specific, Subject (Topical) entries; and Titles.

A single, comprehensive, alphabetical index is generally preferred rather than a main index supplemented by one or more classified ones.* Write out <u>neatly all</u> the entries on 3" x 5" cards or stiff slips, on one side only, and with only one entry to a card, using a style consistent regarding capitalization, indention, and punctuation. "A printer will usually accept a batch of slips if they are neatly written and carefully ordered"[1] otherwise, ingratiate yourself with the typist, for if your MS. entries are illegible to her, the printer will be still more at sea.

PUBLISHING AND BOOKSELLING.

> "I hold every man a debtor to his profession... to be a help and ornament thereunto."[2]

The publisher forms the link between author, printer, bookseller, and the public. As the multiplier of MSS he was already known in classical Rome. But systematic copying then disappeared until Alcuin organized <u>scriptora</u> for Charlemagne (781). For many centuries the publisher was indistinguishable from either the bookseller or the printer. The term <u>stationarii</u> appears for

---

* cf. Letters of Samuel Johnson...ed. by R.W. Chapman. Oxford: Clarendon Pr. 1953. 3v., with <u>seven</u> Indexes occupying 150 pages!
1 (1) CAREY: Making...[469] p.13.
2 (2) BACON.

the first time in connexion with bookshops (1259) at the University of Bologna. The word stationer originally meant a bookseller who had a station, or stand, i.e. he was a shopkeeper as distinguished from a pedlar, or colporteur. About the year 1500 the booksellers organized themselves into separate guilds. The printer-publisher, on the other hand, flourished in the 15 and 16 centuries.[1] Publishing as a trade separate from printing began in the mid-seventeenth century. "About 1730 there grew up a regular system of taking shares in a new book..."[2] To-day a publisher is seldom the owner of a printing plant, and only occasionally is he himself a bookseller.

The aesthetic part of book designing by the publisher falls into the next chapter. When a MS. is received, and backed up by a favourable opinion from his "reader", the publisher will invite quotations from those printers whose facilities he knows will best suit the new title. Similarly his binder will be asked to conform to the standards expected of him.

Though the Relations of Publisher and Author lie beyond the scope of these Notes, we must just set down the main points: Agreements and contracts; the Royalty System; Authors copies; Oversea rights, American and 'Colonial' editions; Rights of

---

1   BÜHLER: Aldus Manutius. (Pap.bibliogr.Soc.Amer. 44(3)205–15, 1951)
2   ESDAILE: Student's...[34] p.121.

translation, Film and Serial rights; arrangements about Re-issues, from standing type, Monotype spools, plates, or by photography; cheaper editions; Publishers Guild Books[1]; Reprint rights (e.g. Everyman's Encyclopaedia from Dent @ 14/- to the Readers Union @ 7/6 per volume) etc.

Relations with the Bookseller.

The Publishers' Association and the Associated Booksellers. The Net Book Agreement (1899). Library discount control. The bookseller is the publisher's distributor and his main agent, selling for him on sale or return, or on consignment, and receiving from 10 to 40 per cent. and more discount. "Remainders" and Second-hand copies; the antiquarian trade.

Coöperative publicity: Advertising in literary periodicals and newspapers; Blurbs, Broadcasting, Cards, Catalogues, Exhibitions; Posters, Prospectuses, Trade lists, Window displays. Other means of advertising and distribution include: Complimentary and Review copies; Advance copies and Dummies; Canvassing for orders by Travellers (in Town and the Provinces); Subscription books[2] at pre-publication prices. The Publishers' Association Export Research Service, and Oversea agents.

---

1   SIMON: British Publishers Guild. (Brit.Bk News. 80:169–71, 1947)
2   SHORES: Subscription books & library reviews. (A.L.A.Bull. 42(13)606–9,1948)
    See also [826]

COPYRIGHT.

The early 'copyrights' expressed the literal meaning of the words and were denoted by the words cum privilegio on the title-page. Works sanctioned by the Roman Catholic Church still receive the imprimatur, or approval, of her authorities (usually recorded on the back of the title-page).[1] The King's Printer, and the Oxford and Cambridge University presses hold monopolies for printing The Bible and the English Prayer Book.

A. Copyright - International.

The Berne Convention, 1886, revised in 1896, again in 1908 at Berlin, at Rome in 1928, and in 1948 at Brussels, provided for a uniform system of copyright. Article 4 of the Convention reads:

> "Authors who are citizens of any of the countries of the [Copyright] Union shall enjoy in countries other than the country of origin for their works, whether unpublished or first published in a country of the Union, the rights which the respective laws grant to natives."

Forty-one states are parties to the Berne Convention; the important abstaining countries are China, Russia, and the U.S.A.

The President of the Board of Trade has announced the appointment of a Committee

---

1 BURKE, Redmond A: What is the index? Milwaukee: Bruce (1952)

"to consider and report whether any, and if so, what changes are desirable in the law relating to copyright in literary...works; with particular regard to technical developments, and to the revised International Convention for the Protection of Literary and Artistic Works signed at Brussels in June 1948, and to consider and report on related matters."[1]

A Universal Copyright Convention, under the auspices of UNESCO, is to be signed in 1952.

B. Copyright - Great Britain.
The first section of the 1911 Act lays down the area of the operation of copyright as being:

"in every original literary, dramatic, musical, and artistic work; and copyright as being: the sole right to produce or reproduce the work or any substantial part thereof in any material form whatsoever",

and the essence of the subject lies in this statutory definition.

Copyright subsists automatically without registration...if (a) in the case of a published work it was first published within such parts of His Majesty's Dominions to which the Act extends, and (b) in the case of an unpublished work the author was...a British subject or resident within such...Dominions... There is no statutory obligation that a copyright work should bear any indication that it is copyright.[2]

---

1 (The Author. 61(4)118 Summer 1951)
2 cf. the U.S.A. law.

The first English Copyright Act was the Statute of 1709 (8 Anne cap.19). The Act of 1842 (5 & 6 Vict.cap.45) gave copyright for the period of 42 years from the date of publication, or until 7 years after the author's death, whichever was the longer. This Act, in turn, was replaced by the Act of 1911 (1 & 2 Geo.V. cap.46). It effected three momentous changes: 1. It increased the period of copyright to the life of the author and 50 years after his death...; 2. It tacitly abolished the Stationers' Hall Register...and so terminated[1] those records that had been kept since 1557; 3. The act altered the nature of the perpetual common law right of an author...in an unpublished work...for its definition of copyright includes the right...to publish.[2,3]

("The Stationers' Company was incorporated by Royal charter in 1557. No-one, not a member of the Company, might print anything for sale in the kingdom unless authorized by special privilege or patent. Moreover, by the rules of the Company, every member was required to enter in the register of the Company the name of any book that he desired to print, so that these registers furnish valuable information regarding printed matter during the latter part of the 16th century. The Company's control of the printing trade waned during the 17th century, to be revived, in a modified form, under the Copyright Act of 1709").[4]

---

1 actually not till 31 December 1923.
2 SKONE JAMES: Copyright law in the British Empire. (Brit. Bk News. 112:181–6,1949)
3 MACKINNON: Notes on the history of English copyright. (In Harvey: Oxford companion to English literature; 3ed. 1946. p.881–90)
4 (ib. p.747)

"There is still in existence a Register established by the Stationers' Company at Stationers' Hall, London, in which Books and "Fine Arts" can be registered. This Register is not a continuation of the former one, and is not kept pursuant to any statute. The entries made therein are for the purpose of record, and for assisting in the proof of the existence of a work on a given date in the case of infringement... "Registered at Stationers' Hall" may be added to any registered work... A copy of every work for which registration is desired must be filed with the Registrar...& certified copies of the entries...are issued."[1]

Delivery of Copies to Libraries. The practice dates from 1666. After changes in the number of copies involved and in the names of the benefitting libraries, the Act of 1911 (Sect. 15) finally requires from the publisher the delivery of copies to: 1. The British Museum; 2. The Bodleian Library, Oxford; 3. The Cambridge University Library; 4. The Advocates' Library[2], Edinburgh; 5. The Library of Trinity College, Dublin; and 6. The National Library of Wales, Aberystwyth. A copy of every book must be sent to the British Museum, within one month of publication, but to the other libraries only those for which a demand...is made within a year of publication... Publication means "the issue of copies of the work to the public." The copy delivered to the British Museum shall be a copy finished in the same manner as the best copies of the book are published;

---

1 Master Print.Annu. 1937. p.494.
2 The 'National Library of Scotland' is substituted for the 'Advocates' Library' by 15 & 16 Geo.V. cap.73.

copies delivered to the other libraries shall be on the paper on which the largest number of copies of the book is printed...and shall be in the like condition as the books prepared for sale. By regulations under the British Museum Act of 1932 some classes of publications need not be sent unless demanded, e.g. those in the nature of calendars, time tables, and trade publications.

Duration. The term for which copyright subsists is normally the life of the author and 50 years after his death. But at the expiration of 25 years from death anyone may reproduce the work for sale on condition of giving notice to the...owner of the copyright...and of paying him 10 per cent. of the published price.

Infringement.

"An important point to be remembered is that there is no infringement unless the matter copied constitutes a substantial part of the publication. This does not necessarily mean a large part. To use the vital section'of a work may prejudice the sale of the original book, although the actual quantity ['lifted'] is small."[1]

No action in respect of infringement of copyright is to be brought after the expiration of 3 years after the infringement (Sect.10).

"Fair Copying" not Infringement. The Act contains a number of exceptions to the general rule. They constitute statutory

---

1   CLOUTMAN: Law...[503] p.103.

defences to an action for infringement of copyright. "Fair dealing" is by far the most important exception. Section 2–[1]

> "Copyright in a work shall be deemed to be in fringed by any person who, without the consent of the owner of the Copyright, does anything the sole right to do which is by this Act conferred on the owner of the copyright: Provided that the following act(s) shall not constitute an infringement of copyright:- [1] Any fair dealing with any work for the purposes of private study, research, criticism, review, or newspaper summary."

As far back as 1935 an agreement on "fair use" of copyright material was signed between the National Association of Book Publishers (now the Book Publishers Bureau) and the [U.S.A.] Joint Committee on Materials for Research... In England,

> "anticipating a demand for microfilmed editions of out-of-print books, the Society of Authors and the Publishers' Association, in consultation with Aslib, issued a "Joint memorandum on microfilms and copyright..."[1]

The following notes are taken from the Fair Copying Declaration.[2]

> "For some time scientists have discussed the problems, created by the Copyright Act, which arise when they wish to obtain reproductions of excerpts from scientific and technical periodical publications... It is assumed that they [scientists] take all reasonable steps to secure the original journals or separates of papers they require... This Declaration does not apply to books and other non-periodic or non-serial publications...

---

1 Bookseller 27 July 1944.
2 Royal Society. Information Services Committee, June 1950.
   See also S.Afr.Libr. 14(2)43–4 Oct.1946; 17(1)45–6,1949; 18(1)29–30,1950; 19(1)16,1951.

We will regard it as fair dealing for the purpose of private study or research when a non-profit making organization, such as a library, archives office, museum or information service, owning or handling scientific or technical periodicals published by us makes and delivers a <u>single</u> reproduction of a part of an issue thereof to a person or his agent representing in writing that he desires such reproduction in lieu of a loan or annual transcription and that he requires it solely for the purpose of private study, research, criticism or review, and that he undertakes not to sell or reproduce for publication the copy supplied, provided:

1. The recipient of the copy is given notice that he is liable for infringement of copyright by misuse of the copy, and that it is illegal to use the copy for any further reproduction.
2. The organization making and furnishing the copy does so without profit to itself.
3. Proper acknowledgement is given to the publication from which the copy is made.
4. Not more than one copy of any one excerpt shall be furnished to any one person.

The exemption from liability of the library, archives office, museum or information service hereon provided shall extend to every officer, agent or employee of such organization in the making and delivery of such reproduction when acting within the scope of his authority of employment. This exemption for the organization itself carries with it a responsibility to see that employees caution those receiving copies against the misuse of material reproduced. We reserve the right to take action against any person or organization copying or misusing for any purpose whatever the whole or part of a work published by us without abiding by the conditions laid down herein unless the person or organization has our special permission in respect of the item to be copied. We reserve the right to withdraw this declaration."

There follows the List of (118) Subscribers to The Fair Copying Declaration, 1 May 1950, and the List of Journals covered by the Subscribers.

> "When original sources are properly acknowledged, the author will be acquitted of literary dishonesty; but this may not free him of liability for damages..."[1]

In case of doubt secure permission from the copyright owner; ask yourself: Am I injuring sale in quantities?; and never reproduce a thing so that the reader will not have to buy or borrow the whole book. All libraries lay down conditions on which photoduplication is done. The following are extracted from The Library of Congress 'Order for Photoduplication':

1. The Library will make photoduplicates of materials in its collections available for research use. It performs such service solely for research and in lieu of loan of the material in question or in place of manual transcription.
2. All responsibility in the use made of the photo-duplicates is assumed by applicant.
3. Copyright material will ordinarily not be copied without the signed authorisation of the copyright owner...
5. Payment in advance is required...
6. The Library reserves the right to decline to make photoduplicates requested...

Stamped in large letters on the back of L.C. photostats appears the following notice:

> "Copyright material. Not to be further reproduced without permission of the copyright owner."

---

1 CLOUTMAN: Law...[503] p.104.

Publication.

"For purposes of Copyright a work is <u>published</u> even if printed copies are gratuitously distributed to the public but, if the work is issued for <u>private circulation</u> only, it appears that it is not published."[1]

Theses.

"...Opinion in university libraries is...practically unanimous that the copyright is not held by the university, but by the author."[2]

A further object of the 1911 Act was to assimilate the law of copyright throughout the British Empire (now Commonwealth) and to that end the Act provides that, where any self-governing dominions accept its provisions, copyright relations with such dominions shall be in accordance with the system of the Berne Convention.

C. <u>Copyright in South Africa.</u>[3,4]

International convention for the protection of literary and artistic works. - Adherence of the Union thereto.

Proclamation No.32 of 1936, in <u>Govt Gazette</u> No.2335, of 14 February 1936, to form part of the Patents, Designs, Trade Marks and Copyright Act, 1916, provides for the application of the British Copyright Act of 1911, and the Rome Convention of

---

1 CLOUTMAN: Law...[503] p.99.
2 PAFFORD: University theses. (<u>J.Docum.</u> 7(2)121,June 1951)
3 SWEMMER: Some aspects of copyright. <u>S.Afr.Libr.</u> 10(2)25–30,1942)
4 UNGERER: Copyright law in South Africa & the four copyright libraries. (ib. 3(2)31–9,1935)

1928 to the Union of South Africa.

Act to consolidate and Amend the Laws relating to...Copyright, No.9 of 1916, as Amended by Act No.22 of 1950.

Delivery of Books for Libraries.

Sect.150.(1). The publishers of every book first published in the Union and whether printed therein or not, shall, within one month after the day on which such book is first delivered out of the press for issue, deliver free of any charge, bound, sewed, or stitched on the best paper and in the best manner in which such book is issued, one copy to the Trustees of the British Museum, and one copy each to the authority having control of each of the following libraries, namely, [1] the Library of the Parliament of the Union of South Africa, Cape Town, [2] the South African Public Library, Cape Town, [3] the Library of the Natal Society, Pietermaritzburg, [4] the State Library, Pretoria, and [5] the Bloemfontein Public Library.

"...Of these libraries only the [South African Public Library & the State Library] are able to fulfil the obligation, implied in the privilege, of preserving all the material received. The Committee is of opinion that two copyright libraries are sufficient for the Union, & recommends that the Copyright Act be amended so as to restrict full copyright privileges to the two national libraries, while giving the other two libraries mentioned the right to receive one free copy of such Union publications as they may wish to have, on application to the publishers within three months of the date of publication."[1]

This recommendation has not been adopted. On the contrary, a fifth South African library, The Library of Parliament, was added on 6 May 1950 to the list of copyright libraries, thus

---

1   UNION of South Africa. Interdepartmental Committee on the Libraries of the Union: Report.1937. C.T: Cape Times 1937. p.21.

creating the anomalous and extravagant situation of two libraries within hailing distance of one another, now needlessly burdening themselves and the publishers with commitments that neither can afford.

In the case of an encyclopaedia, newspaper, review, magazine, or work published in series of numbers or parts, the delivery prescribed by this section includes all numbers or parts of the work which may be subsequently published.

(2). Any publisher who fails to comply with this section shall be liable on conviction to a fine not exceeding five pounds and the value of the book, and the fine shall be paid to the trustees or authority to whom the book ought to have been delivered.

(3). For the purposes of this section, a certificate given under the hand of the librarian of a benefitting library that a book has not been received shall be sufficient evidence of the facts stated in the certificate.

(4). For the purposes of this section the expression "book" includes every part or division of a book, pamphlet, sheet of letterpress, sheet of music, map, plan, chart or table separately published, but shall not include any second or subsequent edition of a book unless such edition contains additions or alterations either in the letterpress or in maps, prints or other engravings belonging thereto.

The British Museum.

"Under the Books Registry Act of 1888, 'Four... copies of the whole of every book which shall be printed or lithographed in this Colony [Cape of Good Hope]...shall...be delivered free of any charge...to such officer as the Governor shall...appoint...one of such copies shall be delivered to the Librarian of the South African Public Library, & another to the Grahamstown Public Library, & the remaining copies shall be disposed of as the Governor shall direct.' It is interesting to note that, by courtesy of successive Governors, a copy of every book received under this Act is sent to the British Museum."[1]

Under the first Copyright Act in England (1709) it was essential in order to secure protection to have a work registered at Stationers' Hall. Further, section 6 of Act No. 4–1888 (Cape of Good Hope): "To provide for the <u>Preservation</u> of copies of books printed in this Colony and for the <u>Registration</u> of such books" reads:

> "<u>A transcript of the entries</u> registered in the registry book either under this Act or under the Copyright Act of 1873 shall be prepared quarterly by the Registrar of Deeds, and <u>shall be forthwith published in the Gazette</u>."[2]

Some 8,000 items were entered in the Deeds Registry Office between 1874 and 1916.[3]

Under the main Union Act (1916) copyright subsists automatically and without registration with the Registrar of Deeds; provision is made for registration, but very few registrations are being made, and the majority of these are for musical and artistic works.[4]

---

1   DYER: Public library systems. Kimberley 1903. p.41.
2   cf. <u>UNION Gaz</u>. 16(497)413–5, 24 Apr.1914. Notice No.499)
3   The British Museum and University of the Witwaterstand Library have copies of the Transcript of the Copyright Register from 1894–1901.
4   UNGERER: - Copyright law in South Africa. (<u>S.Afr.Libr</u>. 3:31–9 1935)

There is no statutory obligation on the copyright libraries either to preserve or to catalogue the publications deposited with them; indeed it is well-known that two of these libraries are unable to do so. It seems highly desirable that the Act[1] be amended:

(a) To make registration, including statement of price, compulsory;
(b) To compel nos. [2] and [4] to catalogue and <u>preserve</u> all South African publications received;
(c) In respect of libraries nos. [3] and [5] to substitute a selective claim on the publishers;
(d) To arrange for the Registrar, in co-operation with the South African Public Library and the State Library, to publish a monthly list of material received under the Act. Such a list issued, say, monthly, and circulated to all libraries could be used by them for ordering printed catalogue cards from the Central Library.

The State Library already issues useful mimeographed monthly lists, but these are necessarily incomplete until the Act is revised.

Annual, and five-yearly cumulations would carry the scheme to its logical, and necessary conclusion.

D. <u>Copyright (U.S.A.)</u>.[2]

"...The Constitution does not establish copyrights, but provides that Congress shall have the power

---

1 UNION of South Africa: Act no.9 1916, sections 141–60.
2 DE WOLF: Note on American copyright law. (<u>In</u> Harvey: Oxford companion to English literature; 3ed. 1946. p.891–906)

to grant such rights...not primarily for the benefit of the author, but...for the benefit of the public... [It] is believed...it will stimulate writing and invention to give some bonus to authors and inventors..."[1]

Copyright Code. Title 17 - Copyrights - U.S. Code. Being the Act approved 30 July 1947, Public Law 281, 80 Congress, chap. 391, 1 Session (H[ouse of] R[epresentatives] 2,083)

Sect.5. Classification of Works for Registration ... (a) Books... (b) Periodicals.
Sect.10. Publication of Work with Notice.
Sect.11. Registration of Claim and Issuance of Certificate.
Sect.13. Deposit of Copies after Publication; ... there shall be promptly deposited...two complete copies of the best edition...or if the work is by an author...of a foreign state...one...copy... No action...shall be maintained for infringement... until the provisions...with respect to the deposit of copies and registration...shall have been complied with. [It is not essential that the deposit be made on the very day of publication... Books, Periodicals...cannot be registered until after they have been published]. (See 1949 Amendment)
Sect.16. (Manufacturing Provisions). Mechanical work to be done in United States...the text of all copies...shall be printed from typeset...or from plates made...or by a process wholly performed...and the printing of the text and binding of the said book shall be performed within the limits of the United States.
Provided however, that said requirements

---

1 From: Rep.No.2,222, 60th Congress, 2nd Session, 22nd Feb. 1909, accompanying the bill embodying the present Act of March 4 1909. (Howell: Copyright...[510] p.220)

	shall not apply to works in raised characters for the use of the blind, or to books of foreign origin in a language other than English, or to books published abroad in the English language seeking <u>ad interim</u> protection...
Sect.17.	<u>Affidavit</u> (attesting their domestic manufacture) <u>to accompany Copies.</u>
Sect.19.	Notice, Form.

The notice of copyright required by Sect.10...shall consist either of the word 'copyright' or the abbreviation 'Copr.', accompanied by the name of the copyright proprietor and, if the work be...printed, the Notice shall include also the year in which the copyright was secured by publication...thus, 'Copyright, 19- [the year of publication] (by) A.B.' [the name of the claimant]. "The inclusion of additional words or phrases, e.g. 'All Rights Reserved', adds nothing to the sum total of the rights secured...provided the essential elements are present. The word 'by' is not essential."

Sect.20.	Notice [Position] of Application...

The notice...shall be applied...upon its title-page or the page immediately following...[i.e. the verso].

Sect.22.	Ad Interim Protection of Book Published Abroad. (201(16)). Affidavit for <u>ad interim</u> Term.

In the case of a foreign author applying for a book in the English language, the same affidavit must be made as in that of an American author, except where a book is deposited for <u>ad interim</u> protection... In such cases the affidavit must be filed when the <u>ad interim</u> copyright is sought to be extended to the full term by the publication of an edition printed in the United States. (See 1949 Amendment of Sect.22.)

Sect.23.	Extension to Full Term. (See 1949 Amendment).

Duration; Renewal and Extension. ...in default of the registration of such application for renewal...the copyright on any work shall determine at the expiration of 28 years from first publication.

Sect.25.   Renewal...
             ...application...within one year prior to the expiration of the original term of 28 years.
Sect.26.   Terms Defined.
             ..."the date of publication" shall in the case of a work of which copies are reproduced for sale or distribution be held to be the earliest date when copies of the first authorized edition were placed on sale, sold, or publicly distributed by the proprietor of the copyright...
Sect.107.   Importation...of Piratical Copies, or of Copies not Produced in Accordance with Sect.16...is prohibited...Provided, however...such prohibition shall not apply...(d) To any book published abroad... when imported under the circumstances stated... when imported...not for sale, not more than one copy of any such book in any one invoice...for any... college, university, or free public library in the United States...
Sect.201.   Copyright Office...
             All records relating to copyrights...shall be kept...in the Copyright Office, Library of Congress...
Sect.201(3). Registration.
             Promptly after the publication of any work entitled to copyright, the claimant should register his claim in the Copyright Office... [cf. Sect.11 and 13]. A certificate of registration is issued to the claimant and duplicates...may be obtained...fee...$1.00.
Sect.201(16). (See Sect.22).
             Notice of Change in the Copyright Law of the United States of America.
             On 30 June 1949 H.R.2285 became effective as Public Law 84, amending S ect.16, 22, 23, and 215 of Title 17 of the United States Code.
             Public Law 84 relates to works published outside of the United States and has the following provisions:

1. It offers an alternative to the requirement of the deposit of one copy of the work, an application for registration, and a $4 fee. The alternative is the deposit of two copies of the book, musical composition or other work, an application and a catalog card, but no fee. Regulations relating to the catalog card will be issued. The alternative can be availed of only if the required items reach the Copyright Office in acceptable form within 6 months after first publication.
2. It extends the period for <u>ad interim</u> registration of a book or periodical in the English language from 60 days to 6 months after first publication abroad. It extends the period for the manufacture of such a book or periodical in the United States from 4 months after registration to 5 years after first publication abroad.
3. It permits the importation into the United States of 1,500 copies, in one or more shipments, of a book or periodical of foreign origin in the English language during the 5 years after first publication abroad. This privilege applies only to works that have already been registered under the new law for <u>ad interim</u> copyright within six months of publication and is in addition to the copies allowed to be imported by other provisions of the copyright law. The Copyright Office is working on regulations to facilitate such importations.
<u>Books or periodicals so imported must bear a valid United States copyright notice.</u>

Dr Luther Evans [680, p.46–7] ..."I should personally prefer to see the manufacturing clause corrected by simple and total elimination from our statute...Failing that I would at least expect to secure support for a revision of Section 16 of Title 17.U.S.C. which would permit the importation of editions of works in English up to the number of 2,000 to test our market, to give our citizens the benefit of access to English scientific and scholarly works, and to revise and clarify that language of the present law which may penalize failure to manufacture within the <u>ad interim</u> period with loss of all copyright as well as merely constituting a restriction on importations."

Copyright Entry and the Printed Catalogue Card. It was R.R. Bowker in 1897 when the L.C. was about to move into its new quarters in Washington, who first voiced a practical plan for using the national library as a distributing bureau for cataloguing items:

> "For a fee of 50 cents additional to a like fee for copyright entry, the Register of Copyrights is obliged to return a record of copyright, and it is the practice of copyright proprietors to pay the double fee and obtain the record in all cases. If, in the new development, it should be arranged that this record shall take the shape of a printed card for catalog entry, and if duplicates of such cards could be supplied to subscribing libraries, a great step forward in practical bibliography would be made."[1]

E. Cognate Legislation.

Censorship. The present Law of the Press and Drama. (Great Britain) The following are the chief heads under which the law to-day punishes the publication of illegal matter: 1. Libel as a civil injury; 2. Libel as a criminal offence; 3. Infringement of copyright; 4. Slander of property; 5. Contempt of Parliament or Court. [6] Dramatic Performances.[2]

---

1 Libr.J. 22:387,1897.
2 FISHER, Jos.R., & Strahan, Jas.A: The law of the press. Clowes 1898.

(Great Britain) Public Bodies Corrupt Practices Act 1889.

Prevention of Corruption Act 1906.

(Union) " " " " A.4-1918.

Designed to prevent the practice of giving secret commissions.

Customs Act. A.35-44.
    Sect.21. Prohibited Goods.

    (1) The following goods are...prohibited...
        (f) goods which are indecent or obscene or on any ground whatsoever objectionable;
        (g) unlawful reproductions of any works which are copyright...
    Sect.21.(2) In the event of any question arising as to whether any goods are indecent or obscene or objectionable, the decision of the Minister...shall be final: Provided that in respect of printed, engraved, lithographic and photographic matter the decision shall be given after consultation with the Board of Censors appointed in terms of sub-section (1) of section two of the Entertainments (Censorship) Act No.28 of 1931: Provided further that if any printed, engraved, lithographic or photographic matter is according to the decision of the said Minister indecent, obscene or objectionable...he may by notice in two consecutive issues of the Gazette publish the name of such publication and every issue...shall...be deemed to be indecent, obscene or objectionable...
    Sect.133. Objectionable Literature.
        Any person who sells, offers, or keeps for sale, or distributes or exhibits any issue of any publication in respect of which a notice has been issued under sub-section (2) of section twenty-one and which has

not been withdrawn, shall be guilty of an offence and liable on conviction to a fine not exceeding £200 or to imprisonment...or to both...fine and imprisonment.

Schedules.

1. Customs Tariff. Class XI. Books...

Item 284 Books, printed, and printed music, newspapers and periodicals...and which are not foreign, unauthorized prints of any British or Union copyright work the importation of which is prohibited... Free of duty.

Item 296(8)(ii): Catalogues, price lists and trade publications of firms or persons having no established place of business in the Union, and no permanent agent holding stocks in the Union. Free of duty.

Printer's Imprint.
(Great Britain)
Newspapers, Printers and Reading Rooms.
Repeal Act, 1869.
Second Schedule: Every person printing any paper or book for publication or dispersal is to print his name and address on the first or last leaf.
The back of the title-page carries other than bibliographical information. As Sir Stanley Unwin says[1]

"Here are to be found such notices as: 'All Rights Reserved', or 'Copyright in the U.S.A.', and last, but not least in importance, the printer's imprint, preceded by the words: 'Printed'; or, as some people prefer it: 'Made in Great Britain', or

---

1 Truth...[498] p.121–2,193–9.

whatever the country of production may be...It is the import or export of copies without the country of origin being clearly printed upon them that brings the fact home and gives the inexperienced publisher his first acquaintance with the Merchandise Marks Act or American customs regulations."

Booksellers in the U.S.A. stamp the following warning on all their orders to oversea firms:

"All books must be stamped with the country of origin: 'Printed in...'; otherwise a 10 per cent, fine will be collected by the U.S. Customs, and must be charged to your account. Also stamp wrapper."

Under this Act of 1869, every printer is required to preserve for six months a copy of every paper he prints, and to write on it the name and address of the person who employed him, (Cloutman: Law...[503] p.72)

(Union) A.14–1934. <u>Newspaper and Imprint Act.</u> Provides for the compulsory registration of all newspapers published in the Union, and for the inclusion of an imprint, sect.7,

"whereby the full and correct name of the printer and the full and correct address at which he conducts his business...are indicated, &c."

The Act, however, makes no mention of the inclusion of the <u>date</u> of printing or publication. As the outcome of representations made to the Minister of the Interior, the following communication, dated

20 July 1934, has been received from the Secretary for the Interior:

"I have to inform you that the Executive Council of the Federation of Master Printers of South Africa has intimated its agreement with the Minister's request that the date of publication be included as part of the imprint on books, pamphlets, etc., & the General Secretary states that a notice to this effect is being sent to all members of the Federation."[1]

Postal Rates.
For Newspapers; Printed Papers; and <u>Literature for the Blind.</u> [See latest 'Post Office Guide'].

Railage.
South African Railways.
Official Tariff Book; [latest]
160. Articles transported at half parcels rates,
(b) Books, printed, of a literary nature...

Printers' Contracts.
There are thirteen <u>Standard Conditions</u> and recognized Customs of the printing trade as issued by the British Federation of Master Printers, and adopted (1947) by the F.M.P. of South Africa. These Conditions should be printed, without alteration, either on the back of the quotation, or

---

1 <u>S.Afr.Libr.</u> 2:66 1934.

the letterhead, and to which the printer should direct the attention of his customer. No.10, concerning Periodical Publications, reads as follows:

> "In the absence of any agreement to the contrary, estimates are given upon the condition that not less than three months' notice is given to terminate the contract for the printing of monthly publications, and not less than one month's notice in the case of weekly publications."[1]

Printers' Liability for Customers' Property.
Law of 'Bailment'.

> "A bailee is a person who accepts goods in custody from another person. Authors, 'editors', and publishers' difficulties usually arise in connexion with MSS, and printers' difficulties usually over plates sent to them for use on a printing job, or from lost or damaged 'copy'." (Cloutman: Law...[503] p.61-9)

BOOK-COLLECTING.

> "Encourage collecting - if more people had hobbies there would be less crime."[2]

Book-collecting, as distinct from the formation of working libraries, began in 1536, prompted by 'book massacres' following the dissolution of the monasteries by Henry VIII. Patrons and scholars were aroused to the rescue and preservation of books.

---

1 The full Conditions may be found in Cloutman: Law...[503] p.28-30, & in the Master Print.Annu.
2 A sign at the Butterfly Store on Manhattan Island. Quoted in Winterich: Grolier...[604] p.36.

Outstanding examples of book-lovers of the Middle Ages and early Renaissance are: Richard de Bury, author of <u>Philobiblion</u> (1345), Leo X, who sent book-hunters all over Europe in search of MSS., and Aldus Manutius.

Sadleir[1] traces a rhythm in the tide of book-collecting from the beginning of the eighteenth century, which marked the rise of the aristocratic collectors, e.g. the Dukes of Devonshire and Roxburghe, through an era of less ostentatious collecting by scholars and antiquarians. With the nineteenth century book-collecting again became the sport of the wealthy, followed by the "Dibdin" period of frenzied speculation by fashionable collectors. It next became the quiet pursuit of genuine bibliophiles. In the mid-90's the third boom occurred and continued till the collapse of 1929.

<u>Aspects of Book-collecting</u>.

Book-collecting may be antiquarian, autocratic (O.W. Holmes), cultivated as a "gentle art", approached as an adventure, or suffered as an affliction; it may provoke atrocities, or fan 'a vice most glorious' and, as we have seen, it may have its fashions and (1) tendencies, its tastes and technique.

---

1 (<u>Libr.Ass.Rec</u>. 3s,3:331–42 Nov.1933)

Reasons and Uses for collecting. For the excitement on acquiring an unusual item: the reward of the bibliomaniac; as a medium of speculation; by friends, trustees, and librarians in order to benefit their libraries and the reading public; and finally as offering the interest, the joy, and the pleasure of a hobby. "Collect what you like, seeking neither profit nor applause..."[1] Whether guided by chronology, colour, or condition; by form, language, or size, e.g. miniature books, and broadsides. But have a definite aim, and a programme. "The best kind of book-collecting is such as is born of a collector's interest in a subject, or love for an author or group of authors.[2]

Condition is very important. Some collectors insist on 'mint', or perfect copies, in the state in which they were first issued: either bound in contemporary calf, or unbound and uncut, as the case may have been; certainly not "re-bound". The older copies must be free from "foxing", and the modern ones wrapped in their dust-jackets. "The caparisoning of books...bewitches the soul of the bibliophile... Nothing so fair as a comely book, and its comeliness is first apparent and last recalled in its outer seeming, where it"[(1)]

    Nimbly and sweetly recommends itself
    Unto our gentle sense[3]

---

1   JACKSON: Anatomy...[521] p.647, 376.
2   TURNBULL: Thrills of book-collecting [Charles Lamb]. (S.Afr.Libr. 5(1)1–15 July 1937)
3   Macbeth i.6.

Some "Mighty women book hunters" include: Diane de Poitiers, Isabella of Spain, Queen Elizabeth I, and Marie Antoinette. Hobbies for modest ladies might include: Christmas books; Books illustrated by an admired artist; Children's books from days gone by; Song books from many lands, etc. etc.

Association Copies are those that have been associated with famous men and women of the past, and may carry their autographs, or other inscriptions. Doubly interesting are those that were once the property of interesting people, or when a former owner was himself a collector of books.

The inner as opposed to the outer, physical form of certain items also has appeal, e.g. Almanacs, Chap-hooks, Penny Dreadfuls, Primers, Prognostications, and Yellowbacks. Local, or Special Collections are rather the responsibility than the recreation of their custodians, e.g. the huge Shakespeare Collection in the Birmingham Reference Library. On a still larger scale we have: Americana, Canadians, Africana, etc. with the appeal of locality.

Rarities and First Editions are not confined to titles issued only in limited editions, éditions de luxe, or even to first editions. Other circumstances may have operated, e.g. censorship, fire, and flood. These are not for the impecunious amateur. But to-day modern books, and particularly contemporary books are being actively, and enthusiastically collected, perhaps because their first editions are within the reach of everyone. Book-collecting has become democratic. Does anything remain for the newcomer, that "is despised and rejected of men"? A stray incunable may still crop up; items from some remote part of the world are for those that seek; neglected and forgotten books are everyman's quarry. In his "Sanctuary of Printing" Dr John Johnson now enjoys perusing the ephemera of typography that he began harvesting during a full life while still Printer to the University of Oxford.[1] The output of one of the (private) presses offers fun for the enthusiast; Bulmer, and Chiswick press items may still be found; South African missionary literature is far from exhausted. Is anyone interested in sartorial, or tonsorial literature, or facetiae?

A book-collector should acquire some essential qualifications. He should be, or become familiar with the physical side of book production, and add to that a knowledge of the science of book-collecting especially. The essential, basic qualities include: patience, common sense, a good memory, and a sense of beauty. Book-love lasts throughout life, it never flags or fails, but like beauty itself

> ...is a joy forever:
> Its loveliness increases; it will never
> Pass into nothingness; but still will keep
> A bower quiet for us, and a sleep
> Full of sweet dreams, and health, and quiet breathing."[2]

---

1 JACKSON: Printing...[537] p.251–64.
2 KEATS: Endymion I,1–5.

"A sense of beauty and fitness ought to be satisfied in the form and aspect of the books we read, as well as by their contents."[1]

XIII

MODERN FINE PRINTING

The result of book designing should be a book harmonious in its proportions and with some relation in its looks to its subject matter, this irrespective of whether it is produced by hand by a private press, or composed on a machine in a commercial printing office.[2]

The first designers of books were, of course, the printers themselves, but quite early in the history of printing, the publisher-printer appeared on the scene, and the distribution and financing of books gradually became divorced from their actual production. The various processes connected with bookmaking, e.g. binding, and the engraving of plates were done by specialist firms. Perhaps this is the reason why the nineteenth century was not a happy time for the art of the book, and perhaps the success in beauty, if not in money, of the earliest private presses and the revival of printing in the 90's derived

---

1 ARNOLD, M.
2 MEYNELL: A printer considers the book, (Monotype Rec. 32 (3)9–16, 1933)

from the fact that these presses were small enough to be supervised by one man. The typographic designer, the man who plans all details of the book before actual production begins is, however, only now entering his prime. Smaller houses have their publications planned by the publisher himself, and for some of the great publishers planning has been associated with expensive, private press books. One, if not the largest, of all publishing concerns in the United Kingdom: H.M.S.O., has only within recent years appointed Sir Francis Meynell as typographic adviser and, of course, with salutary results. Stanley Morison has been typographic adviser for various publishers for the last twenty to thirty years.

A prerequisite for a typographic adviser is a knowledge of the various processes of printing and illustration, down to their last detail, and then to combine them in the right way, not too startling to divert attention from the reading matter of the book - for which the design is only the body, after all - but not excluding some novel and pleasing details.

The first thing to decide on is the type. There are numerous faces to choose from, and very rarely is a special face cut for a special job. It will, however, be appropriate to pay some attention to the design of type-faces as this explains much about the factors governing our reading habits. The English-speaking world as a whole prefers what we call the roman type-faces, those associated with the Renaissance; while Germany still prints a large proportion of her reading-matter in Gothic, and the first books, as we have already seen, were printed in this script, copying the Bible-hands of the time of the invention of printing from movable type. Gothic faces are not easy to read: f and s are easily confused, but a page of these types gives a beautiful, compact entity, not easily obtained by roman. The English-speaking reader, therefore, will expect a roman type-face in his book. The average person, however, will pay little attention to the kind of type he reads, whether old-face or modern, and even if he can see that something is "wrong", he can probably not explain why. The first thing we demand of a typeface is that it be easily legible; no unusual forms of a letter should mar the smooth reading; the letters must not be readily confused one with another. These are practical considerations. The aesthetic considerations include the optical effects of letters on a line.[1,2] Letters are not geometrically constructed because of this optical effect: the round sorts should be larger than the square sorts; upper part of the lower-case "s" is smaller than the lower part; the dot over the "i" must not be centred, because it would look as if it were too much to one side, and so on. The style of the fount is a matter of individual taste, but each letter must be in harmony with the rest of

---

1   GRESS: Art...[591]
2   LEGROS: Typographical printing-surfaces, Longmans 1916.

the fount to give equality of "colour". An old-face type should have "hanging" figures, i.e. some figures descending below the others, but most printers prefer to use "ranging" figures with all faces.

When the type-face has been chosen, and here the designer takes into consideration whether illustrations are to accompany the text or not, it must be matched with the appropriate paper, as already outlined. Old-face founts that were cut before the use of calendered paper should not be printed on such; they would give too dark an impression, because they were meant to be pressed <u>into</u> the paper, not just "kissed" <u>on</u> to it. The proportion between the width of the letters and the length of the ascenders and descenders imparts the dark or light effect to the page; some faces with long descenders demand no "leading", while others must be leaded. (See chapter VIII). The human eye must have some light space in which to travel from one line to the next: fitting ten to twelve average-length words to a line of about 5 inches, or 30 'picas', is suitable.

The best setting, whether by hand or machine, must be demanded for a well-printed book: no "wrong fount", no turned letters; and the spacing is most important for the pleasing appearance of the page. Too wide spaces between words produce ugly rivers meandering down the page. Certain proportions between type area and the rest of the page must be maintained. The type area should be about half of the whole page. The economy measures during the war demanded not less than 58 per cent., and very good book-work was done, all the same. Some typographers say that the height of the type page should equal the width of the paper, but this need not be strictly adhered to. Certain conventional proportions for margins are usually maintained: inner 1½, top 2, outer 3, foot 4.[1]

So much for the compositor's work. Whether it will show up or not depends upon the press work, for which the inking and impression should be even and clean throughout.

Autographic illustrations in books are rare, except perhaps wood-engravings. If they are reproduced, the planner should take care to select the process which will reproduce them most faithfully and to select the paper conformably. The type-face should be selected to match, e.g. old-face goes well with wood-engravings (it was designed to do so) but a thin, modern face goes better with line-engravings, or reproductions of thin, pen and ink drawings. If the illustrations are printed with the type and placed in the type-area, they should not be smothered in the text but be allowed some white around them.

Headings and title-page can be printed in a larger point-size of the same type-face than the text, but most typographers prefer, rightly, to try and combine other faces and so give a contrasting effect. Ornaments may be used at ends of chapters

---

1 TSCHICHOLD: Correct measurement of book proportions. (Print. Rev. 14(46)21–6,1948)

and large initials at the beginnings. The title-page gives most scope for the inventive typographer: the style may be orthodox or asymmetrical.

The binding is important for the impression the book will give when on the shelf. Most publishers' books in the English-speaking world are "cased"; continental books on the other hand are paper-covered and carry such illustrations there (and text-matter) that an English book would have on its dust-jacket. Good work must be taken for granted but design can make a vast difference to the appearance of the book. Casings are often embossed with some pattern - the Victorians overdid it. The dust-jacket is often more striking than tasteful, mainly because it is supposed to be discarded within a few months of purchase. Endpapers can be coloured in harmony with the cloth used on the cover.[1,2,3,4]

Anatole Claudin defines a private printing press as "one set up in a [university], monastery, a palace, a residence or a private house, not the office of a printer. In fact it is a

---

1 DAVIS: Design in British book production. (Print.Rev. 15: 34–7,53,1950)
2 DE LA MARE: Author to public: thoughts on the principles of book production. (J.roy.Soc.Arts. 92(4675)573–82,1944; Libr.Assistant. 38(2)19–30,1945; abridged in Print.Rev. 12(38)5–8,32,1945; extracted in Sch.Libr.Rev. 4(2)25–9,1944)
3 MEYNELL: Making of books. (In Barker, E., ed. Character of England. Oxford: Clarendon Pr. 1947, p.389–96)
4 TARR: The use of space in typography. (Typographica 1(1) 19–23,1949)

press reserved for personal and not for public use, patronised, held, owned, or hired for the occasion by a private person at his own house...whether they were...for sale...makes no essential difference."[1] Eric Gill said that "a private press prints solely what it chooses to print, whereas the public press prints what its customers demand of it."

In their beginnings the Oxford and Cambridge presses were, and remain the property of their respective universities.

T. Rood printed at Oxford from 1478–85, and a second press lasted from 1517–20, But the present Oxford University Press dates only from 1585. Until 1669 the printing was done at the private houses of the University printers. In that year the press was installed at the Sheldonian Theatre built by the munificence of Archbishop Sheldon at the instance of Dr Fell, Dean of Christ Church and Bishop of Oxford, who made a collection of type-punches and matrices, largely from Holland (some of which were cut by Granjon) from which the handsome, so-called Fell types are still cast at Oxford[2] (operating a type foundry since 1667) and which, after 150 years' disuse, were uncovered by Dr Daniel in 1876. They have been used as models in some of the modern type revivals: the "Poems of Richard Lovelace" were

---

1 RANSOM: Private...[554] p.16.
2 MORISON: The roman, italic & black letter bequeathed to the University of Oxford by Dr John Fell. Oxford: Clarendon Pr. 1950.

printed in them at the press in 1925. Early in the 18th century the press was moved to the Clarendon building, built for it chiefly out of the profits from the sale of Clarendon's "History of the Rebellion", the perpetual copyright of which is vested in the Press.

Printing in <u>Cambridge</u> began in 1521 when Erasmus brought over John Siberch from the Continent to found a press. Armed with charters from Henry VIII and Charles I, the University resisted numerous attacks by the Stationers' Company on its rights to print "all manner of books", and since 1583 its history as printer and publisher has been uninterrupted. In 1698 the scholar, Richard Bentley, did for the Cambridge University Press what Fell had done for Oxford. He had the buildings enlarged, new presses set up, and founts of fine type imported from Holland. In 1831 the present Pitt building was erected, part of the surplus of a fund collected for erecting a statue of William Pitt being given towards its cost. The most famous of the Cambridge University printers was John Baskerville. (See later). Both Bruce Rogers and Stanley Morison have acted as typographic advisers here.

In the second half of the 16. century, while printing on the Continent deteriorated, in England it improved, and in <u>John Day</u> we have an English printer who, with the support of Archbishop Parker, set himself to obtain good types, especially a fine fount of italics, pictorial initials, and other ornaments, mostly from abroad, and used them with skill. In 1567 Day used the first fount of Anglo-Saxon. Gothic was displaced in England by roman (after Granjon) in 1572, when Day printed for Parker the first privately printed book brought out in England: De Antiquitate Britannicae Ecclesiae, the first limited edition on record. Day is generally admitted to be the best English typographer of the 16.century.[1]

Samuel Richardson, successful author of "Pamela" and other novels, was a master-printer in London.[2]

William Caslon, the first, greatest English type-founder, in 1734 brought out his famous first type-specimen sheet, that exhibits results of his labours since 1720, thereby creating founts of old-face roman type, that raise English type-founding from mediocrity to perfection, e.g. in Selden's "Works" (1726). Caslon emancipated English printers from dependence on Holland for their types. The popular favour subsequently accorded to the modern types of Bodoni, Didot, and other post-Baskerville designers, relegated the Caslon types to disuse from about 1810. But after the revival of the old-style, or Caslon founts, about 1844, by Whittingham and Pickering (see later) it came slowly back to that degree of favour it has retained ever since. Its almost continuous use for over 200 years is almost a record for a type-design. That is why William Caslon, more than any single

---

1 JOHNSON: John Day. (Penrose Annu. 41:54–7,1939)
2 SALE: Samuel Richardson: master printer. Ithaca, N.Y: Cornell Univ. Pr. 1950.

individual, is the most significant figure of his century in the history of the printed book. The foundry still exists.

Robert Foulis in 1743 was appointed printer to the University of Glasgow. He and his brother Andrew raised printing there from insignificance to an excellence which equalled, or perhaps surpassed the standard attained at London, Oxford, or Cambridge or, indeed, for the moment, anywhere in Europe. Historically their chief importance is that they proved that care and enthusiasm for fine printing were re-awakening, and that printers with high ideals would not lack support. Their 1744 "Horace" was hung in proof in the University, with the offer of a reward for every misprint detected (in spite of which 6 remained!)[1]

John Baskerville, printer, type-founder, writing-master, innovator of methods in the manufacture of ink and paper, hot-pressed and wove, father of fine printing in England, and maker (ca 1752) of most influential type designs second in importance in England only to Caslon's. His first production was a quarto "Virgil" (1758); 1763, his Cambridge "Bible"; 1770 "Horace". He influenced book production in France, Italy, and Germany; his type designs have been successfully revived by the Monotype Corporation. The merit of Baskerville's type is its distinctness;

---

1 GASKELL: The early work of the Foulis Press & the Wilson foundry. (Libr. 5s, 7(2)77–110,1952)

its fault is the reappearance in a slightly different form of the old heresy of Aldus, that what is thought to be good in penmanship must, necessarily, be good in type. His great merit was that he relied on his types and his presswork to make fine books, instead of on ornaments; he thus revived the dignity of the craft.

Sir Horace Walpole's STRAWBERRY HILL PRESS (1757–89) at Twickenham, on the banks of the Thames, produced some 32 books in Caslon types, e.g. Whitworth's "Russia" (1758) and Lucan's Pharsalia (1760). "Present amusement is all my object... I hope future edition-mongers will say of those of Strawberry Hill: they have all the beautiful negligence of a gentleman".[1]

John Bell, type-founder, designer, and publisher, whose faces are, perhaps, the first English "moderns", and of considerable influence upon journalistic typography. (Mrs Beatrice Warde calls the 1931 Monotype Corporation's Bell no. 341 facsimile reproduction: "The quintessentially British roman and italic"). He effectively introduced the short "s" into English printing in his 1785 "Shakespeare", and used instead the final form "s" in all positions in a word. (Ames' "Typographical antiquities" (1749) is said to be the first book to discard long "s", the medial form of "s")[2,3] He and the following two printers were the exponents

---

1 DOBSON: Horace Walpole's printing-press. (Libr. 1s, 1:313–9, 1889)
2 MCKERROW: Introduction...[36] p.309–10.
3 ULLMAN: Ancient...[186] p.219.

of the "classical" style in printing, inspired by Bodoni and the Didot brothers.[1]

Thomas Bensley began his long career in 1783. He shares with his rival, Bulmer, eminence in the history of his craft as being purely a "commercial" printer, who preserves a high artistic integrity, e.g. in Macklin's "Bible", and ."Virgil" (1800), Hume's "History of England", and an octavo "Shakespeare". Bensley originated some mechanical adjustments adopted by The Times, 1814.

William Bulmer was Bensley's contemporary and one of the most characteristically English printers.[2] His famous Boydell 8-v. folio "Shakespeare" (1792–1802) and the charming "Poems" by Goldsmith and Parnell (1795) illustrated by his friend, Thomas Bewick, were printed from memorable types designed by William Martin. In 1800 he tested for its 1798 inventor, Stanhope, the first commercial, iron printing press, and printed Dibdin's "Bibliographical Decameron" (1817) 3v, and Ames' "Typographical Antiquities" (1810–9) v.1–4.

Bell, Bensley, and Bulmer bridge the gap between Baskerville, and William Morris.

Sir Egerton Brydges, bibliographer, founded his LEE PRIORY PRESS, near Canterbury, in 1813, and up to 1823 issued 50 reprints of rare English pieces, John Johnson, one of his two printers, till 1817, published his Typographia, a classic (1824) in 2 vols.

---

1 BEILENSON: The nineteenth century. (Dolphin 3:233–67, 1938)
2 CROFT, Sir Wm: Achievement of Bulmer & Bensley. (Signature ns 16:3–28; 17:31–54, 1952–3)

In 1789 Charles Whittingham, "the uncle", founded the press, from 1810 known as the CHISWICK PRESS; 1824 he took his nephew, Charles Whittingham, into partnership; but in 1828 Whittingham began independently and, in 1830, became associated with William Pickering, a publisher of excellent taste. In 1840 Whittingham took control of the Chiswick Press until his retirement in 1860. This press became one of the most venerable of English proprietary presses, justly famous for the excellence and beauty of its printing, having borne the highest standards of each period, and lasting till to-day. In 1830 Pickering persuaded the nephew to procure specimens of the fine capitals and border-pieces of the 16 century French printers. As early as 1840 Whittingham and Pickering had been experimenting with the old-face type of Caslon, and it was an important event in the history of English typography when, 1844, Whittingham printed two books in that type. These were George Herbert's "Temple", published by Pickering, and "Lady Willoughby's Diary", brought out by Longmans, Although the latter has long been cited as the vehicle of the successful revival, which was the earlier is still a matter of discussion. The 18 century "modern" faces thus received their first serious blow.

Other famous publications of the Chiswick Press were: the "Diamond Classics", 1821–31, for which cloth as a binding material was probably first used; the Aldine edition of the British poets; the "Book of Common Prayer"; the 1847 "Euclid", "That gayest of all school books, with illustrations in colour", and other volumes reviving the use of woodcut borders, are "a monument of what could be achieved by good taste and craftmanship in the ordinary way of business before ever the self-conscious products of private presses had obscured the issue by suggesting that commerce and fine printing were incompatible."[1]

After the Great Exhibition of 1851 much of the good work disappeared in blatancy and, on the other hand, right up to 1890 many books, well laid out, were spoiled by the greyness of pages lightly printed with cheap ink. The books printed at the Chiswick Press under the management of C.T. Jacobi stood out from this greyness. In 1889 William Morris accepted the Chiswick Press edition of his story "The Roots of the Mountains", as the best printed book produced in England for many years.

The most truly private of all the English private presses was the DANIEL PRESS owned by the Rev. C.H.O. Daniel, who began as a printer at the age of nine. His "personal press" followed him from Frome (1845–59, with 11 productions) to Oxford (1874–1906 with 59) where, as a student, he set up in his college rooms, and where, 1876, as Provost, he uncovered the Fell types after 150 years of disuse. In 1876 he printed a "New Sermon..." from old-face type cast from these matrices. It was, however,

---

1   KEYNES: William...[578]

in 1881, by an edition of 36 copies of "The Garland of Rachel", that the Daniel Press won its renown. While neither his types nor his presswork was exceptionally good, Daniel succeeded in investing his little books with a charming appropriateness which gives them a special place of their own in the affection of book-lovers. A hand-printing press used by Daniel from 1880–1906 is in the Bodleian, and "The Daniel Press Memorials of C.H.O. Daniel" (1921) was printed on it.[1]

The Caxton celebrations in 1877 revived interest in printing as an art. Herbert P. Horne and Selwyn Image issued their handsome quarterly "The Hobby Horse" (1886–92) printed, of course, at the Chiswick Press, in which a high literary standard was combined with much care for typography. Its physical features constituted a landmark in the history of modern printing of an importance similar to that of the return to old-face type about 1844. (Horne designed three type faces: "Montallegro" (1904) for Updike of the Merrymount Press, Boston; "Florence" for Chatto and Windus; and "Riccardi" (both 1909) for the Medici Society. All were cut by E.P. Prince, who cut most of the "revival" faces in England, including those for William Morris and Emery Walker).

---

1 The DANIEL Press. (Bodleian Libr.Rec. 3(30)57–8,1950)

The progress of the movement can be followed, firstly, in the Catalogue of the Exhibition of the Arts and Crafts Exhibition Society, 1888, with an article on printing by Emery Walker; and secondly in three books by William Morris: "House of the Wolfings", "Roots of the Mountains", and "The Gunnlaug Saga", printed under the superintendence of the author and Emery Walker at the Chiswick Press, 1889–90.

Aesthetic leadership, during the last quarter of the 19 century, especially the 90's, lay in the hand of three groups: firstly, enlightened practical printers such as Charles T. Jacobi of the Chiswick Press, William B. Blaikie of T. and A. Constable, and the Ballantyne-Hanson Press. They were most important when co-operating with outside publishers and designers, e.g. W.E. Henley, and J.M. Whistler, whose "Gentle Art of Making Enemies" (1890) was an early and exquisite example of taste operating free of book making traditions. As far as the printing of books is concerned, the principal figures of group two, the art noveau groups, were the publishers: John Lane and Elkin Mathews, and the artists and designers who worked with them: Beardsley, Ricketts, L. Housman, Home, and Image.[1]

William Morris's KELMSCOTT PRESS was the first of the "big six" private presses of the revival: The Kelmscott Press, The

---

1   SYMONS: An unacknowledged movement in fine printing, the typography of the 1890's. (Fleuron. 7:83–119,1930)

Vale Press, Eragny Press, Essex House Press, Doves Press, and the Ashendene Press.

The Kelmscott Press was set up in 1891 close to William Morris's own residence, William Morris had not been satisfied with the production of his books, immediately preceding the setting up of his own press, but his press grew naturally out of the Arts and Crafts movement with its respect for fine craft-manship. Morris went into the minutest detail of the production of his books: the paper was made specially for the press, hand-presses were used, and the printed pages were dried slowly and not pressed, so as to prevent the ironing out of the indentions made in the paper by the type, which always is a mark of hand-printing, and should be preserved as far as possible. (This is also why a smasher should never be used in the binding of fine books). He went thoroughly into the theory of design[1] and laid down rules for the proportion between the margins, and he first showed that two facing pages in a book should form a unit when the book is opened. He took great care that the ratio between black and white in the illustrations was the same as that of the text, and that there was a just proportion between the thickness of lines in the types and in the illustrations.

Three type-faces were cut for the Kelmscott Press: the

---

1 MORRIS: The ideal book. (Trans.bibliogr.Soc. 1:179–86, 1893)

first, a 14-point roman, was based upon Jenson's and intended for the "Golden Legend", but was first used in "The Story of the Glittering Plain"; the second, an 18-point black-letter, originally intended for the Press's edition of "Chaucer", was found to be too big, and was eventually called the Troy, because it was first used in parts of the "Historyes of Troye" (1892). The type eventually used for the "Chaucer" and called after it, was a 12-point reduction of the Troy. Morris designed his own types with the help of Emery Walker and had them cut by Prince. He also designed some of the borders, initials and marginal ornaments used for the 53 books published by the Press. Other drawings were made by the other great member of the Pre-Raphaelites, Burne-Jones; they were cut, however, not by the designer, but by W.H. Hooper and Catterson-Smith, Morris "did make books it was a pleasure to look at - as arrangements of type and fine pieces of printing - but he did not make books that it was a pleasure to read... he led the printer of his particular movement to see how imposing...masses of strong type, closely set and well inked, combined with fine decorations may be. [He] taught a lesson in the unity of effect in books for which the modern printer is deeply in his debt - a unity now influencing volumes very far removed from those rather precious productions in which it was first exemplified... Morris's reforms have extended to illustrations, which are at present almost always by one hand, and not, as in old-fashioned books, by half a dozen different designers and drawn without any relation to the type-page. These newer and better fashions in book-making may be directly traced to [Morris's] sounder conceptions of what a book ought to be..."[1]

"No other printer since printing began has ever produced such a series of books,...and no book that has ever been printed can be compared for richness of effect with the "Chaucer" (1896) which was the crowning achievement of the press."[2] "This is the most magnificent printed book ever produced in England."[3] "For monumental splendor and vivid beauty it has not been and can hardly be surpassed. Type, decorations, the Burne-Jones illustrations, press-work and binding blend into a Book beyond the reach of adjectives."[4]

The punches, matrices, and some type from the Kelmscott Press are now at the Cambridge University Press, while the wood-blocks are preserved in the British Museum.

William Morris inspired most of the private presses since his day, not so much with his books as models, because they are now generally regarded as glorious pieces of design but sinning against one of his own dictums, legibility, and they are too

---

1 UPDIKE: Printing...[291] II, p.207–9.
2 POLLARD: Fine...[569]
3 GIBSON: English...[562]
4 RANSOM: Private...[554] p.50.

heavily leaded. But his principles, and insistence on good, careful craftmanship, are still followed.

The VALE PRESS, which operated from 1896–1903, was not its owner's, Ricketts' first effort, the first number of "The Dial" (1–5,1889–97) having been printed seven years before, with Hacon's help, Ricketts designed his own types. The Vale and the Avon (1899) were formed on the pre-Aldine letters and were meant to form counterparts to William Morris's roman. Pollard said that Vale was not very far behind the Chaucer. King's was based on roman and semi-uncial letters. Ricketts' aim was to show what could be achieved with the material ordinarily at the disposal of the printer. His books were all printed at the Ballantyne Press under his personal supervision, and not, like Morris's, on a hand-press. He was thus one of the first of the modern fine printers to show that fine printing does not depend on whether it is done on a hand-press or as any commercial printing, but on the designing and fine presswork which goes into it. The most famous production of the Press is the 39-v, "Shakespeare" (1900–3), printed, of course, in the Avon type. After the winding-up of the Press the punches and matrices were thrown into the Thames.[1]

---

1   FEGAN: Modern fine printing since the Kelmscott Press. (Libr.Ass. Rec. 15:301-27,1913)

The ERAGNY PRESS (1894–1914) was named after the hamlet in Normandy where Lucien Pissarro spent his boyhood. Later he was fired with enthusiasm for the revival of printing in England and emigrated there. His press, where he and his wife, Esther Pissarro, did the designing and the printing entirely with their own hands, used Ricketts' Vale type, until Pissarro was warned that it was going to be destroyed, when he designed Brook, based on the Vale. He also designed the Disteltype for the Kunera Press, The Hague, in 1923. It is, however, for the wood-engravings in colour that the publications of the Eragny Press are justly famous[1]. They heralded a new era in wood-engraving after the quick decline which followed Bewick's superb execution; Pissarro's text was indeed conceived rather as accompanying the illustrations than the reverse. The punches of the Brook type were thrown into the Channel after his death, but some of the type is preserved at the Cambridge University Press. The most famous of the Eragny Press books is <u>Livre du Jade</u> (1911).

The ESSEX HOUSE PRESS (1898–1909) was started by C.R. Ashbee, and run by him, together with Dr A.K. Coomaraswamy, from 1906 to the end. Influenced by the Kelmscott Press, Began with an ordinary Caslon fount, but Ashbee later designed the Endeavour (1901) and Prayer Book (1903) of a large design, that was first used for

---

1   MANSON: Notes on some wood-engravings of Lucien Pissarro. (<u>Imprint</u>. 1:240–7,1913)

"The Prayer Book of King Edward VII", the best production of the press, lavishly decorated with wood-cuts and initials.

T.J. Cobden-Sanderson and Emery Walker,[1,2] both of whom had been associated with the Kelmscott Press, started the DOVES PRESS in 1900, Emery Walker retiring from it in 1909, while Cobden-Sanderson carried on till his death in 1916, after which the types were thrown into the Thames at the wish of Cobden-Sanderson, The Doves Press apparently grew out of the Doves Bindery, where Douglas Cockerell served his apprenticeship under Cobden-Sanderson. The roman type in which the masterpiece of the Press, the "English Bible", 5v. (1903-4) was printed, was based on Jenson's "Pliny" (1476) but lighter than the Kelmscott Golden.

> "The books of the Doves Press are characterized by a majestic simplicity of design, meticulous typesetting, flawless presswork on the finest of papers, and workmanlike binding. Free from all ornament, save for an occasional colored initial, they form a contrast to the works of Morris and show the influence of the Kelmscott Press chiefly in their close spacing."[3]

> "When it is said that they approach dangerously near to absolute perfection in composition, presswork, and page placement, everything has been said. Their peculiarly individual quality is entire absence of decoration..."[4]

> "It was Emery Walker who produced for the Doves Press, with Prince as type-cutter, the lovely version in which that chef d'oeuvre of the private presses, the Doves "Bible" was composed."[5]

---

1 NEWDIGATE: Contemporary printers. II. Emery Walker. (Fleuron. 4:63-9, 1925)

2 POTTER: An appreciation of Sir Emery Walker. (Libr.Quart. 8(3)400-14, 1938)

3 MCMURTRIE: The...[168] p.468,471.

4 RANSOM: Private...[554] p.41,264,56.

5 THORP: A significant period of our printing, 1900-14. (Print.Rev. 12(40)5-28,1945) p.19.

The last of the great private presses of the "Revival of Printing" movement was the ASHENDENE PRESS owned by C.H. St John Hornby, who was also a director of the commercial printing firm of W.H. Smith & Son. The Press used five types. The first three were Caslon, Long Primer (O.U.P.) and Fell; the last two were cut specially for the Press, and the punches are now at the Cambridge University Press. Emery Walker and S. Cockerell designed Subiaco, first used for the famous "Dante" (1909) in 1902, after the type used by Sweynheim and Pannartz for their 1467 "Augustine" which, in turn again, was derived from a script of about the year 1,200. The Ptolemy type (1925) derived its name from its prototype: Halle of Ulm's "Ptolemy" (1482) and was used for the Ashendene Press's "Don Quixote" 1925–7. The press operated from 1894 to 1935.

Other, minor presses from this period are:

1899 PEAR TREE PRESS (James Guthrie and John Freeman). With the closing down of the Ashendene Press in 1935 the Pear Tree Press became the oldest existing press. Produced the "Book Craftsman" 1934–5. 4 nos.

1902 DUN EMER PRESS, renamed CUALA PRESS in 1907. Founded in County Dublin by Elizabeth and Lily Yeats, sisters of the poet, and by Evelyn Gleeson, with the object of stimulating Irish industries and giving employment to young women.

1904 SHAKESPEARE HEAD PRESS, founded by A.H. Bullen, at Stratford-on-Avon, to print the poet's works in his native town, using Stratford men only to do the production. 1920–44 the Press was operated by that scholar-printer, B.H. Newdigate[1,2]. It now belongs

---

1 BLACKWELL: Bernhard Newdigate. (<u>Print.Rev.</u> 13(41)21–8,1946; also in: <u>Signature</u>, ns.1:19–36,July 1946)
2 THORP: The work of Bernhard H. Newdigate. (ib. 8(29)803-9, 1938)

to Basil Blackwell and has been moved to Oxford. Its chief title was the "Froissart". 8v.

1909   The RICCARDI PRESS, the imprint of the publishers to the Medici Society, for whom H.P. Home designed the Riccardi type.

(1863)   John Curwen established a press at Plaistow for the purpose of printing music. It became distinguished

1916   when Harold Curwen, grandson, entered the firm in 1916. Aided in artistic endeavours by C.L. Fraser and Oliver Simon, In 1928 the "Specimen Book of Types and Ornaments" used at the CURWEN PRESS was issued by The Fleuron, Ltd, and is notable for its exhibition of typographic inventions of Percy J. Smith, C.L. Fraser, John Nash, Albert Rutherston, and Edward Bawden, who make type ornaments of high distinction and freshness.

After the first world war enthusiasm for fine printing continued and many new presses were started[1,2,3,4,5,6,7,8,9] 1916–25? PELICAN PRESS. Study alongside the Nonesuch.

1916   ST DOMINIC'S PRESS is ably conducted by H.D.C. Pepler, author of "The Hand Press" 1934; repr.[1953]. Beedham's "Wood-engraving" first printed there in 1920.

1917   The CYRIL W. BEAUMONT PRESS. Beaumont, a bookseller, specialized in contemporary literature.

– Bruce Rogers and Emery Walker at their MALL PRESS printed for the Grolier Club of New York Dürer's "Just shaping of letters."

---

1   CARRINGTON: Fine printing. (Brit.to-day. (134)13–7,1947)

2   NEWDIGATE: Fine printing in Great Britain 1925–34. (Gutenberg Jb. 1935:334–41)

3   SIMON: British book-production between the two world wars. (Brit. Book News. (64)211–9,1945)

4   – To "The Fleuron". (Signature. ns (13)3–29,1951)

5   THORP: A significant period of our printing, 1900–14. (Print.Rev. 12(40)5–28,1945)

6   WARDE: British book production since 1922. (Yearb.Ldn Sch. of Print. 15:11–25,1936/7)

7   – The British typographical reformation,1919–39. (Print.Rev. 13(42) 5–17,1946)

8   – Fifty wartime books from Britain. (Brit.Book News (58) 53–7,1945)

9   – Fifty-nine well-dressed books. (ib. (71)208–11,1946)

FINE PRINTING: OTHER PRIVATE PRESSES

- The HOGARTH PRESS, now semi-commercial, was started as a private press by Leonard and Virginia Woolf, "Two [self-styled] amateur and incompetent printers".

1919 J. Howard Whitehouse, author of "The Craftmanship of books" (1929) (dedicated to the memory of William Morris) started his YELLOWSANDS PRESS.

1920 H.M. Taylor founded the GOLDEN COCKEREL PRESS, which Robert Gibbings took over in 1924, bringing out many handsome books, illustrated with wood-engravings by himself and Eric Gill. In 1933 the Press was moved from Waltham-St-Lawrence to London, operating under the direction of Christopher Sandford, and F.J. Newbery.

1922 C.W. Hobson founded the CLOISTER PRESS in Heaton Mersey, Manchester, with Stanley Morison as typographic designer and Walter Lewis as printer. Issued the <u>Manchester Guardian</u>; Printing Supplement, 1922.

- The GREGYNOG PRESS is set up near Newtown, Montgomery, Wales, at the instance and cost of the Misses Davies, Until 1930 the Press was worked by R.A. Maynard, himself also a wood-engraver. The Press has (recently) been taken over by Loyd Haberly. Many fine bindings have also been done at the Press, following the designs of contemporary artists.

1923 The NONESUCH PRESS started under Birrell & Garnett's bookshop, seizing advantage of the increased interest in fine books. The Nonesuch Press is a publishing enterprise. Of the (private) presses established since World War I, the Nonesuch Press is one of the most interesting. It was founded by Viola Meynell and Francis (later Sir Francis) Meynell, with David Garnett as literary editor, with the purpose of serving the need of "book collectors who also use books for reading". Much of the "official printing" is done at various English presses, e.g. Kynoch (1924) O.U.P., Chiswick, Mayflower, and Westminster. The 5v. "Bible", and 7v. "Shakespeare" are outstanding among its many titles.

1927 The CRESSET PRESS begins. "One of...that group of publishers which is striving to preserve the highest standards in book-production".

1946 DROPMORE PRESS, a revival of Lord Carlow's Corvinus Press, begins. "The Press was founded with the simple but unusual intention of designing, printing, binding and publishing books of uncommon literary merit for those who take pleasure in good literature finely produced" (by Robert Harling) e.g: Howe, Ellic: The London bookbinders 1780–1806; with wood engravings by Gwendolen Raverat. 1950; and the Book handbook 2(1–3)1951. [55]

The success of the private presses has spurred the "commercial" printers on to greater efforts. A survey of the publishers of books selected by the National Book League for their Exhibitions since the first in 1945 gives the following results (the figures in brackets reflect the total number of volumes selected for the seven exhibitions to date): Faber and Faber (65); Penguin books (39); Cambridge University Press (37); Oxford University Press (28; for 1950–1, divided between Clarendon: 4, and Cumberlege: 11); Cape (20); Chatto (19); Collins (18); Longmans (15); Macmillan; Murray (13 each); Cassell (10); Folio Society, Lehmann, Methuen, Phaidon (9 each); H.M.S.O. (8); Allen and Unwin, Architectural Press, Dent, Golden Cockerel, Harrap (7 each); Grey Walls Press, Hart-Davis, Lund, Humphries, Transatlantic Arts (6 each); Country Life, Eyre and Spottiswoode, M. Joseph, F. Muller (5 each).

William Morris's influence was actually felt nearly as strongly on the Continent and in the U.S.A. as in Britain. In Germany the Cranach Press of Count Harry Kessler operated from 1913–33; a roman type resembling Dove's was used.

Across the water the éclat of Morris's books induced the Riverside Press (1903-12) of Cambridge, Mass, to form a special department for finely printed books in limited editions, and in that special department Bruce Rogers made wonderful experiments in printing books.[1,2]

Some other big names to note in the U.S.A. are those of Th. De Vinne,[3] W. Gilliss, F.W. Goudy (Village Press 1903–47), Grabhorn Bros, John H. Nash, W.D. Orcutt, Pynson Bros (Elmer Adler), D.B. Updike (Merrymount Press).

Walter Gropius founded the Bauhaus in Weimar, and later moved it to Dessau. The movement originating from here has influenced the latest typography immensely with its asymmetric designs. One of its exponents in England was Jan Tschichold, but he has again returned to Switzerland.

Other Friends of the Book are corporate bodies such as bibliographical societies and private book clubs. Their task includes: 1. Surveying fields for study; 2. To arrange for the compilation of new bibliographies in fields found to be incompletely covered; and for the publication of such bibliographies when completed. Usually the works published by a bibliographical society should be of the type that an ordinary

---

1 HOFER: The work of W[illiam] A[ddison] D[wiggins]. (Dolphin. 2:220–56,1935)

2 WARDE: Bruce Rogers. (Fleuron. 4:99–121,1925)

3 ROLLINS: T.L. De Vinne. (Signature. ns(10)3–21,1950)

publisher would not undertake (because he could not possibly make them pay); 3. To publicize bibliographies and especially those just, or about to be published. This is carried out mainly through papers, discussions, and the publication of news in the journal of the society. Most bibliographical societies devote too much attention to points of antiquarian bibliography; 4. Elevation of popular taste in the technique of book-making; 5. Provision of libraries on the arts of the book and of exhibitions illustrative of these arts; 6. Sharing of mutual pleasures in such a way that all choice spirits know the joy of the book hunter.[1,2,3,4]

Of English corporate bodies for book-lovers the following are important: Arts Council; Bibliographical Society; Design and Industries Association; Double Crown Club; First Edition Club (1922); Monotype Corporation; National Book League, Roxburghe Club; and in America: American Institute of Graphic Arts (1914+, Annual Exhibition of 50 books of the year 1923+); American Type Founders' Company; Bibliographical Society of America; Bibliographical Society of the University of Virginia; Book Arts Club of the University of California; Caxton Club (Chicago);

---

1 BARWICK: Bibliographical societies & bibliography. (Libr. 4s, 11:151-9,1931)
2 COPINGER. On the necessity for the formation of a bibliographical society, etc. (ib. 1s, 4:1-7,1892)
3 GRANNISS: What B. owes to private book clubs. (Pap.bibliogr.Soc. Amer. 24:14-33,1930)
4 PEDDIE: Some possible bibliographical activities of the Library Association. (Libr.Ass.Rec. 11:187-92,1909)

Club of Odd Volumes; Grolier Club of New York (1884); Limited Editions Club (New York); Typophiles of New York. Die Suid-Afrikaanse Akademie vir Wetenskap en Kuns will start annual exhibitions of 25 outstanding books in Afrikaans, from 1953.

The various lecture series will be found in the corresponding part of the bibliography to this chapter.

> "...and so there ain't nothing more to write about, and I am rotten glad of it, because if I'd 'a' knowed what a trouble it was to make a book I wouldn't 'a' tackled it, and ain't a-going to no more".[1]

---

1 TWAIN: Huckleberry Finn.

APPENDIX

EXAMINATION QUESTIONS

No questions of the "write-short-notes-on-the-following"-type are included. Students would do well to learn the definitions from the Index.

L.A. = Library Association Examination Question.
S.A.L.A. = South African Library Association Examination Question.
C.U. = Cape Town. University. School of Librarianship Examination Question.

★ The questions marked thus should not be attempted before these <u>Notes</u> have been mastered.

PART 1.

CHAPTER I.
What is meant by the statement "True [descriptive] bibliography is the bridge to textual, that is to say literary, criticism"? (Greg)
What do you understand by the term "analytical bibliography" and what are the wider purposes which it serves? (L.A. 1945)
"Bibliography" has been variously defined. To what different kinds of activity do you consider the term may properly be applied? (L.A. 1950)

*"...yet without this sort of editing there is no security that we are reading what the author intended us to read". (Esdaile) What sort of editing is probably meant, assuming the work to be a 16 century text? (L.A. 1950)

CHAPTER II.

If you had to deal with a library containing many early printed books, what bibliographical aids would you consider essential? (L.A. 1941)

Describe in detail the scope and arrangement of three bibliographies of bibliographies. (L.A. 1944)

In what main bibliographical works is English Literature down to the year 1800 recorded? (L.A. 1944)

Trace the development of modern English trade bibliography, including a critical commentary on its resources. (L.A. 1944)

Name and describe briefly the main general bibliographies of German literature. (L.A. 1946)

Write a brief review of the main published catalogues of the British Museum. (L.A. 1951)

(a) What is the distinction between "primry" and "secondary" bibliographies? Give two examples of each.

(b) What in your opinion are the most important gaps in the primary bibliographies of this country. [Union of South Africa] (S.A.L.A. 1949)

Discuss, in relation to South African conditions: "It is to a large extent true of bibliography...if you take care of the present, the future will not have to take care of the past". (Luther Evans) (S.A.L.A. 1951)

CHAPTER IV.

"Bibliography is the basis of all intellectual coöperation" (Committee on intellectual coöperation of the League of Nations. 1922). Explain.

Describe the procedure to follow in the compilation of a bibliography.

What do you understand by the "natural history method" of bibliography? (L.A. 1942)

What are the points to which you would pay particular attention before commencing the compilation of a bibliography? Explain why you consider them important. (L.A. 1944)

How would you set about evaluating a new bibliography? Describe the main features you would look for, illustrating with special reference to a recently published work. (S.A.L.A. 1946)

Enumerate all the forms of bibliographical arrangement known to you. Give an example of each. (S.A.L.A. 1948)

CHAPTER V.

Demonstrate the value of bibliography to the cataloguer, classifier, and reference librarian.

*What means are available of establishing the order of publication of the books of an early printer, some only of which are dated? (L.A. 1939)

Pagination, signatures, and catchwords are each important to bibliographical research. Explain this statement and show how they are inter-related. (L.A. 1940)

What is the purpose of "full bibliographical description" of a book? Enumerate, in their correct sequence, the divisions of such a description, and describe the information to be given in each. (L.A. 1940)

Explain fully what you understand by the following: 12°, *, A-L^4, pp.[1-8] + 9-96, Pl[i] + vii 28 lines + headline and signature and catchword line. 90(95)× 57mm. (L.A. 1941)

How would you distinguish an octavo from a quarto? Name the main divisions of a "full standard description" and indicate briefly the information to be recorded in each. (L.A. 1941)

*Outline the history of the development of the title-page. (L.A. 1941)

*How would you proceed to assign a date (a) to a 15 century and (b) to a 19 century, unrecorded book? (L.A. 1942)

*In the early days of printing changes in technique were fairly frequent. Many of them proved of great importance to bibliographers. State which these were and describe their particular importance. (L.A. 1945)

Give an account of the origin and history of the colophon. (L.A. 1946)

Sketch the origin and development of the imprint. (L.A. 1948)

What parts of a book are usually known as the "preliminaries"? Show the purpose of each part. (L.A. 1948)

*"But if we make it our rule to follow the printer step by step in his work, considering at every point what would be the most convenient thing for him to do...we shall seldom go far wrong". (<u>McKerrow</u>). Relate this advice to the task of collating a 16 century book which you wish to describe bibliographically. (L.A. 1951)

"The description of a <u>copy</u> of a book should never be confused with that of the <u>edition</u>". Explain. (S.A.L.A. 1936)

★Your collation of an old book results in an imperfect succession of watermarked and unwatermarked leaves. What may have happened? (S.A.L.A. 1936)

"The modern bibliographer may properly be called the anatomist of the book". (Dr Cole). Explain and illustrate this statement. (S.A.L.A. 1943)

"Only by working from facts can we help to keep bibliography in the position of a scientific study" (<u>Duff</u>). Comment and illustrate. (S.A.L.A. 1945)

"Omnes sunt quaterniones praeter P & S qui sunt duerniones". How many pages are represented by the following signature equations: (i)a^6, b-z, A-H^8, I^4; (ii) $[A]^4$ B-M^4, N^2? 'Since every leaf is half or part of a folded sheet, each has its conjugate leaf'. Explain.

Tabulate:
    (a) Syluarum$^{(1)}$ Quaterniones nouem.
        <u>Silvae</u>. 4×9 : a.b.c.d.e.f.g.h.i.
    (b) Thebaidos$^{(1)}$ Quaterniones xxi: k.l.m.n.o.p.q.r.s.t.u.x.y.z.
                                    A.B.C.D.E.F.G.Sed[but]
                                      G est duernio.
        <u>Thebais</u>. $4 \times 20 + 1[G] \times 2$.
    (c) Achilleidos$^{(1)}$ Quaterniones tres: A.B.C.Sed [but] C eat
                                        duernio.
        <u>Achilleis</u>. $4 \times 2 + 1[C] \times 2$.

(d)⁽²⁾ A a - x. Omnes sunt quaterni preter[!] A qui est duernus. All are quaternions except A which is a duernio: 1[A] × 2 + 21 × 4.

(e)⁽³⁾ [Registrum]: ★ a - [alpha - omega]. Omnes sunt quaterniones praetor ★ unionem & [omega] ternionem. All are quaternions except ★ (as) a single fold & [omega] (as) a ternion. ★x 1 + 23 × 4 + 1 × 3: ★2, 2 - 8 [alpha - psi], 6 [omega]

(1) 5(a)-(c) are titles(1502) by the Roman poet P. Papinius STATIUS (c.40-96? A.D.); (d) is from a 1509 Herbal; (e) from a 1523 Aldine.

(2) Remember that the Latin alphabet had only 23 letters, as I interchanged with J; U with V, & W was omitted.

(3) The Greek alphabet has 24 letters.

PART 2.

CHAPTER VI.

"...Swash and ligatured letters...are the most obvious reminders our books contain of the fact that all books were once written by the pen." (Pottinger). Explain.

Give a brief account of the materials used for recording events before the advent of paper, (L.A. 1939)

"Gutenberg's accomplishment...was the co-ordination of a number of techniques". Explain this statement. (L.A. 1940)

★Trace the evolution of the physical form of the book from early times to Caxton's day. (L.A. 1944)

Estimate the extent and duration of the influence of the MS. upon the early printed book. (L.A. 1941)

Write a short account of block–books, and discuss their relation to typography. (L.A. 1942)

★Describe briefly the stages by which the printed book developed its independence from the influence of its manuscript predecessor. (L.A. 1946)

Discuss the claims of Gutenberg to be considered the inventor of printing from movable types. (L.A. 1946)

Write a short account of materials that have been used for writing surfaces during the Christian era, and explain how their characteristics have affected the form of the physical book. (L.A. 1946)

*Explain the difference in the types of book issued from the first presses of Paris and Westminster. (L.A. 1947)

Give a short account of the introduction and development of printing in South Africa, (S.A.L.A. 1938)

CHAPTER VII

Name the types of paper which should never be used in good book production, and state reasons for their exclusion. (L.A. 1945)

Outline the processes of hand-making paper. (L.A. 1946)

What are the chief materials used in the manufacture of paper? Name and describe briefly the main types of printing paper into which they are made, explaining which are the most durable, and why. (L.A. 1946)

What do you know of the invention of paper and of its introduction into Western European countries? (L.A. 1948)

What qualities in materials decide their suitability for paper-making? With reference to these, describe the preparation of "half-stuff" from wood. (L.A. 1950)

Describe five important differences between hand-made and machine-made paper. (S.A.L.A. 1949)

CHAPTER VIII.

*"The cultured accents of a pleasantly readable type face effect their object where the asthmatic raucousness of a type face with meaningless frills or obesities fails." (Tarr) Explain.

How do type faces differ? Illustrate.

*Outline the history of roman type. (L.A. 1939)

What were the origins of the three great families of type faces? (L.A. 1941)

What are the advantages and disadvantages of monotype in relation to linotype and hand setting? (L.A. 1942)

Describe briefly the main parts of the early printing press and the manner of its operation. (L.A. 1945)

Describe the classes of Gothic types, indicating the type of text for which each was used. (L.A. 1946)

Enumerate the main parts of the printing press, indicating the function of each, and describe their manner of operation in platen; flat-bed; and rotary presses, (L.A. 1948)

Name and describe FOUR specific type founts in common use at the present time. Pay special attention to the characteristics by which each may be identified. (L.A. 1951)

What is the difference between Old-Face and Old Style? Sketch the vogue and desuetude of the latter. (L.A. 1951)

CHAPTER IX.

Explain why some illustration processes use a negative print and others a positive. Give examples.
  (a) Name four non-photographic book illustration processes, one relief, two intaglio, and one planographic.
  (b) Describe the process of one of them. (C.U. 1949)

How may the standards of good book production be observed when photo-mechanical methods of illustrating are used in books? (L.A. 1940)

What is the principle underlying the processes of aquatint and photogravure? How do the two processes differ? (L.A. 1941)

State what you know of the revival in the use of woodcuts for book illustration during the past fifteen years. (L.A. 1942)

How are the graduations of tone represented in an illustration by (a) mezzotint; (b) half-tone; and (c) photogravure; and by what essential processes is the effect obtained? (L.A. 1946)

Give an outline account of the use of colour in book-illustration, excluding photo-mechanical processes. (L.A. 1947)

How would you establish the following:
  (a) Whether an illustration in a modern book is a photolitho, half-tone, or photogravure plate? The work is of good quality, tone values being excellent.
  (b) Whether an older book has metal-engraved or etched line illustrations? (L.A. 1950)

CHAPTER X.

In his review of Carter & Pollard Esdaile said: "Of these new methods of bibliographical authentication, the book...will probably long remain a classical example." (L.A.R. Aug. 1934). Write what you know of "these new methods", as applied to this case or a similar one.

If you suspected the presence of forged pages in a copy of a sixteenth-century book, to what points would you pay particular attention? (L.A. 1942)

What methods of composition and printing are available for producing, at a moderate cost, (a) a first edition, (b) a reprint, and (c) a revised edition, of an important work? Outline the advantages and disadvantages of each. (L.A. 1946)

When and by whom was stereotyping first (a) experimented with, (b) perfected, for printing? Describe the process. (L.A. 1946)

*Write a specification for a reprint of a classic novel suitable for library use, giving reasons for your choice of materials, etc. (L.A. 1947)

Suggest THREE methods by which a university thesis may be reproduced economically in a very short edition. Describe these briefly and comment in each case on the likely quality of the result. (L.A. 1951)

What do you understand by the "contact method" of documentary reproduction? Show your familiarity with TWO examples. (L.A. 1951)

"All facsimile work was...on a firmer basis when photography was added to the illustrator's resources." (Esdaile). Discuss. (S.A.L.A. 1936)

CHAPTER XI.

(a) What kinds of pests attack books? How would you prevent such attacks?

(b) Describe how books should be shelved in order to avoid damage to the books themselves. (C.U. 1948)

Discuss the merits and faults of at least four leathers for binding a much-used reference book. How would you preserve and care for leather-bound books in general? (C.U. 1951)

Describe briefly the use made of gold in binding decoration to the end of the 16 century. (L.A. 1942)

Describe carefully the bookbinding methods employed to attach the separate sections of a book to each other and to the covers. (L.A. 1946)

Prepare a specification (a) for binding a book of permanent value, (b) for a normal library binding. (L.A. 1946)

Outline the research that has been made in the last half-century into the causes of the decay of binding leather. What is the present position of knowledge on the subject, and what are the latest methods recommended to prevent it? (L.A. 1947)

Describe any new methods and materials that you know of, which have been applied to library binding. Estimate their possibilities. (L.A. 1950)

What factors influence the librarian's decision when he considers the rebinding of a work? Discuss the range of binding materials from which he may select. (L.A. 1950)

CHAPTER XII.

By what stages did the rights of authors come to have statutory protection? Give a short account of the modern position of copyright law. (L.A. 1941)

Contrast publishing methods to-day with those of Elizabethan days. (L.A. 1945)

Show how various methods of sharing the publication of books have prevailed in succession at different times. (L.A. 1946)

Your libraries committee have decided to publish a history of the borough. Outline the processes involved in publication, from manuscript to finished production. (L.A. 1946)

List twelve of the conventional signs used in proof correction and indicate their meaning. (L.A. 1947)

What are the recommendations of the Interdepartmental Committee on Libraries of 1937 concerning Copyright Libraries in South Africa? Describe, with reference to similar libraries overseas, how the present provisions might be improved. (S.A.L.A. 1942)

CHAPTER XIII.

(a) The actual type design is not so important as the use that is made of it...

(b) The essential of a fine book is unity in its structure and unity in the "colour" of its pages. (<u>Meynell</u>) Explain.

"Imposition determines the margins of a book." (<u>Updike</u>). Give the common rules for well proportioned margins.

What main factors in book-making are sought by a collector but shunned by a librarian, and why?

Write an essay on English book production between World Wars I and II.

"Any disposition of printing material which, whatever the intention, has the effect of coming between author and reader is wrong." Comment on the implications of this statement. (L.A. 1939)

How far are modern machine methods compatible with the principles of good book production so far as these relate to (a) binding, (b) paper, and (c) illustration? (L.A. 1939)

Write a short account of the work of the private presses since the year 1890, and estimate the worth of their achievement. (L.A. 1941)

A number of publishing houses maintain a "design office". Write in reasonable detail on what you take to be the duties of such a department. (L.A. 1951)

"The ultimate aim of type is to be read." Name some potent factors which make for legibility. (S.A.L.A. 1941)

What differences would you expect to find between a book published in the 15 century and a modern edition of the same book? Comment on the reasons for these differences. (S.A.L.A. 1942)

Describe any progress towards better book production in this country [Union of South Africa] during recent years. (S.A.L.A. 1947)

Write an essay on PATRA's work for the printed book. (S.A.L.A. 1948)

Name <u>six</u> characteristics of good typography. Mention <u>two</u> books and <u>two</u> periodicals published in South Africa during the past two years that in your opinion conform most closely to the requirements of a well-printed item. (S.A.L.A. 1950)

INDEX
(Authors, Presses, and Titles)

Numbers enclosed within square brackets [ ] occur in Chapters II and III, or as A[DDENDA] p.xii–xiv; others on the pages indicated followed by 'n' if footnote reference.

A.S.L.I.B. [44–5]
ARSKATALOG för svenska Bokhandeln [737]
ARSKATALOG over norsk Litteratur [734]
ADAMS, Randolph Greenfld [683e]
– Scott [803]
ADLER, Elmer 319
Advocates' Library, Edinb. 269
AITKEN, Revd P.Henderson 145n
ALDIS, Harry Gidney [156]
ALDUS Manutius 142,289,303
ALPHABET & Image [39]
ALTICK, Richard Daniel [605]
AMERICAN Bk-Prices Curr. [819]
– Catalogue of Books [708]
– Doctoral Dissertations [827]
– Documentation [40]
– Inst.of graphic Arts [279]
– Library Ass. [41–2, 423, 432, 747–48a, 817]
– Paper & Pulp Ass. [227]
– Standards Ass. [464]
ANNUAL of Bookmaking [43]
ANTHOENSEN, Fred. [590]
APPLETON.Inst.Paper Chem. [223]
ARBER, Edw. 1836–1912 [695]
ARCHER, Fredk Scott 183, 195
– John, jt-auth. [450]
ARMITAGE, F.D. 247n
– Merle [558]
ARMS, John Taylor [307]
ARNIM, Max [773]
ARRIGHI, Ludovico degli 174
ART of the Book [157]
ASHBEE, Chas Rbt 313
Ashendene Press [585] 315
Aslib [44–5]
ASSISTANT Librarian [80]
ASSOCIATED sci...Soc.S.A. [479]
ASSOCIATION Mkrs Esparto [256]
– Suisse d.Composit. [A266a]
Atkinson, Basil F.C. 135n
AUDIN, Maurice 141n
AUNGERVILLE, Richard [514] 289
AUSTIN, Roland 113n
AUSTRALIAN Books [713]
AUTHOR [481]

AYER'S Directory [802]

BALD, Rbt Cecil: Forme-unit 11
BALSTON, Thos [338,354,391,581] 186n
BARNARD, Cyril Cuthbert 115n
BASKERVILLE, John 1706–75
    [573–4] 145, 171–2, 300, 302–3
BASTIEN, Alfred [294]
BATESON, Fredk [Noel] Wilse [143]
BAWDEN, Edward 196, 316
BAXTER, Geo.Colour proc. 184, 206
BAY, Helmuth [675]
BEARDSLEY, Aubrey 196, 308
BEAUJON, Paul. See WARDE, Mrs B.
Beaumont (Cyril W.) Press 316
BECHTEL, Mrs Louise Seaman [677]
BEDFORD, Francis 1799–1883. 233
BEECK, Peter [461]
BEEDHAM, R.John [339]
BEILENSON, Peter 304n
BELL, John [576] 173, 303
BEMBO, Card. Pietro 1470–1546. 173
Ben.Day screens 196, 204
BENBOW, John [465]
BENDIKSON, Lodewyk 220n
BENESCH, Otto [318]
BENNETT, Colin Noël [392]
– Henry Stanley [658]
– Paul Arthur [158]
– Wm [573]
BENSLEY, Thos [577]162, 304
BENSON, John Howard [195]
BENTLEY, Richd 1662–1742 300
BENTON, Linn Boyd 162
BERNE Copyright Conventn[506]266
BERRY, Wm Turner [295]
BESTERMAN, Theodore
    [Nathaniel] [105,760,762] 11
BETHE, Erich [192]
BEVAN, Edw.John, jt-auth. [233]
BEWICK, Thos 1753–1828 [356,
    359–60a, 606] 182, 186, 304
BIBLIO [745]
BIBLIOGRAPHIC Index [767]
BIBLIOGRAPHICA [46]

333

INDEX

BIBLIOGRAPHICAL Aids to Res.82n
– Society [3,47–8,600]
– Society of America [49–50]
BIBLIOGRAPHIE de...France [744]
– d.deut.Bibliothek [726]
– d.Bibl.-u.Buchwesens [8]
BIBLIOTHEEKLEVEN [51]
BIEGELEISEN, Jacob Israel[402–3]
BIGGS,John R. [280, 308]
BIGHAM, Clive [601]
BIGMORE, Edw.Clements [144]
BINDERS Board Mfrs Ass. [424]
BINNS, Norman E. [A151a]
BIOGRAPHY Index [774]
BINKLEY, Rbt Cedric [410]
BLACKWELL, Basil [659] 315n,316
BLADES, Wm 1824–90 113,126
BLADO, Antonia 1490–1567 177
BLAIKIE, William Biggar 308
BLAKE,Wm 183, 186, 188, 194
BLAND,David [309]
BLISS,Douglas Percy [340] 187
BLOCK,G.D,M. 194n
BLUM, Andre [252]
BLUNT, Wilfrid [195a, A405a]
Bodleian Library 269,307
BODONI,Giambattista 171, 174
BOEK [52]
BOHATTA, Hanns [761]
BOHN, Henry Geo., ed. [698]
BOLLAND, Wm Craddock [636]
BOOK Collector [53]
– Collector's Packet [54]
– Collector's Quarterly [55]
– Craftsman 315
– Handbook [53] 318
– Prices current [818]
– Review Digest [822]
– Trade Handbook [482]
BOOKBINDING & Book Produc. [56]
BOOKLIST Books [748]
BOOKMAN [57]
BOOKMAN'S Glossary [22]
BOOKS (N.B.L.) [58]
– About Books (N.B.L.) [12]
– In Print [712]
– Of the Month... [751]
BOOKSELLER [703]
BORCHARDT,D.H. 141n
BOSWELL,David B. [A32a]

BOWERS,Fredson T. [124] 12,129n
Bowker memorial Lect. [668–82a]
BOYD, Anne Morris [786]
BRADSHAW,E.M. 189
– Henry 1831–86 113–4
BRANDSTETTER,Oscar 219
BRANDT, Joseph August [676]
BRINKMAN'S Catalogus [730]
BRIQUET,Chas Moise [263]
BRITISH Book News [752]
– Drama League [778]
– Fed.of Master Printers [145,457]
– Leath.Mfrs' Res.Ass. [452]
– Museum [311,560–1,688–9,691,792] 124,269,27
– National Bibliography [705]
– Printer [59]
– Society for int.B. [60]
– Standards Instn
  [112,411,A411a,466–7,530]
BROWN,Jas Duff [17,113] 5,111n
– Zaidee [114]
BROWNE,Arthur,trans. [687]
BROWNING,Earl W., jt-auth. [432]
BRUCE,David (1834) 162
BRUNET,Jacques Chas. [685]
– Pierre Gustave [796]
BRYDGES,Sir Egerton 304
BUCK,Mitchell Starrett [425]
BUCKLAND-WRIGHT,
  John [A360b]
BÜHLER,Curt Ferdinand
  [125] 13,128,264n
BULL,Alfred J. [393]
BULLEN,Arthur Henry 315
BULLETIN de Docum.bl. [766]
– for Libraries [61]
– of Bibliography [764]
BULMER,Wm [577] 292,304
BURBRIDGE,Peter Geo. [A467a]
BURCH,Rbt M. [399]
BURGER,Konrad [788]
BURKE,Redmond Ambrose 266n
BURNE-JONES,Sir Edward 310–1
BURRIDGE Broadsheets [301]
BURTON,Margaret [1]
BUSENBARK,E.J., jt-auth. [402]
BUTLER,Samuel 1835–1902 [607]

CAMBRIDGE.University. PTO.

INDEX

CAMBRIDGE.University.
-- Fitzwilliam Museum [159]
-- Library 269
-- Sandars Lectures 68-72
- Bibliographical Society [62]
- University Press 300,315 [468]
CAMPBELL,Revd Frank B.F. 4
- Marinus Fredk And.Ger. 113
CANADIANA [714]
CANNON, Herbert Graham [406]
CANNONS,Harry Geo.Turner [2]
CAPPELLI, Adriano [220]
CAREY,Arthur G., jt-auth. [195]
- Gordon Vero [469]
CARNEGIE Inst.of Technology [146]
CARRINGTON,Noel 192n,316n
CARROUSEL for Bibliophiles [608]
CARSON, F. 242n
CARTER,Harry [Graham] [172]
- John [Waynflete]
    [156,415-6,515-7,596,654]
- Thos Francis [188]
CASLON, Wm 1692-1766 161,301-2
CATALOGUE generale de la
librairie française [741]
CATHARINE de Medici 231
CAXTON, Wm 1422?-91 161
CERNY,Jaroslav [A192a]
CHANTICLEER [587]
CHAPMAN, Dr Rbt Wm [133,517]
129n,212,224n,249n,263n
CHAPPELL,Warren [196]
CHASSANT,A.A.L. 1808-1907 [221]
CHICAGO...Print.Ho.Craft. [210]
CHILDREN'S Catalog [750]
Chiswick Press [578-9] 292,305-6
CHIVERS, Cedric [426] 234n
CHURCHILL,Wm Algernon [264]
CIM,Albert [33]
CLAPPERTON,Rbt Henderson
    [231-2,253,662]
CLARK,John Willis [621]
CLARKE,Archibald Leycester [470]
CLAUDIN, Anatole 298-9
CLEETON,Glen Vriel [160]
CLERC,Louis Philippe [385]
CLEVERDON,Douglas [355]
CLODD,Edw. 1840-1930 [178]
CLOUGH,Eric A. 242n
CLOUTMAN,Brett [503]
CLOWES' Book types [298]

Club of odd Volumes 321
COBDEN-SANDERSON,Thos
    Jas. [531-2] 233,314
COBLANS, Herbert 221n
COCKALORUM [589]
COCKERELL, Douglas 1870-1945
    [427-427a] 151n,233-4,314
- Sir Sydney 233
COHN, Max Arthur,jt-auth. [403]
COLE,Dr Geo.Watson 1850-1939
    [3] 8,82n,115n,125,130n
COLLINS,Fredk Howard [462]
COLLISON,Rbt Lewis [106,A470a]
COLOPHON [63]
- New [87]
COLUMBIA University [18,152]
COLVIN,Ian D., ed. [715]
COMPTON,Frank Elbert [671]
CONNER,Martha 1874-1933 [115]
CONOVER,Helen Field [118]
COOK,Dorothy Eliz. [A781a]
COOMARASWAMY,Dr Ananda K. 313
COPINGER,Walter Arthur
    1847-1910 [504,788] 4
CORNS,Albert Reginald [832]
CORVINUS,M.,King of Hungary 231
COTTON G.B. [A781b]
COURTNEY,Wm Prideaux [759]
COUTTS,Henry Thos [428]
COWELL'S Types [296-7]
COWLES,Barbara [23]
COWLEY, Arthur Ernest [631]
- John Duncan [126] 11,124
CRAIG,Edw.Gordon [341]
- F.A. 146n
Cranach Press 318
Cresset Press 243n,317
CRESWICK,Harry Richardson [653]
CROFTS, Fredk S. [670]
CROSS,Chas Fredk [233]
- Tom Peete [4]
CROUS,Ernst 114
CRUTCHLEY,E.A.,i.e. Brooke C.
jt-auth. [156]
Cuala Press 315
CUMULATIVE Book Index [710]
CUMMING, David [381]
CUNANE,Thos H. 146n
CURRENT Literature [704]
CURWEN,Harold [386] 316
- John 316

335

CUTNER,Herbert [361]
CUTTER,Chas Ammi 1837–1903 5

DALLISON,C.R. 192n
DANCER,John Benjamin 1812–87.221
DANIEL,Revd Chas Henry Olive
   1836–1919 [580] 299,306–7
DANSK Bogfortegnelse [731]
DANSKE Bogmarked [732]
DARTON,Fredk Jos.Harvey [320–1]
DAUMIER,Honore 1808–79 193
DAVENPORT,Cyril Jas H. [362]
DAVIES,Hugh Wm [137]
DAVIS,Alec 298n
– Elmer Holmes [672]
– K.R. 247n
– Raymond Caz. 1836–1919 3
DAWE,Edw. [234–5]
DAWSON,Thos [505]
DAY,Benjamin 1838–1916. 196, 204
– Fredk T. [236] 155n
– John 1522–84 300–1
DEIGHTON, Harold [197]
DE LA MARE,Richard [664] 298n
DELISLE,Leopold Victor [127]
DE MORGAN, August.1806–71. 129n
DENT,Joseph Malaby 1849–1926. 73
– Rbt Kirkup,jt-auth. [574]
Dent Memorial Lectures 73
DE RICCI,Seymour [643]
DEROME,Nicolas Denis 232
DE ROOVER, F.E. 136n
DESCHAMPS, P.C.E.1821–1906 [685]
DEUTSCHE Bibliographie [726]
– Buch, Das [727]
– Nationalbibliographie [725]
DEUTSCHES Bucherverzeichnis[723]
DE VINNE,Theodore Low [140] 319
DE WOLF,Richard Crosby
   [508–9] 278n
DIANE DE POITIERS 231,291
DIAL (1889–97) 312
DIBDIN,Thos Frognall 2,289
DICKINSON & Co. [257]
DICTIONARY nat.Biogr.D.N.B. 82
– Printing terms [153]
DIEHL,Edith [429] 233n
DI GEMMA,Joseph [405]
DILL,Francis Parsons [532a]
DIRECTORY...Microfilm Serv.[412]

DIRINGER,David [179,A204b]
D'ISRAELI,Isaac 1766–1848 1n
DISSERTATION Abstracts [830]
DOBELL,Bertram [A820a]
DOBSON,Austin 303n
– Margaret Stirling [342]
DOCTORAL Dissertations [828]
DOCUMENT Reproductie [64]
DOLPHIN [65]
DONNELLY & Sons' Rod [430]
DOUGLAS,Lord Archibald [73]
Doves Press 314
DRAMATIC Index [779]
DREWERY,Rbt Forrester [431]
DRIVER,Godfrey Rolles [189]
Dropmore Press 318
DUBLIN Univ.Trinity Coll.
   Library 269
DUFF,Edw.G. [212,620,630] 123
DULKA,John 209n,216n
DUNN,Geo: Incunabula Coll. 114n
DWIGGINS,Wm Addison [533–4]
DYER,Bertram L. d.1908 277n

EASTERN Corp.Type [299]
EBERT,Frederick Adolf [687}
EDE,Chas,ed.[157]
EDMAN,Irwin [682]
EDMOND,John Philip 1850–1906 124
EDMONDSTON,Elizabeth [518]
ELENCO del libro suiazero [729]
ELIZABETH I,Queen of Engl. 291
ELLIOTT,R.C. 163n
ELZEVIRS,Holl.Print.–Publs. 224
ENCYCLOPAEDIA Britannica
   (Co.) [237,265,269–70,288,311]
ENCYCLOPEDIE française [484]
ENGLISH Catalogue of Books[699]
– Romanesque Illum. [206]
Eragny Press '[584–a] 313
ERASMUS [66]
ERICKSON,Edgar L. 221n
ESDAILE,Dr Arundell James
   Kennedy.[34,640,792]vi,10,124
ESSAY & gen.Lit.Index [781]
Essex House Press 313–4
EVANS,Chas 1850–1935 [706]
– D.M. 247n
– Dr Luther Harris [680] ii,13,108n,282
EVE,Nicolas & Clovis 231

INDEX

EVELYN,John 1620–1706 [647] 151n
EWART,K. [A505a]
EYRE,G.E.Briscoe,ed. [695a]

F.I.D. [67,97]
FAIRBANK,Alfred J. [198–9]
Fanfare Press (1932) 213
FARLEIGH,John [343] 187
FARMER,Bernhard Jas [519]
FEDERATION int...Docum. [67,97]
– ...Process Engravers [387]
FEGAN,Ethel S. 312n
FEIPEL,Louis N. [432] 9n
FELL,Dr John 1625–86 299–300
FERGUSON,John P.1857–1916. 5
FICTION Catalog [782]
FIGENBAUM,Muriel C. 181n
FIRKINS,Ina Ten Eyck [780]
FIRST Editions Club [557,603]320
FISHER,A.Rigby [161]
– Dorothy Canfield [678]
– Jos.R. 283n
FLETCHER,Wm Isaac,ed. [810]
FLEURON [68]
FLOWER,Desmond [55]
FORMAN,Henry Buxton 212
FORTESCUE,Geo.Knottesford [691]
FOULIS,Andrew & Rbt [572] 302
FOURDRINIER,Henry & Sealy 146
FOURNIER,Pierre Simon 175
FOWLER,Henry Watson [471]
FRANÇOIS I,King of France. 231
FRANKLIN,Benjamin [683]
FRASER,Claud Lovat 196,316
FREEDMAN,Barnett [383] 193,206
FREEMAN, John 315
FREER,Percy [A717a,807]
FRENCH,J.Ellery 242n
FREY,Ralph Wylie [447]
FRICK,Bertha Margaret, ed. [152]
FRY,Roger Eliot [200]
FULTON,Dr John F.[683i] 115n,254
FUMAGALLI,Giuseppe,ed. [24]
FUNKE,Walter,jt-auth. [761]
FURNIVALL,Dr Fredk Jas 217
FURST,Herbert[E.A.][344,363]186n
FUST,Johann.d.1466. 141

GARAMOND,Claude 173,175,177
GARDNER,Frank M. [823]
GARNETT,David (1923) 317

GARNETT,Porter,jt-auth. [532a]
– Dr Richard 1835–1906 [134]
– Rbt Singleton [609–10]
GASELEE,Sir Stephen
  [649] 110n,211n
GASKELL,Philip 302n
GAYLORD Bros [433,448–9]
GEBERT,Clara,ed. [136]
GED,Wm 1690–1749 161
GELB, Ignace Jay [A179a]
GENTRY,Helen, jt-auth. [19]
GESAMTKATALOG d.deut.
  (preuss.) Bibliotheken [722]
– d.Wiegendrucke [793] 124
GESNER,Konrad 1516–65 1,1n
GIBBINGS,Rbt [354] 187,203,317
GIBSON,Strickland [562] 123
GILL,Eric,1882–1940 [355,535]
  176,186–7,194n,299,317
GILLETT,Chas R. [770]
GILLISS,Walter 1855–1925 319
GILLOT,Chas 183
GLEESON,Evelyn (1902) 315
GLENCROSS,Alan,jt-auth. [A781b]
GOLD-tooled Bookbindings [455]
Golden Cockerel Press[587–9]317
GOLDSCHMIDT,Ernst Ph. [213–4]
GORDON, Cosmo Alex [650]
GORIER,B.de 223n
GOSSOP,Rbt Percy [665]
GOUDY,Fredc Wm 1865–1947
  [201,281,594–a] 319
GOULD,Canon Charles [480]
– F.C. 239n
Grabhorn Press 319
GRAESSE,Johann Geo.Theo. [686]
GRAHAM,Bessie [5]
GRANGER'S Index...Poetry [816]
GRANJON,Rbt 177,179,299
GRANNISS,Ruth Shepard
  [602] 121n,320n
GRANT,John Cameron 295n
– Julius [247] 147n
GRAPHIS [69]
GRAVES,Eileen C. [808]
– Haslehurst [520]
GRAY,Basil [325]
GREAT BRITAIN.Board of
  Trade. [500–1,A501a,506]
– H.M.S.O. [785–a]
GREENHOOD,David [19]

337

INDEX

GREENWOOD,Herbert Wm [A410a]
GREG,Sir Walter Wilson [129,632]
6–8,11n,83n,121n,124,212
Gregynog Press 317
GREGORY,Winifred[775,784,800,806]
GRESS,Edmund Geiger [591]
GREIG,Geo. 144
GRIFFITS,Thos Edgar [400]
GRIFFO,Francesco 140,173,177
GRIGGS,Wm 1832–1911 190,217
GROLIER,Jean 1479–1565 231
– Club of New York [604] 321
GRONEMAN,Chris.Harold [434]
GRONENDAAL,M.H. [282]
GRONINGEN,Bernhard A.van [190]
GROPIUS,Walter [Adolf] 319
GULL,Cloyd Dake 81n
GUPPY,Dr Henry 1861–1948
 vi,5,124,138n,143n
GUTENBERG,Johannes
 1399–1468 141,161
– Jahrbuch [70]
GUTHRIE,Jas [J.] 1874–1952 315

HAAS,Irvin [551–2]
HABERLEY,Loyd 317
HACKLEMAN,Chas Wm [162]
HAEBLER,Konrad [128,215] 114
HAIN,Ludwig Fried.Theodor [787]
HALBJAHRSVERZEICHNIS d...
 deut. Buchhand.erschien.Buch. [724]
HAINES,Helen Elizabeth [563]
HALKETT,Samuel 1814–71 [768]
HALL,Fredk Wm 127n,139n
HALLAM,Henry 1777–1859 2
HAMMELMANN, H.A. 190n
HAMMERMILL Paper Co. [258]
HAMPDEN,John,ed. [485]
HANDBUCH d.Bibliothekswiss. [6]
HANSON,T.W. 235n
HARCOURT,Alfred [669]
HARDIE,Martin [326]
HARLING,Rbt 318
HARRISON,Fredk [163]
– Thos 233n,245n
HARROD,Leonard Montague [25]
HART,Horace 1840–1916 [7,472]
HARTHAN,John P. [435]
HARTNETT,John B. [Ap.202n(3)]
HARTRICK,Archibald St. [382]
HASKELL,Daniel Carl [797]

HASSALL,Joan [337] 187
HAYTER,Stanley W. [364]
HAYWARD,John,jt-auth.[517]
HAZEN,Allen T. [575] 211n,226
HEAL, Sir Ambrose 133n
HEAWOOD,Edw. [266]
HENDERSON,Wm,jt-auth. [232]
HENRI II,King of France 231
HENRY Huntington Library [564]
HERBERT,John Alex. [207]
HERBST,Hermann, jt-auth. [421a]
HIGGINS,Marion Villiers [115–6]
HILL,A.Barbara 194n
– Thos Geo. [407]
HILTON,Jas [135]
HIND,Arthur Mayger [310,345]
HINMAN,Charlton 129–30n
HINRICHS Halbjahrs-Katalog[721]
– Katalog [720]
HLASTA,Stanley C. [283]
HOBBY-Horse (1886–92) 307
HOBSON,C.W. 317
– Geoffrey Dudley [420,641]
HODES,Frank,jt-auth. [761]
HODGE & SPALDING [262]
HODGSON,Sidney 9
HOE,Richard M 1812–86 162
HOFER,Philip 181n,319n
HOFFMAN,Hester R.J.,ed. [5]
Hogarth Press 317
HOLBEIN,Hans 1497?–1543 185
HOLDEN,John A 1855–1941 [22]
HOLLISTON Mills [259]
HOLMAN,Louis Arthur [312]
HOLME,Chas,ed. [157,365–6]
HOLSTEIN,Mark 224n
HOLTROP,Jan Willem 1806–70. 113
HORNBY,Chas H.St John [585] 315
HORNE,Herbert P.[436] 307–8,316
– Thos Hartwell 1780–1862 2
HOSTETTLER,Rudolf [154,A283a]
HOUSMAN,Laurence 308
HOWARTH,R. 247n
HOWE,Ellic [536] 318
HOWELL,Herbert A. [510]
HUBBARD,Eric Hesketh [367]
HUGHES,J.Horace 170n
HULLMANDEL,Chas Jos. 203
HULME,Edw.Wyndham [635] 9
HUNT,Kenneth G. 135n
HUNTER,Dard [238,254–5] 146n

INDEX

HURT,Peyton [117]
HUSUNG,Maximilian Jos. 114
HUTCHINS,Margaret [18]
HUTTON,C. 193
HYETT,Sir Francis Adams 109n

I.I.D.Communications [97]
ILIN,M.,pseud. of Marshak [612]
ILLIG,Moritz Fr. b.1777 146
IMAGE,Selwyn [356] 307–8
IMAGE,Alphabet & Image [39]
IMPRIMATUR (Cinn.) [71]
– (Hamb.) [72]
IMPRINT [73]
INDEX Bibliographicus [760]
– Librorum prohibitorum [771]
– to S.Afr.Periodicals [815]
– to Print.Tr.Periodicals [147]
– Translationum [831]
INLAND Printer [74]
INNES, R. Faraday 245n
Institut int.de B. 79
Institute of hist.Res.
Bibliographic aids... 82n
INTERNATIONAL Congr...Publ. [26]
– Index to Periodicals [813]
– Printing [75]
INTERNATIONALE B.d.Haus-
    Druckereien [553]
- B.d.Zeitschriftenlit. [812]
– B.d.Buch- u.Bibliothekswes.[8]
–ER Jahresb.d.B. [765]
IRWIN,Raymond 13
ISAAC,Col.Frank [791]
ISABELLA, Queen of Spain 291
IVINS,Wm [313]
IWINSKI,M.B. 79

JACKSON , F. Erne st 192n
– Holbrook [327,521,537]
JACOBI,Chas Thos[267,556]306,308
JACOBSON,Fred. 243n
JAHANS,Gordon A. 145n
JAHRESVERZEICHNIS d.deut.
Hochschulschriften [829]
– d.deut.Schriftums [724]
JAMES, F.E.Skone [504] 268n
– Montague Rh. [624,637] 139n
– Philip Brutton [328]
JANNON, Jean 1580–1658 175
JARROLD, H.J. 204n

JENKINS,Rhys 145n
JENKINSON,Francis J.H.
1853–1923 [627] 114n
JENNETT,Sean [164]
JENSON,Nicola(u)s 1420–80 142
JOHN Rylands Libr.Bull. [76]
JOHNSON,Alfred Forbes
    [141,277,284,295] 301n
– John (1933) [661]
– John: Typographia 304
– Wm Harding [165]
JOHNSTON,Edw.1872–1944 [202]
JOINT Exec.Comm.Pulp & Paper
Industry of the U.S.A. [239]
JONES,Geo.W.(Dolphin Press)
designs Granjon type. 171,179
– Herbert [285]
JORDELL,D.,ed. [741]
JOSEPH, Michael [486]
JOURNAL of Documentation [77]
JOY,Thos. [A486a]

KANTROWITZ,Morris Samuel [224]
KARCH,Rbt Randolph [166]
KAUFFMANN,Desire [314]
KAYSER,Christian Gottlob [719]
KELLY,Jas,ed. [708]
Kelmscott Press [583] 309–12
KENNEDY,Jas,ed. [768]
KENT,Norman,jt-ed. [353]
KENYON,Sir Fredc Geo. [193,622]
KERR,Elizabeth Margaret [824]
KESSLER,Count Harry 318
KEUSCH,Harry,jt-auth. [395]
KEYNES,Geoffrey L.[578,647]194n
KING,Howard N. 166n
KIPLING,Rudyard [611]
KIRCHHOFF,Albrecht,jt-ed. [720]
KIRCHNER,Joachim [9]
KIRGATE,Thos 1734–1810 226
KLAETSCH,Hermann [278]
KLEBS,Arnold Carl 125
KLIC (Klietsch) Karl 183
KNIGHTS,Chas C. [167]
KOENIG, Fredk 1774–1833 162
KOELHOFF,Johann (1472) 161
KRABBE,Wilhelm [20]
KROEGER,Alice Bertha,ed. [755]
KÜP,Karl,jt-ed. [13]
KVARTALSFORTEGNELSE over
norsk Litteratur [735]

339

INDEX

KYLE,E. 206n

LABARRE,Emile Jos. [228]
LADAS,Stephen Pericles [502]
LAFONTAINE,Gerard H. [229]
LAING,John,jt-auth. [768]
Lamb,Chas. 290n
LANGDON-DAVIES,Bernh.N. [487]
LANGWELL,W.H. [A247a]
LASKY,Joseph [473]
LAVER,Jas [368]
LAWLER,John [488]
LAWRIE,L.G. 237n
LEAGUE of Nations [122–3,248]
Lee Priory Press 304
Leesburg Experiment 166n
LEGROS,Lucien Alphonse 295n
LEHMANN-HAUPT,Hellmut [148,216,592] 136n
LEIGHTON,Clare (V.H.)[346–7] 187
– Douglas [437,456,663]
Leo X. Pope 289
LE PRINCE,Jean Bpte 1733–81. 182
LESLIE,Shane [683c]
LEVY,Max & Louis 183
LEWIS,Bernard [595]
– C.T.Courtney [329]
– Freeman [A682a]
– John N.C. [A296]
– Walter (1922) 317
– Wilmarth Sheldon [575a]
LEXICON des Buchwesens [9]
LEYH,Georg,ed. [6]
LIBRAIRIE française [743]
LIBRARIAN & Book World [78]
LIBRARY [79]
– Assistant [80]
– Association [11,16,35,81,249,754,814]
– Ass.Record [81]
– Binders' Memo. [457]
– Journal [82]
– Literature [10]
– of Congress [110–1,118,413,511,693–b] 283
– Quarterly [83]
– Science Abstracts [11]
LIBRI [84]
Limited Editions Club [65] 321
LINDSAY, Wallace Martin[629,A629]
LINOTYPE & Machinery,Ltd [155]
LIPPMANN,Friedrich. d.1903[369]

LITHO-Media,inc, [394]
LIVRES de l'annee [743]
LLOYD,Alan Charles Gore 143n
LOGASA, Hannah [780a]
LÖFFLER,Karl [9]
LONDON,Stationers' Company. [85,695–a,A695–a] 268–9
– School of Econ... [489]
– of Print...Yearb. [85]
LORENZ,Otto,ed. [741]
LOWE, Elias Avery [633] 136n
LOWNDES,Wm Thos 1798?–1843[698]
LUCK,Francis Wm.jt-auth. [503]
LUKER,Leslie G. [268]
LUMSDEN,Ernest S. [370]
LUTHER,Fredc 221n
LYDENBERG,Harry Miller [450]
LYELL,Jas Patrick Ronaldson 73

MCCOLVIN,Lionel Roy [A521a]
MCCORMiCK ,Ken [679]
MACDONALD,Hugh 211n
MACKENZIE,F.W. 206n
MCKERROW,Ronald Brunlees [36,138,642] 9,124,128
MACKINNON,Sir Frank 268n
MCLEAN,R. [538]
MCMURTRIE,Douglas C. [168,211]
MACNAB,Iain [348]
MADAN,Falconer 1851–1935 [205,628] 4,123–5,130n,168n
MADDOX,Harry Alfred [240]
MAGGS Bros [180]
MAIOLUS or Mahieu,Thos 231
MALCLES,Louise Noelle[736,A763]
MALLABER, K.A. [37]
MANCHESTER Guardian.Print.Sup. (1922) 317
MANN,Geo. [169]
MANSION,Colard. d.1484 182
MANSON,J.B. 313n
MANUTIUS,Aldus 142,289,303
MARCHMONT,Fredk [769]
MARIE ANTOINETTE 291
MARINACCIO,Anthony [170]
MARROT,Harold Vincent [577]
MARSHAK ,Ilia I.("M.Ilin") [612]
MASON,John 233n
MATTHEWS,W. [438]
– Wm: Diaries [776–7]

INDEX

MATTHEWS,Wm F. [439]
MAYNARD,R.A.(1922) 317
MAINE,J. [383]
MEARNE,Samuel fl.1660–83 232
MEHR nicht erschienen [832a]
MEISENBACH,Georg.1841–1912 183
MEJER,Wolfgang [421–a]
MENDELSSOHN,Sidney [715]
MENTELIN, Johann .d.1478 142
MERGENTHALER,Otto 162
Merrymount Press 319
MERSEY,Cl.Bigham,2d Visc. [601]
MERTLE,Jos.Stephen [395]
MEYNELL,Sir Francis [539,565]
   [586] 213,293n,294,298n,317
– Gerard [73]
– Viola 317
MICROCARD Bulletin [798]
MICROFILM Abstracts [830]
MIDDLETON ,Bernhard
   C.234n, 236,245
– John Henry [208]
– Rbt Hunter [286]
MIDDLETON-WAKE,Revd Chas
Henry [618]68n
MILKAU,Fritz,ed. [6]
MILLER,Eric Geo. [648]
MILLER,Wm [490]
MILNE,Jas [491]
MINNS,Sir Ellis Hovell [639]
MINTO,John,1863–1935 [754]
MONOTYPE (Corporation)
   [86,300,540–a] 162–7n,171n
– Recorder [86]
MONRO,Isabel S,jt-auth. [A781a]
MOORE, T.Sturge [A584a]
MOORHOUSE,Alf.Chase [181,A181a]
MORISON,Stanley [68,73,203,269–
   72,287–9,541–a,566–7,576,596,645]
   133,140,142n,178,294,299n,300,317
MORLEY,Christopher D. [683a]
MORRIS,Wm 1834–96 [583]
   233,306,308–12,318
MORRISON,Paul G. [694a]
– Wm R. [222]
MOTH,Axel [27–8]
MUDGE,Isadore Gilbert [755] 8
MUELLER,Hans Alexander [357]
MUIR,Percy H. [522–4]
MUMBY,Frank Arthur [492]
MURRAY,David,1842–1928 [572] 9

MURRAY,Sir Jas Augustus H. 2
MYRICK, Frank B. [A170a]

NASH,John 196,316
– John H. 319
– Paul 1899–1946 187,206
Natal Society's Library,PMB.275
NATIONAL Ass.Paper Mer. [260]
– Book League [12,58,330] 320
– Gallery [331]
– Library of Wales 269
NEW Colophon [87]
NEW York.Public Library[88,797]
NEWBURY,Francis J.(1920) 317
– K.M. 223n
NEWDIGATE,Bernhard II.1869–
   1944 [157,557,597] 314n–6
NEWELL,Leslie Fredk [A272a]
NEWKIRK,Louis V.jt-auth. [165]
NEWTON,Alfred Edw. [683d]
NICHOLSON,Margaret [507,512]
NICOLSON,Donald [396]
NIEPCE,J.N., 1765–1833 183, 194
NINETEENTH-C.Engl.Bks [684b]
NODIER,Chas.1780–1844 225n
Nonesuch Press [586] 317
NORRIS, F.H. [241]
NORSK Bogfortegnelse [733]
– Bokhandlertidende [735]

O.P. Market. Adams [803]
OATES,J.C.T. [658a]
OSTERREICHISCHE B. [728]
OFFICIAL Yearb.Sci...Soc. [825]
OGG,Oscar [182]
OLDHAM,Jas Basil [656]
ORCUTT,Wm Dana [542] 319
ORNE,Jerrold [463]
ORTON,Rbt Merritt [821]
– Vrest [595a]
OSBORN,Burl Neff,jt-auth. [170]
OSLER,Sir Wm 1849–1919 254
OSWALD,John Clyde [568]
OTLET,Paul 1868–1941 79n
OXFORD Soc.Proc. [89]
– University Press 299–300

P.A.T.R.A. [93–4,149,250,452]
PADELOUP,A.M.,le jeune 232
PAFFORD,John Henry Pyle 274n
PAGLIAINI,Attilio [A745a]

341

PALAU y Dulcet,Antonio [746]
PALTSITS,Victor Hugo 11
PANNARTZ,Arnold,fl.1465–73 142
PANZER,Georg W.1729–1805. 113
PAPER & Print [90]
PAPER Makers' Ass. [242]
PARIS,Bibliothèque Nat. [692]
PARKER,Bertha Morris [183]
PARLEY,Norman 153n
PARTINGTON Wilfred Geo. [417]
Pastonchi,Francesco.Ital.poet.
– type (1923) 179
PATON,Hugh [371]
PATRA [93–4,149,250,452]
PAYNE Roger (1739–97) 232
Pear Tree Press 315
PEDDIE,Rbt Alex.1869–1951 [690]
PEIGNOT,E.Gabriel 1767–1849 2
PENNELL,Jos.(1860–1926) [372]
PENROSE Annual [91]
PEPLER,H.Douglas C.(1916) 316
PERTELOTE [588]
PETRINA,John [315]
PETZHOLDT,Julius 1812–91 [756]
PRISTER,Albr.fl. 1460–4 161,182
PHILIP,Alex.John [440]
PHILLIPS,John (1631–1706) 2
Philobiblion [514]289
PI-SHENG fl.1041–9 161
PICKERING,Wm (1796–1854)
 [578] 174,301,305
PINKER,H.L. [194,A502a]
PINTO, Dr Olga [29,107]
PIPER,Myfanwy [358]
PISSARRO,Lucien (1863–1944)
 [A584a] 185,203,313
PITKIN,Chas W., jt-auth. [160]
PLANT,Marjorie [496]
PLANTIN,Christophe 1514–89
– Musee Plantin, & Type 177
PLATT,John Edgar [349]
PLENDERLEITH,Harold Jas [451]
POE,Edgar Allan [613]
POLAIN, (M.) Louis [795] 124
POLLARD,Alfred Wm 1859–1944
 [119,129,142,322,569,634,694] [792]
 5–6,112n,114–n,124,126,213n
– Graham jt-auth. [415–6]
POOLE'S index...Per.Lit. [810]
POORTENAAR,Jan [171,316]
Portrait Index [817]

POTTER,Mrs Greta Lagro 314n
POTTINGER, David Thos [570]
PRAETORIUS,Chas.fl.
 1880–9.217–8
PRIDEAUX,Sarah Treverbian
 [373,422,441] 233
PRINCE,Edward P. 307,314
PRINT [92]
PRINTING...Res. Ass.
 [93–4,149,250,452]
– Review [95]
– Tr.Craft Lect. [85]
PROCESS Yearbook [91]
PROCTOR,Rbt Geo.Collier
 [790–a] 113–4,226
PRODUCTION Yearbook [96]
PUBLISHERS Association [493]
– Circular [700]
– Trade List Annual [712]
– Weekly [494,711]
PUTNAM,Geo.Haver [495]
Pynson Printers [63] 319

QUÉRARD,Joseph Marie [739–40]
QUILLER-COUCH,Sir Arthur [474]

RANDALL,David A.,jt-auth. [529]
RANSOM,Will [554–5]
RATCHFORD,Fanny E. [418]
RATDOLT,Erhard (1476–1527) 184
RAVERAT,Gwendolen 318
RAYMOND,Harold [666]
RAYMOND & Raymond [401]
READERS' Guide...Per.Lit. [811]
RECORD,P.D.,ed. [A830a]
REDGRAVE,Gilbert Richard,
 jt-comp. [694] 216n
REED,Talbot Baines 1852–93[277]
REFERENCE Cat...cur.Lit. [701]
REICHARDT,Günther 153n
REICHLING,Dietrich [789]
REID,Forest [332]
REIMER,Imre [350]
RENKER,Arnim [243]
REPERTOIRE de B.franc. [742]
– du livre suisse [729]
Reprints in Series.Orton. [821]
REVIEW of Documentation [97]
– Digest, Book [822]
REVUE de la Documentation [97]
REYNOLDS,Graham [359]

Riccardi Press [556] 316
RICHARD de Bury See Aungerville
RICHARDSON,Samuel 1689–1761 301
RICHES,Phyllis M. [772]
RICKETTS,Chas 1866–1931
    [582] 185,308,312
RIDENAUER,Louis N. [684a]
RIDER,Fremont [414] 221
RIDGWAY,John Livesy [408]
RILEY & Co. [442] 247n
RIPS,Rae Elizabeth,jt-ed. [786]
RITTER,Johan Christian 143
Riverside Press 319
RIVIERE,Rbt 1808–82 & Son 233
ROBERT,Louis (1798) 146
ROBERT,Wm 1862–1940 [139]
ROBERTSON,Edward 142n
ROBINS,Wm Palmer [374]
RODENBERG,Julius,jt-auth. [571]
Rödar (C.G.) Prozess 219
ROGERS,Bruce.Riverside
    Pr.,C.U.P.O.U.P. [598–a–9]
    173–4,300,316,319
ROOD,Theodoric,1.Oxf.Pr. 299
ROORBACH,Orville Augustus [707]
ROSENBACH,A.S.W. [683–i,A683]
ROSNER,Chas [273,458] 248n
ROWLANDS,Wm 1802–65 2
ROWLES,Geo.E. [614]
Roxburghe Club (1812–1927) [601]
ROYAL SOCIETY [A474a] 176n,271n
– of Arts [251,453]
RUSCH,Adolf.15c.R-printer 142
RUTHERSTON,Albert 196,316
RUZICKA,R. [360]

SADLEIR,Michael
    [459,517,525,651,660,783] 289n
ST Bride Foundation Cat. [150–1]
St Dominic's Press 316
SALAMAN,Malcolm Chas [333,351]
SALE,Wm Merritt 301n
SANDARS Lectures 68–72
SANDERS,Francis Douglas [497]
SANDFORD,Christopher 186n,317
SANGORSKI, F. & Sutcliffe,G. 233
SCHXFFER,Jacob Christian 146
SCHAFFERT,R.M. 202n
SCHEELE,Karl Wilhelm (1774) 146
SCHMIDT,F.A. 141n
SCHMOLLER,Hans P. 171n,179

SCHNEIDER, Georg [130–1] 9
SCHOEFFER,Peter [216] 141,161
SCHOLDERER,Dr Victor
    [217,644,792] 114,142n,143n
SCHOONBERG, V.A., sen. 143
SCHWEIZER Buch [729]
– Bücherverzeichnis [729]
SCIENTIFIC...Soc:Off.York [825]
SCOTLAND.Nat.Libr.Edinb. 269n
SCRIBNER, Bourdon Walter 153n
SELECTION of recent Books [752]
SENEFELDER Alois 1771–1834 183
Sequels - Sequence [823–4]
SHAABER,Matthias Adam 121n
Shakespeare Head Press 315
SHAPIRO,S.R.,ed. [820]
SHAW,Geo.Bernard: Farleigh 187
– Thos Shuler [120]
SHEPPARD, L.A. [792]
SHORES,Louis [108] 265n
SHORT,Sir Frank [375]
Short-title Catalogue [694]
SIBERCH,Johann (1521–2) 300
SIGNATURE [98]
SILCOCK,E. 167n
SILVER,Harry M. 220n
SIMON,Herbert [172] 265n
– Oliver [68,98,173,571] 316
SINDALL,Rbt Walter [244] 146n
SINGER,Hans Wolfgang [376]
SISSON,Chas Jasper [652]
SKETCHLEY,R.E.D. [334]
SLEIGH,Bernhard [352]
SMITH,Anna H. 144n
– F.Seymour [526]
– Frank H. [388]
– Harry Harwood 143–4
– Percy J. 141n,316
– Wm Jos. [389]
SONNENSCHEIN,Wm Swan [753]
SOUTH African Cat.of Bks [717]
– – Libraries [99]
– – Public Libr.[716,A717a] 275
– – Publisher & Bksllr [718]
– – Pulp...Industr. [261]
SPALDING & Hodge [262]
SPARKE,Archibald,jt-auth. [832]
SPARLING,Henry Halliday [583]
STANDARD Catalog [749]
STANHOPE,Chas,3d Earl 162,304
STANILAND, Lancelot N. [A408a]

343

INDEX

State Library.Pretoria [716] 275
STATIONERS' Co. See
   under LONDON
STEEL,Kenneth [377]
STEELE,Rbt (Reynolds) [556]
STEER,Vincent [A289a]
STEEVENS,Geo.1736-1800 211
STEEVES,Henry Allan [305]
STEIN (Fredc A.) Henri [741,758]
STEPHEN,Geo.A.,jt-auth. [428]
STERNBERG,Harry [404]
STEVENS,Henry 1819-86 3,15,117n
STEVENSON,Allan H. 122n
- Wm Henry [619]
STILLWELL,Margaret Bingham
   [132,218,794] 124
STOKES,Fredk Abbot [668]
STONE,Reynolds [358] 187
STORM,Cotton [527]
STRAHAN,Jas A., jt-auth. 283n
STRANG,Wm, jt-auth. [376]
STRAUS,Ralph [574]
STRAUSS,Victor [Ap.206n(2a)]
Strawberry Hill Press [575-a] 303
STROMER,Ulman (1389) 145
STURT,J.,facsimilist 211
SUBJECT Index to Periodicals [814]
SUBSCRIPTION Books Bull. [826]
SUID-Afrikaanse Biblioteke [99]
SUTCLIFFE,G.& Sangorski,F. 233
SWEMMER,B.Northling 274n
SWEYNHEIM fl.1465-73 142
SWIFT,Jonathan [683c]
SWINNERTON,Frank Arthur [667]
SYMONS,Alphonse Jas A. [55] 227n
- Julian [615]

TALBOT,Wm Henry Fox
   1800-77 183,195,215
TARR,John C. [174,204,302,543-4] 298n
TATE,John d.1507 145
- Vernon D. 221n
TAUBE. Mortimer [118]
TAYLOR, Harold M. (1920) 317
TER HOERNEN,Arnold (1470) 161
THACHER,John B. 225n
THOMAS,David [290]
- R.N. 126n
THOMPSON,Anthony [31]
- Sir Edw.Maunde 1840-1929
   [191,617,626]

THOMPSON,Elizabeth Hardy [30]
- Henry Yates [623,625]
- Jas S. [674]
- Jas Westfall 136n
- Laurence S. 245n
THORP, Jos.[175,545,597] 314-6n
THORPE,James [335]
TILLOTSON'S...Type-faces [303]
TIMES.The [274,801] 178
- Literary Suppl. [100] 118n
TODD,Wm B. 130n
TOMKINSON,Geoffrey St. [557]
TONNON,J.C., jt-auth.
TORY,Geoffroi 1480-1533 231
TOUSSAINT,A. 144n
TOWN,Laurence [443]
TRITHEIM,Johannes (1494) 1
TSCHICHOLD,Jan [184-5,546]
   297n
TULLIS Russell & Co. [245]
TURNBULL,John 290n
TYPOGRAPHIC Stand.Type [304]
TYPOGRAPHICA [101]
TYPOGRAPHY [102]

UNESCO [109-11] 82n,267
- Bull.du droit d'auteur [513]
- Copyright Bull. [513]
UHLENDORF,B.A. 143n
ULLMAN,Berthold Lovis[186] 135n
LLLYETT,Kenneth [390]
ULRICH, Carolyn F. [13,808]
ULRICH'S Periodicals Dir. [808]
Unfinished books,B.of [832]
UNGERER,J.S.F. 274n
UNION Catalogue of...Per. [805]
- List of Microfilms [799]
- of South Afr.Libr.of
   Parliament. [715] 275
UNITED States Catalog [709]
- - Cumulative Bk Auction
   Records [820]
- - Govt Print.Off. [275,444]
UNWIN,Sir Stanley [498] 250,257,285
UPDIKE,Daniel Berkeley 1860-
   1941 [291,547-8,599] 319

VAIL,Rbt Wm G. [683h]
Vale Press 312
VALLÉE,Leon Alex 1850-1919[757]
VAN HOESEN,Dr Henry B. [38] 10

INDEX

VAN PATTEN,Nathan 10
VARLEY,bouglas H 143n
VAUGHAN,Alex.J. [445]
VEITCH,F.P. [447]
VEREENIGING ter Bevord.v.de Belang.d.Bkhandels:Cat. [14]
VER NOOY,Winifred,jt-ed. [780a]
Vertical File Serv.Cat. [833]
VICENTINO,L.degli Arrighi 174
VICTORIA & Albert Museum [378]
Village Press 319
VOLK,Kurt Hans [292]
VORSTIUS,Joris [15,104,765]
VOSBURGH,Marion E.,jt-ed. [1]

WADE,Arthur Cecil [549]
WALKER,Sir Emery 1851–1933 [638] 10,308,314–6
WALKER & Robertson 143
WALL,E.W. 233n
WALPOLE,Sir Horace [575–a] 303
WALTER,Frank Keller [32,38] 10
WARDE,Beatrice ["Paul Beaujon"] [276] 172n,175n,177n,316n,319n
– Frederic 174
WARNER,John 243n
WARREN,Arthur [579]
WATKINS,Ann [673]
WATSON,Ernest W.,ed. [353]
WATT,Rbt 1774–1819 [697]
WEBER,Carl Jefferson [460]
– Chas Gould,jt-auth. 242n
WEDMORE,Fredk [379]
WEEKLEY,Montague [A360a]
WEEKS,Edw. [681]
WEITENKAMPF,Frank [306,323] 209n,225n
WEITZMANN,Kurt [209]
WENGENROTH,Stow [384]
WEST,Aubrey [204a]
– Clarence Jay,comp. [225–6]
– Levon [380]
Westminster Press [73]
WHEELWRIGHT,Wm Bond [230,246]
'WHEN found, make a note of' 78n
WHETTON,Harry,ed. [176]
WHISTLER,J.McNeill 189–90,308
WHITAKER'S cum.Booklist [702]
WHITE,H.L.,comp. [713]
– Jos.W.Gleeson [336]
– W.H: Chronograms 125n

WHITEHILL,Clayton [293]
WHITEHOUSE,John Howard[177] 317
WHITMAN,Alfred [317]
Whittinghams,The [579] 301,305
WILEY'S Author's guide [475]
WILLIAMS,Geo.Edw. [476]
– Sir Harold [603,657] 10
– Henry Smith [187]
– Iolo Aneurin [528] 124
– Reginald Gordon [21]
WILLIAMSON,Hugh [550]
WILLING'S Press Guide [809]
WILLY,Clifford Mason [397]
WILSON,Frank Percy 12
– John Dover [646]
– John G. [499]
– Thos Arden [398]
– Company,The H.W. [477,488]
– Library Bulletin [103]
WINCHELL,Constance M. [755]
Windsor,Phineas L:Lectures 75–6
WING,Donald Goddard [696]
WINSHIP,Geo.Parker 1872–1952 [219,683f,794]
WINTERICH,John T. [529, 604,684]
WISE,Thos [419] 212,227
WISTAR Inst.Style Brief [409]
WÖCHENTLICHES Verzeichnis [725]
WOMALD,F. [655]
WOODBINE,Herbert vi, 188
WOOLF,Leonard & Virginia 317
WORDS into type [478]
WORLD–List of sci.Per. [804]
WORLEY,Parker 82n
WOTTON,Thos 1521–87 232
WROTH,Lawrence Counselman [65,125,593,683b] 13
WYER,Jas Ingersoll [121]
WYLD,Henry Cecil Kennedy 11
WYMAN,Chas Wm H.,jt-auth. [144]

YEAR'S Wk...Librarianship [16]
YEATS,Elizabeth & Lily 315
Yellowsands Press (1919) 317

ZAEHNSDORF,Jos.Wm [446] 233
ZAINER,Gunther (1471) 182
ZENTRALBLATT f.Biblwesen [104]
ZIGROSSER,Carl Daniel [324] 206
ZURCHER,Geo. [A276a]
ZWEIG,Stefan [616]

www.ingramcontent.com/pod-product-compliance
Lightning Source LLC
Chambersburg PA
CBHW060548080526
44585CB00013B/484